FAMILY THERAPY
WITH
COUPLES

FAMILY THERAPY
WITH
COUPLES

The Family-of-Origin Approach

DAVID S. FREEMAN

JASON ARONSON INC.
Northvale, New Jersey
London

Production Editors: Judith D. Cohen and Adelle Krauser
Editorial Director: Muriel Jorgensen

This book was set in 12 point Goudy by Lind Graphics of Upper Saddle River, New Jersey, and printed and bound by Haddon Craftsmen of Scranton, Pennsylvania.

Library of Congress Cataloging-in-Publication Data

Freeman, David S.
    Family therapy with couples / by David S. Freeman.
        p.   cm.
    Includes bibliographical references and index.
    ISBN 0-87668-471-1
    1. Family psychotherapy.   2. Marital psychotherapy.   I. Title.
    [DNLM: 1. Family Therapy—methods.   2. Marital Therapy—methods.
    WM 430.5.F2 F855f]
    RC488.5.F738   1992
    616.89'156—dc20
    DNLM/DLC
    for Library of Congress   91-33209

Manufactured in the United States of America. Jason Aronson Inc. offers books and cassettes. For information and catalog write to Jason Aronson Inc., 230 Livingston Street, Northvale, New Jersey 07647.

To my family,
my wife Virginia,
daughter Amy, son Dan,
and brother Izzy

Contents

a reflection of unfinished business than expressions of a lack of commitment, caring, and love. The ability to be intimate in marriage is developmental and will be influenced by peoples' ages at the time of marriage.

Preface

Family Therapy with Couples is not a text about couple therapy. The objective of the book is to present a model of family systems therapy that focuses on the adults in the family. It is based on the premise that change in a family has to be sustained by the most powerful members of that system. Family therapy with couples allows the therapist to enter the family at several different levels. The therapist first establishes a relationship with the adults in the family; establishing this relationship opens the door to involving additional family members as indicated. The majority of couples who seek therapy define their problem as resting in their relationship. However, some marriages stabilize by focusing on a problem child. It is prudent to start with the parents and listen to their story about the difficulties they perceive in the family before deciding whom to involve in treatment.

This text describes the different ways to work with the adults in the nuclear family to effect family change.

The accepted family therapy practice is to begin therapy with the entire family. There is a premise that when there is a problem with a child it is most often a reflection of some family dysfunction. The common view is that to understand the problem it is necessary to observe how the family members interact with each other. It is true that when the entire family is seen the therapist obtains a quick overview of how the parts interact with the whole. Ordinarily, the family plays out before the therapist the familiar ways they behave together at home. Unfortunately, many of these families leave the session feeling confused and pessimistic, primarily because their experience with their therapist was so similar to their home reality.

In my first text, *Techniques of Family Therapy*, I discussed the importance of working with the entire family, and I continue to believe that it is sometimes helpful to see the whole family. However, I have come to question the wisdom of beginning family therapy with the entire family, that is, the nuclear family. When the family is seen together the needs of the parents and the needs of the children must be balanced. Ordinarily the parents will have a need to explain to the therapist why they are good parents and how they have done the best they could to meet the needs of their children. On the other hand, the children need to feel that their own struggles and expectations are understood and not overshadowed by their parents' concerns. If the therapist aligns with the parents in the first session, he will lose the children, who will feel that the therapy will replicate home life. However, if the therapist aligns with the children, he undermines the need of the parents to feel validated. The struggle for structure occurs in setting up the first interview. It is at the time of this initial contact that the therapist has the first opportunity to shift the focus to working with the adults in the family.

This text is about how to begin the therapy process with the adults. The approach allows the therapist to focus on the selves of the adults quickly. Helping the couple understand what each partner brings into the relationship from the past leads to a better sense of connection, intimacy, and positive honoring of the past in the present.

The first two chapters of this text deal with the theory that underpins a systemic approach to family therapy with couples. Chapter 1 provides the groundwork for understanding the reason for beginning family therapy with the adults and highlights some of the basic assumptions that govern relationship dynamics. Chapter 2 presents a theoretical framework for understanding relationship problems. It discusses the development of a relationship, developmental differences, the difficulties with intimacy, and the impact of unfinished business on the functioning of the family.

Chapter 3 deals with understanding relationship problems systemically. It highlights the functional nature of relationship problems, how problems can actually stabilize the family system. Chapter 4 discusses beginning the therapy process. It describes in greater detail the rationale for beginning with the couple. It further discusses how to initiate the first session, whom to involve, and how to reframe the presenting problems.

Chapters 5 through 9 are clinical chapters. Each of these chapters contains a complete interview with commentary. Chapter 5 focuses on how to conduct a beginning session with a couple. It provides a guideline for understanding the dynamics of the beginning, middle, and ending stages in the first session. Chapter 6 concentrates on the beginning of the middle phase of therapy. It highlights how to help the couple deal with self issues. Chapter 7 discusses the process of shifting into the middle-middle phase of family therapy with couples. This chapter emphasizes how a therapist builds on work done in previous sessions. Chapter 8 is about ending the middle phase of family therapy and focuses on the importance of involving the parents of adult children in the therapy.

Chapter 9 deals with the termination process, and Chapter 10 outlines several special issues concerning family therapy with couples.

A unique feature of this text is its concentration on the middle phase of therapy. It is important that therapists conceptualize the complexity of middle-phase work. Chapters 6, 7, and 8 provide the reader with an in-depth analysis of the middle-phase process.

My hope is that the reader will find this book a useful guide for working with families. A major objective was to provide a text that fostered an understanding of the complexity of family life and also provided a framework for helping family members form deeper connections with each other. The goal is that the reader will understand the importance of connecting the past with the present so the future can be more hopeful and successful.

This text is meant for both students and teachers of family therapy. I hope that people not directly involved in the family therapy field will also find this text a useful guide for rethinking their own history, making peace with unresolved issues, and honoring their families in the present in a more positive and powerful way.

1

Introduction to Family Therapy with Couples

Overview

It is unusual in the field of family therapy to find a book titled *Family Therapy with Couples*. In some ways it is a contradiction in terms. How is it possible to understand the family by first getting to know the parental subsystem? Isn't it wiser to meet with the whole family, hear each person's story, get a feel for the total dynamics of how the family members interact with each other? Most family therapy models support that point of view. Family therapists encourage the whole family to come in and experience how the members interact with each other in front of a stranger—the family therapist. When you bring the entire family together there is a heightened degree of anxiety. The parents are defensive and protective about their position in the family. It is important for the parents to establish quickly with their therapist that they have done the best they can, given the current situation. Usually the parents will express their frustration and dismay by highlighting their difficulties with one or more of the children. The parents might also talk about mutual differences regarding how each feels the children should be dealt with.

The children, by and large, do not want to come into anything called family therapy. If they are adolescents they want to be with their peers, in school, or anywhere but with adults talking about the family problems. Many children realize that their family's problems are not really because of them but have to do with their parents' difficulties in their own lives and/or relationships. Usually children do not want to come into family therapy because they think they are going to be blamed, put on the spot, and/or made to talk about things they believe are best left unsaid. Basically, the children feel threatened and anxious about the negative repercussions a family session might have.

If the family has had a previous experience in family therapy that was negative and/or hurtful to one or more of its members, this also complicates starting with the whole family. After such an experience the family becomes very cautious about exposing itself to another experience that might take on some of the same manifestations. Another dilemma in starting with the whole family involves one of the first goals of family therapy: reframing the problem, to refocus the problem away from one member of the family who may appear seriously dysfunctional and is perceived as the central problem to an understanding of how the family as a system is functioning. When the entire family is seen in the first session, the family members are usually convinced that the problem rests with one of their members. It has always been curious to me that the therapist involves the whole family as a way of redefining the problem while the family views this structure as reinforcement of the idea that one or more members of the family truly does have a problem.

The way a family is organized—its roles, structure, and the hierarchical arrangement of various components within it—rests with the parental subsystem. How the parents experienced family life in their own growing-up years, the issues they have or have not worked through with their own parents and siblings, and what I call the "unfinished business" that they have taken from their original family and introduced into their new family are all vital dynamics that add to the dilemmas families have in the here and now. Most parents are not aware of this principle. They believe that by getting married and starting a new family, they start with a clean slate. Generally there is little recognition that each parent as an emotional being brings into the current situation his or her own complicated history. The degree to which husbands and wives understand this dynamic will determine how connected they are in being able to bring the best of their past into the present in order to make the future different. It is difficult for parents to appreciate this when they are focusing on concerns about their children or when each is angry, upset, or disappointed about how the other is dealing with important family issues.

Many parents will either put the responsibility for problems on what they see as their spouse's ineptitude or emotional overinvolvement or lack of concern with family matters, or will focus on the child as the real source of the problem. They will not realize that what they bring from the past has a powerful dynamic on what they (1) define as the problem; (2) try to do to resolve the problem; and (3) perceive as their general frustration in not being able to make a difference regarding the problem. The degree to which each adult in the family understands the influence of the past on the present will determine how "stuck" he or she is in the problem.

There is general agreement among family therapists that defining the problem is more important than the problem itself. It is a basic principle that a problem's solution accompanies its definition. Defining the problem differently, allows for a greater range of options for resolving it. One of the first tasks of the family therapist is to challenge, gently but provocatively, the adults' perception of the problem in the family. When the entire family is present and the members are anxious, unsure of themselves, and defensive regarding their own stance, they are not as open to rethinking the meaning of the problem. In fact, the very structure of having a family in therapy, at the beginning, reinforces, heightens, and makes more powerful each member's need to hold on to his or her emotional definition of the problem.

The therapist has to challenge the definition of the problem without alienating, frightening, and/or criticizing members of the family. With this goal in mind, I have found it more helpful to begin the family therapy process with the adults. Starting this way allows the therapist to form a positive relationship with the parents. This positive relationship is central to the timing of when to involve the children in the therapeutic process. When the parents feel comfortable and trusting toward their therapist, they can allow the children to tell their story to the therapist without fearing the therapist will take sides, use the story to invalidate what they have said, and/or undermine how they want the family to be structured.

The Difference between Couple Therapy and Family Therapy with Couples

It is important to differentiate between family therapy with couples and couple therapy. When there is a relationship problem — that is, a marital problem — it can have a negative impact on the entire family. When couples have problems in their relationship, it does not necessarily follow that the family is in dysfunction and/or that the problems will have severe negative effects on the children. However, when the parents project their relationship problems with each other onto one or more of the children and/or use the children to stabilize their relationship with each other, this can create serious problems with the children.

The family therapist must assess what parts of the family are in dysfunction. Is the problem primarily marital, and are the parents using the children to deal with their unfinished business with each other? Is the problem more about one of the parents' having severe difficulties in his or her own life and not being able to take a positive parental role with the children? Is the problem in the extended family, where one or more members are having difficulties and the parents are unable to balance the needs of their own children with those of their family of origin? Is the problem that siblings are acting out in their relationship what they are not getting from their own parents? Is the problem economic or social, wherein the family is not able to get the resources it needs from the community and/or is being discriminated against, thus making it difficult for the family to function as such? The family therapist must be aware of all these different levels of dysfunction and not be too quick to assume that the problem rests just within the family and/or the couple. If the problem is seen as one involving the relationship between the husband and wife, and if the therapist approaches it as such, one can call this couple therapy. In contrast, a more systemic approach would focus on where the family defines its problems — self, the marital relationship, children, the siblings, extended family members, and/or the community, etc. — and tries to understand how these problems have affected the overall functioning of the family.

Couple therapy is too restrictive. It holds that the problem rests within the couple relationship, and the relationship itself should be treated. There is not much appreciation that what isn't working between the husband and wife is quite complicated and is influenced by a combination of dynamics. One contributing factor is what the adults bring into the relationship from their past families and how that gets played out in their current life together. It is also complicated by the adults' expectations from the world and what they want from work, peers, and leisure-time activities. How well the adults deal with their own needs, fears, anxieties, and problems with intimacy will determine the degree of balance they bring to their parental, spousal, and extended-family responsibilities.

Family therapy with couples allows the therapist to use the adults as the center subsystem to move up, down, or across a generation to help produce family change. It is important for the therapist to understand that how the partners arrange their relationship will determine the balance the children have regarding their involvement within the family, with each other, and with their relationships outside the family. How well the partners have been able to work through their attachment issues with their own families and develop intimately with each other will affect their ability to meet the needs of their children.

The therapist does not focus primarily on the relationship between the husband and wife but tries to understand how their relationship has developed over time to allow the husband and wife to feel special, nurtured, and understood by each other. Using the adults as an entry point into the family allows for a greater appreciation of what one brings from the past to the present that influences the future direction of the family. The relationship is not what is under scrutiny or what is being treated; nevertheless, the relationship should be used to help the family become a more positive resource for its members.

A basic theoretical assumption of this text is that as the husband/wife relationship improves and becomes more solid, each spouse can provide a more solid, balanced involvement with the children. The ideal is for the parents to become resources to each other in being able to meet the multidimensional needs of their children. It is also assumed that if there is severe dysfunction in the husband/wife relationship, to some degree that dysfunction will be acted out toward the children either by one or both parents becoming overly involved with or distant from the children, and/or the children misinterpreting the lack of involvement or criticism of the parents as an indication that the children are not lovable enough to have their needs met by their parents.

In Family Therapy with Couples, Who Is Treated?

When we think of problems systemically, it is important to understand that no matter where a family places the problem, it can affect all family members in different ways. The problem does not affect all family members equally; however, all family members are affected to some degree by any major concern in the family. It is helpful to view the family from a multigenerational perspective. The therapist must understand what is happening in the extended family, between the husband and wife, and with the children. All these subsystems dovetail with each other. In making a systemic assessment the therapist needs to survey the unresolved issues that each parent has with his or her family of origin. A therapist should not assert that therapy leads to change only with individual members, couples, or families; all these units must be in mutual harmony. The therapist needs to choose which unit to work with. However, he or she also must understand that a change in one family unit affects the entire family. In family therapy with couples it is assumed that when there is change with the couple there is also change with the individual members within the relationship, which frees their ability to meet the needs of their children on the one hand and their extended-family members on the other. The choice is not which subsystem one should be working with—the individual, the couple, or the family; rather, the assessment should determine the most powerful unit for change in the family and then use that unit as a way to influence the multigenerational family positively.

Another theoretical assumption of this text is that the parental unit is the most powerful unit most of the time and that it should be the entry point for systemic change. Occasionally extended-family members may be more powerful or more influential than the parents in the family. In these cases, the extended family members should be involved in the therapy early in the process.

Basic Assumptions Governing Family Dynamics

The major premise governing this text is that the adults in the family are responsible for transferring to their children their hopes and expectations. These legacies from the past in turn serve as useful guides for the future. On the other hand, couples also transfer to their children their losses, anxieties, and unfulfilled dreams. Children, often without knowing it, carry as their personal burdens their parents' struggles and losses. It is assumed that the adults in the family are the basic links between the past and the future. Their challenge is to help their children embrace the future without excessive anxiety. The following assumptions describe some of the reasons parents have difficulty meeting this challenge.

Assumption 1: One cannot come out of family experiences without a certain degree of emotional unfinished business.

Unfinished business is a present emotional reaction shaped by a past experience. It is a reactive response guided by strong emotional feelings based on past experiences of anxiety. Unfinished business does not allow for a thoughtful, creative response to a here-and-now situation; rather it triggers an emotional reactive response to it. Who we bring into our life, our major life decisions, how we embrace important people, and the amount of closeness or distance we need emotionally are all shaped by the degree of unfinished business we carry into our adult life.

The unfinished business we carry from our family of origin gets played out to some degree in whom we choose to marry, the type of family we structure, and the needs we feel should be met by our spouse and our children. This dynamic of unfinished business is quite profound in all of us. It is not possible for anyone to come out of his or her original family without some unresolved issues around attachment and separation. Built into normal family life is a certain degree of loss, deprivation, and anxiety. The degree to which our parents were able to minimize the amount of anxiety we experienced as children greatly affects the degree of unfinished business we carry into our adult relationships. This concept is made more complex by the fact that our parents' success in raising us was determined by the success of their parents in raising them. To understand the amount of unfinished business we carry as children, it is important to understand our parents' relationships with their own parents. The degree to which parents felt safe and loved in their own families influences how safe and special they are able to make their own children feel.

The concept of unfinished business is a multigenerational one. One cannot understand unfinished business by conceptualizing only the parent/child interaction. Parents continually deal with their children in terms of unresolved issues from their original families. It is not unusual for parents either to attempt to raise their children in ways significantly different from their own experiences or to try to replicate exactly the experiences they had in their own families. Many parents will say, "It was good enough for me as a child, it should be good enough for my children." Others will say, "I grew up in a home that wasn't safe or loving, and I am going to make my new family different. I will give the love and caring to my children that I did not get from my parents." On the surface this latter statement seems like a positive stance coming out of a negative family experience. However, the way that parent might try to love his or her children and make life safe for them may not meet their needs in terms of their own realities, temperamental styles, and situational experiences. One of the major dilemmas of unfinished business is that it restricts our options. When a situation in the present stirs up anxiety, we try immediately to find some way to reduce the anxiety. We do not become thoughtful about what is going on or expansive in ways that allow us to deal with that anxiety differently. Our tendency is to react to the anxiety either by withdrawing from it or doing battle with it.

Assumption 2: We look for a spouse to help complete emotionally what hasn't been completed in our own family of origin.

This assumption is connected with assumption 1. It is always interesting to ponder what was behind someone's selection of his or her mate. What were the attractive features of the person that made one think he or she could be a partner for life? What did self need from that significant other that felt right, safe, and loving? I have discovered in my clinical practice that many people respond to the question "What was it in your partner that made you think he or she was right for you in ways that no one else appeared to be?" with the answer that the partner appeared to be able to complete emotionally the parts of self that were felt unfinished. Another way of understanding this dynamic is to ask clients what they wanted from their partners that they felt they were not able to give themselves. The answer usually elicits descriptions of those areas of emotional need that self felt most deprived of in the original family. Many people get married out of need. They carry the fantasy that with the right partner they can finally feel whole, safe, and loved. This hope places tremendous demands on the marriage. When a partner is not able to live up to the covert contract of completing those missing pieces, a loss is experienced in the relationship. One begins to feel unloved, unspecial, and unsafe. These feelings, in turn, lead to distancing, shutting down emotionally, and a general withdrawing from the marriage. This dynamic undermines the basic integrity of the relationship and usually leads to severe family conflict, often with one partner becoming overly involved with the children and the other becoming more distant from and peripheral to the relationship.

Assumption 3: We carry into our new family a degree of debt, loyalty, and attachment issues that we have not made peace with and through our new family try to resolve and honor.

Each partner brings into the marriage a degree of loyalty from his or her original family. The challenge in a new marriage is for each partner to integrate the best of his or her original family into the marriage. The task is for the couple to begin to develop a sense of family that is uniquely theirs without having to give up the best parts of their own personal histories. Many relationship problems originate from a lack of understanding of this principle. When there is high anxiety around certain developmental issues, life challenges, and issues of death and loss, individuals usually bring methods from the past to the problem-solving. The way in which they deal with high-anxiety situations is based on what they learned in their original families. How well each partner is able to be curious rather than reactive about how the other deals with significant emotional and social issues determines the degree of intimacy and connection the couple will be able to achieve around these differences.

Assumption 4: We cannot give to others what we have not emotionally received from our own families.

This assumption addresses the issue of how people take care of each other. The underlying premise is that we cannot give emotionally to our spouse and children what we have not received from our original families. Although we may earnestly try to give what we did not receive, we are able to do this only if we feel safe, secure, and loved. Behavior on the part of our spouse or children that appears critical, distant, or unloving, will trigger anxiety and doubt in us and block our ability to be loving and nurturing. In contrast, a person who is his or her own hero can be loving to others even in situations that are not emotionally safe. When we enter relationships as a way of making up for our own losses we need more from the other than we are able to give the other. When our partner does not appear emotionally safe to us, we will respond by withdrawing or attacking. Many of us enter marriages because we want someone to be our hero. In other words, we want someone to be there to take care of us and make us feel safe. We lack that safety inside ourselves. In part this is a developmental issue that needs to be understood in terms of how one develops a solid sense of self over the life cycle. Nonetheless, the degree to which an adult comes out of his or her own family feeling emotionally unsafe determines the degree to which he or she will need a partner to make up for those losses. When one feels emotionally unsafe and one's partner behaves in a way that seems unloving, one is not able to become curious about one's partner's reactions. Rather, one becomes defensive and reactive toward those behaviors that remind one of earlier losses, abandonment, and betrayal. Once these dynamics are set in motion one can no longer give emotionally or be nurturing; the defensive stance takes over and one withdraws or shifts into anger and conflict.

This assumption upsets many people because it seems so pessimistic. However, when one begins to work through some of his or her basic losses with the original family, self becomes able to embrace the other's anxiety in a more positive, caring, way.

Assumption 5: Individuals cannot be intimate with their mates until they have worked through their unresolved attachment issues to their original families.

This assumption connects with the previous one. We search in our mates for the emotional experiences we felt were missing in our original families. We cannot become our own heroes until we have had appropriate heroes in our lives. Our first and most important heroes should have been our parents. It was their responsibility to make us feel safe, special, and nurtured. Individuals are not able to provide themselves with feelings of safety and specialness unless they have received them from their original family and/or caretakers. To be truly intimate with our partners we have to feel safe within ourselves. The ability to be intimate is developmental and commences around the mid-thirties. Prior to this we are learning how to be intimate. It is only after we have worked through our basic attachment issues with our original families that we can begin the process of becoming intimate.

If we have left our families reactively through anger and hurt, it will be difficult for us to feel safe in other relationships. Many people leave their families prematurely or because of some conflictual issue. These individuals then look for family substitutes. The hope is that the new relationships will make up for their previous losses. These individuals enter adult relationships based on what they need to receive to feel safe rather than in terms of what they can give. They are still working through their basic attachment issues. How we separate from our original family will determine how well we are able to connect in relationships as adults. When we have left home out of anger and hurt, it is necessary to rework these events as adults; once we are able to understand them differently, we can begin to embrace differences positively.

Assumption 6: There are basic developmental differences between men and women that can be misinterpreted as relationship problems.

Men and women are different in many ways. Besides the obvious, men and women respond to the world differently emotionally. Much research has been conducted on the different expectations parents and society at large have for how to raise boys and girls. These differences in early experiences lead to life-long differences. Boys relate to the world in ways quite different from girls. Boys are more active, goal-oriented, and competitive. Girls are more interested in caring, nurturing, and connections. These differences should not be viewed as good or bad but as different ways of approaching the world. When they become battlegrounds in marriages they undermine the integrity of the family. Differences do seem to attract, but over the long run have a tendency to undermine as well. Men seem to be slower in learning how to connect; women, on the other hand, are more aware of the importance of family relationships. When people come into marriage with a significant degree of unfinished business they have a tendency to misinterpret these differences as indications of lack of caring and attentiveness. As we begin to feel more solid about ourselves, we truly can become more curious about the other's differences. It is essential in healthy male/female relationships that each person understands that the differences he or she brings into the relationship can add to the connections. One begins by understanding that reactions to the partner's differences can be more about one's own feelings concerning self than about other.

Assumption 7: Relationship problems are more a reflection of unfinished business than expressions of a lack of commitment, caring, and love.

This assumption is directly connected with assumption 6. Although there are differences between males and females, the degrees to which these differences show themselves in relationships and in the family are based on the amount of unfinished business each person brings into the marriage. It is important to understand that individuals who come from families in which the parents were respectful and loving toward each other will be likely to use this as a model for their own marriages. However, those individuals who come from families in which the parents were abusive, rejecting and undermining each other, lack a positive model for how male/female relationships should be. The opposite-sex parent is an important one for learning how to be in a marriage. When fathers treat their daughters with respect, caring, and interest, their daughters are likely to see themselves as women entitled to being loved, respected, and taken seriously. Boys who felt safe and encouraged by their mothers have a tendency to become curious and interested in how their wives function as women individually and in the world. When parents have been abusive or acted inappropriately toward their children, the tendency is for those children, when they grow up, either to position themselves in similar ways with their mates or to need excessive emotional closeness or distance from their mates to feel emotionally safe.

Assumption 8: The ability to be intimate in marriage is developmental and will be influenced by people's ages at the time of marriage.

Most people believe that when they marry they are able to form intimate relationships. However, true intimacy appears more often to occur in our late thirties and forties. People in their twenties are usually working through fundamental attachment issues. Basically, during the first thirty years of our lives we are in training to be intimate. When people marry in their twenties, what they need from each other is quite different from what they need in their thirties, forties, and fifties. One of the dynamics I have discovered in my clinical practice is that as soon as a couple gets married they begin an elaborate process of "mythology-making" about each other. If we take into consideration the first seven assumptions, it should become obvious that there is the potential for tremendous misunderstanding between couples. What they feel is going on in their relationship may differ dramatically from what is actually happening. As soon as a partner in a relationship begins to behave in ways that seem hurtful or unloving, the other partner develops some explanation about what is wrong with him or her. The story that self constructs about his or her partner is "mythology-making." By the time a couple begins therapy, they have developed an elaborate mythology about each other. People use this mythology to justify maintaining safe emotional distance. It is difficult to be intimate with someone when you have an elaborate mythology about the person that prevents you from being curious and open to learning about him or her.

To be intimate in a marriage, one has to be able to embrace the partner's differences. When a partner behaves in an unusual way, a person who is solid will become curious about that way to understand it better. However, when anxiety kicks in, self begins to bring in his or her mythology about the partner and to use that mythology to explain what is going on. This leads to a general reactive stance, and that reactivity contributes to emotional distancing. Over time many partners become so distant from each other that they cease to have a relationship.

2 ══════════════

Framework for Understanding Relationship Behavior

Why Do We Form Relationships?

Many people believe that our society is organized mainly for couples. In restaurants and in many social activities, the general assumption is that you have a partner. Many single people tell me how awkward it is to ask for a table for one or go to an event alone and be looked at as if something isn't quite right, as if there is a missing part. We seem to think in twos and assume that unless you have a partner, something is wrong. Even though there is societal pressure to form a relationship, I am not certain this is the primary reason why we form intimate relationships. It might be inconvenient not having a partner, or we might feel strange going to a restaurant alone; however, I think there is a deeper need to pair off.

Many people define themselves by the type of people with whom they are involved. Our social network significantly influences how we see ourselves in the world. First, we get a sense of identity from our primary association with the family. From the beginning of life we learn about ourselves in interaction with others. We learn how to relate through a subtle set of experiences beginning with our primary caretakers. How our family conducts their business of life teaches us how to be not only socially but also emotionally in the world. Parent/child interaction is fundamental to our learning about ourselves in the world. Our relationships with each of our parents and our siblings are all profound guides for how we will relate to our peers and later on, in our most intimate relationships. Observing how our parents interact with each other, how they express emotion, convey important ideas, show affection toward each other, solve problems, and so on are all powerful messages about how one should be in the world. Children who grow up in families in which they do not have an opportunity to observe siblings or parents interacting, or do not have solid parental role models, express difficulty in knowing how to behave in adult relationships. Some of us have to learn later in life how to relate as mature adults both with the opposite sex and in same-sex relationships.

As we grow up, we begin to select certain people with whom to relate. In school we pair off with our special friend; we begin to discriminate regarding whom we want to be with and whom we want to avoid. We gravitate to certain people and feel uncomfortable with others. It is not accidental whom we bring into our world. There is a complicated selection process that goes on in all of us. Most of us do not ask ourselves the questions "Why am I attracted to this person and want to avoid that person? What makes this person seem desirable and the other person boring? Why do I value this relationship and feel it is worthy of me, while I see another relationship as not worthy of me and, in fact, am embarrassed if I associate with this type of person?" These are important questions we should ask ourselves, because almost from the beginning of forming peer relationships we are testing our concept of self in the world in our relationships with others.

Our early experiences with peer relationships lay the groundwork for future adult relationships and have a powerful influence on whom we form our most intimate relationships with. We can learn a lot about ourselves by understanding whom we bring into and exclude from our world. What we have not worked out emotionally is reflected in the types of people with whom we are comfortable and with whom we associate. The characteristics we most admire about others say something about what we feel we most lack.

Feeling Special

One of the most compelling reasons for forming a relationship is to be made to feel special. Most of us want to be admired, liked, and needed, and we cherish and value the relationships that convey those feelings to us. When people are asked what they need from the other to make the relationship work, they will usually describe what they did not get enough of from their own family and/or those experiences in their own family they want to replicate in their current relationship. The basic principle of relationship formation is that we are attracted to people who can give us and/or complete in us what we have not gotten from our own family experience. Two major dynamics get played out in most relationships. First, one enters a relationship to make up for one's losses in one's primary family; secondly, one tries to replicate the experiences from one's primary family.

The first dynamic is particularly powerful, that is, looking for a relationship to make one feel whole and right in the world. These relationships are formed out of mutual need—what one can give the other to make the other feel safe and secure in the world. There is not a sense of what one can give but what one needs. These relationships are reactive and quickly become negative and disappointing to the couple. The degree to which a person feels unloved and/or unlovable based on his or her family of origin will influence the degree of neediness brought into new relationships.

The second dynamic, that is, trying to replicate the experiences from one's own family, has its own difficulties. These difficulties are highlighted when the other is not able to behave in the way that fulfills one's expectations. If one comes out of a family of origin experience feeling special and cared for in a certain way and has a mate who doesn't act that way, then disappointment and disillusionment set in. We should not underestimate the importance of forming relationships as a way to feel special. One of the reasons we exclude a whole range of people as potential partners is that they seem too different, too weird, too unfeeling or uncaring, or are unavailable to us. Many times the people we actually bring in as potential partners offer us the least of what we need. The central question of what we need from the other to make self feel okay is of prominant importance in understanding relationship formation and the eventual disenchantment that can develop in a relationship.

Intimacy

The second major reason we form relationships is to satisfy the emotional need to be intimate. Intimacy is partly feeling special and partly knowing that with at least one other person we can share a part of ourselves in safety. Very few therapy texts define intimacy, even though in most the word is used, and it is seen as a major dynamic in all relationships. It is important to understand what an intimate relationship is, how it shows itself, and how men and women differ developmentally in their ability to be intimate.

First, what is meant by intimacy? Lerner (1989) says, "an intimate relationship is one in which neither party silences, sacrifices or betrays the self and each party expresses strength and vulnerability, weakness and competence in a balanced way" (p. 3). Intimacy should be viewed developmentally. At different points in our life intimacy takes on different forms. Attachment is sometimes mistaken for intimacy but in fact there is a difference between attachment and intimacy. As children we are more attached to than intimate with our parents. The attachment is developmentally appropriate. Intimacy should occur between two adults who are developmentally at or about the same level. In a family children need to be taken care of, protected, and helped to grow and mature by their parents. It is to some degree inappropriate for parents to be intimate with their children by sharing certain thoughts, fears, concerns, and worries. Developmentally, children are not able to hear their parents' anxieties, fears, and worries separately from their own need to be taken care of, protected, and helped to move beyond family attachment.

The ability to be intimate with another adult is partially determined by how well we have worked through our original attachment–separation issues with our parents. Bowlby's early work on attachment and separation (1969) is classic in its description of how important it is for the child not to suffer undue separation anxieties or experience extreme attachment and dependency on the parent. Bowlby's research showed that the child's ability to grow and develop over time is connected with the separation and attachment issues the child has worked through with his or her own parents.

Once we leave our family of origin, the type of intimacy we need changes. In our twenties our need to form relationships are quite different from how we use and need relationships in our thirties, forties, fifties, and later in life. Achieving true intimacy is a midlife task that begins to develop in the late thirties. The first thirty years of life constitute a training ground for the ability to be truly intimate with another.

To be intimate one has to let go of outcome, that is, needing other to be different to make it safe for self to talk about self to other. Malone and Malone (1987) say, "But to love is to be alone, at least initially and momentarily, since it is unilateral and not dependent on response from the loved one" (pp. 10–11). Many people will say that they can be intimate, but are prevented by others' behavior. They believe they need other to be different before self can be a certain way. One of the lessons many have learned from their original family is that it is unsafe to talk about certain subjects or that certain behaviors will result in criticism or lack of love. We become cautious about how we present ourselves and which part of ourselves we show. We have to go through many experiences in life before we can feel safe inside ourselves without outside validation.

Developmentally, before we can let go of needing people to validate us we have to be validated by others. One of the primary jobs of family is to validate the child's basic sense of being worthwhile and loved. That is the foundation of self that the child takes into the world. If the child leaves the family feeling shaky and unloved, it is very hard for that person to risk sharing certain parts of himself or herself, for fear of being invalidated and undermined emotionally. These individuals are very cautious in relationships and preoccupied with judgment, concerns of acceptance, and worries about being good enough. They look for validation in relationships and continually experience the opposite. This type of person has tremendous difficulties in being intimate in the way I have defined. They have to be certain of the outcome before they can risk talking about those parts of themselves they feel vulnerable about. The more solid we feel about ourselves the less concern we have about revealing our vulnerable side.

Developmental Differences between Men and Women

Developmentally there are some differences between how men and women enter relationships. Much has been written about the differences between men and women, how they position themselves in families, and their expectations for family life. Carter and McGoldrick's 1988 text on the changing family life cycle highlights some of the main differences between men and women and how these differences interfere with family life. However, not much has been written about how men and women differ developmentally in how they seek intimacy. We know that boys and girls have different experiences in the family. Boys are encouraged to be more aggressive, to use themselves physically differently, to be more competitive and to avoid expressing their feelings. Girls are encouraged to express their feelings, to show their vulnerability and to be nurturing. Research has indicated that girls are more verbal at an earlier age than boys, while boys are more active (Carter and McGoldrick 1988). These differences seem to show themselves throughout the life cycle and have somewhat serious implications for how men and women relate to each other as couples and as parents. A basic assumption of this text is that many relationship problems are not based on lack of love, caring, or commitment but on the misinterpretation of the differences that men and women bring into a relationship. How we define these differences and the meaning we give them seem to create greater obstacles to couples' feeling intimate with each other than the actual differences themselves.

An example of the impact of these differences was illustrated in the work of the eminent family therapist, Dr. Carl Whitaker, with a farm family. This family was comprised of middle-aged parents and four young adult children, three of them daughters. The children complained that their father was involved with his farm but really did not seem to be involved with them. They complained bitterly that they seldom felt his love and caring for them. The wife confirmed these feelings as well. She said that the husband was much more involved with his cows and their condition than he was with her. As the sessions went on, it became clear that the way that the husband showed caring was being misinterpreted by the rest of the family. True, he was very involved with his farm, but he was trying to keep the farm going as a way to take care of his family.

As the therapy concluded there was a very moving session

in which the father talked about building a special summer home for his family. The session ended with the father saying, "I guess I have not been a very good father or husband. I have not been able to meet the needs of my children and wife. However, the only way I know how to show how much I care for them is by building this summer home. I hope when they are in this home they will feel the love and caring that I have for them. I wish I could do it a different way." This is a powerful example of how some men show caring—not by talking about it to any great extent, but by taking care of things. Unfortunately, many family members do not have the opportunity to hear their fathers or husbands express as clearly as this man the love and caring that was behind his work.

Men show caring and feel important, especially in young adulthood, by performing. Work accomplishment, material possessions, business successes, and career improvements indicate to many men that they are successful in the world and are taking care of their families. Women, on the other hand, see relationships as important indicators of one's connection and meaning in the world. Having family, being connected to others, taking care of things, and being available are all important indicators to women that they have meaningful involvements in the world. Both sets of behaviors are important and should complement each other. Unfortunately, for some couples these differences are battlegrounds. Men may feel that no matter what they do, it is not enough; women may feel unappreciated and diminished by their men. The extremity of these positions is connected with one's own family of origin experiences. The man who has an excessive need to prove himself or the woman who worries excessively about being good enough are acting out losses and messages they experienced in their own families. These differences interfere with couples connecting intimately. Each person in the relationship feels misunderstood. These developmental differences then get acted out around specific issues in the couple's relationship and have a profound impact on how the family operates as a unit. These differences will affect the bonding between the husband and wife. They can undermine family solidarity and affect how well each parent connects with the needs of the children and each other.

Fear of Being Alone

People also form relationships because they fear being alone. This very powerful dynamic keeps people in relationships that are not emotionally satisfying. Many people who come out of their family of origin feeling unloved and unwanted seek out relationships that will help them feel loved, desired, and safe. However, since they feel basically unlovable, they may read into the relationship the opposite of what is actually happening. They often feel terrified that they are unloved, and will work even harder to gain their partner's love. There are many perverse ways in which a person deals with feeling unlovable in a relationship. One is by getting angry and defensive and rejecting the partner as a way of protecting those feelings inside self. Another is by being overly accommodating and available, even when the partner is abusive, rejecting, and cruel. It is confusing to the outside observer why some people stay in relationships that are obviously not working and are basically destructive. It is helpful to understand that people who come out of their families with serious questions about their self-worth seek out relationships that reinforce their doubts. They have a great deal of difficulty leaving a relationship even when they know the relationship is not right for them. The fear of being alone is far more terrifying than anything happening in the relationship. These individuals are not able to leave the relationship until they become involved in another relationship. If they have children, they may become over-involved in the lives of their children to substitute this connection for the lack in their adult relationship, thus stabilizing their relationship with their mate.

How Do We Learn to Be a Couple?

What models do people bring into their adult relationships from their past that serve as a behavioral guide? Where have we learned how to be a partner? What are the concepts we bring into our adult relationships that have been useful guides in the past? As I pointed out earlier, the training ground for adult relationships is the early experience of the parent/child interaction. How our mother and father related to us teaches us about ourselves. We learn how to take care of the other by how we've been taken care of.

We also learn how to develop and maintain relationships by observing our parents' relationship with each other. It is common to hear people say that their relationship is going to be totally different from their parents'. Several clients have told me they never observed their parents being affectionate with each other or showing any interest in each other's experiences. They used these negative lessons to guide them in their own relationships. Attempting to do things differently, they force themselves to be more affectionate. They try to be more curious about their partner and involve their partner more in their own activities. Others describe their parents' relationship as ideal and try to emulate it in their own lives. One couple entered therapy because they were worried that their relationship was not working. The husband revealed he had never seen his mother and father fight. In all the years he lived at home, his parents always seemed to agree and get along. In his marriage his wife seemed very unhappy and continually brought up things that were not working. The wife indicated that in her family her parents argued often in front of the kids, and one of the things she learned was that a fight can make things better. Her raising issues with her husband was her way of working things through. It was of great concern to her that her husband was so unhappy when she raised areas that she felt needed improvement. For his part, the husband said that the most powerful lesson he took from his family was that it was important to agree. Having disagreements meant there was something terribly wrong. This couple had never really talked about or been aware of the different lessons they brought into the marriage. As a result, the husband interpreted his wife's insistence on talking about problems as not caring and being unhappy in the relationship. The wife interpreted the husband's lack of willingness to talk as an indication of his lack of caring and commitment.

The models we have been exposed to in our families serve as blinders to developing alternative ways of dealing with issues. It is not possible to come out of family without a model for how the job of living should be done. We take this model as a given, and we respond to problems and concerns with the model in mind. It is not something we express clearly to our mate. When our mate responds in ways different from ours, we rarely become curious about why there is this difference in attitude, perception, or understanding. Rather, most of us feel misunderstood, confused, or criticized, and we seek to protect ourselves from these feelings by withdrawing from the relationship and/or getting angry and defensive.

Sibling Relationships

Sibling relationships also serve as training grounds for learning how to function in relationships. Many issues get worked out in sibling relationships—how to share, how to deal with conflict, how to work out differences, how to be in control and/or be controlled, and how to fight. In the past few years several studies have been conducted on the impact of sibling relationships on personality development (see Bank and Kahn 1982, Richardson 1984, and Toman 1969). For example, being the older brother of sisters helps one understand girls and how to be a caretaker to girls. Being the oldest in the family trains one in how to take on responsibility and be in control. On the other hand, being the last born in the family provides one with the sense that there is someone there to help out and take control or responsibility. If we want to understand fully the intricacies of relationships between husbands and wives and parents and children, it is essential that we learn the power of sibling relationships. So much of how we see ourselves in the world is determined by the way our parents and siblings have related to us on the basis of our ordinal position in the family. Only children are deprived of this experience, which has a profound impact on how they conduct their family life when they marry and have children.

I worked with a family in which the father was an only child whose parents were in their late thirties when he was born. He grew up in a family in which there was little activity. Daily life was quiet and uneventful. He talked about being able to go into the bathroom and read for hours without being interrupted. This man married a woman who was the oldest of three siblings. Her family experience was quite different. She came from a family in which there was a lot of activity, a fair amount of conflict, and a lot of noise. This couple had five children—four girls and a boy. When the father came home from work he would be overwhelmed by the activity and the noise. The children would be fighting about using the bathroom, when to have dinner, what to watch on TV, and so on. The constant noise was irritating to him, he constantly criticized his wife for not keeping the kids quiet, and he would get angry at his children for having so much conflict. When this couple came to see me, the husband described his children as having severe sibling problems. He further indicated he was having a lot of conflict with his wife about how to run the family. When I saw the entire family together it was clear that the relationships among the siblings were quite normal. The children, for their part, did not understand why their father was so critical of and angry with them. When they heard him tell about how he experienced his own family, they began to appreciate what made large-family life so unpleasant for him. This family's experience illustrates how easily parents who try to replicate their own family experiences can misinterpret the reactions and behaviors the other puts out to make the family work.

Role of the Media

Another training ground for learning how to be a couple is the mass media — TV, radio, movies, literature. The role models in the mass media can be an aid or a hindrance to learning how to be a functional couple and a balanced family. Many of the TV shows that depict family life are quite unrealistic. They show middle- to upper-middle-class families getting along with minimal conflict, the parents generally being in agreement, the siblings with minor irritations, being supportive of each other. The sitcoms of family life in the 1980s show both parents working, all their children going to school, everything in balance. In reality, schedules in dual-career families are difficult to balance: The adults' time schedules, the children's school schedules, and the various activities in which family members are involved besides work and school generally conflict with each other. How family members deal with these differences and competing demands makes family life seem unworkable at times. There are very few models depicted in the movies or on TV that help families realistically balance these competing agendas. When families compare their lives with what they see in the media they often feel as if they have failed.

Education and/or Religious Factors

Another source of learning for how to be a couple and a family is education and religious training. Schools are taking increasing responsibility for offering high-school courses on family life education. Regrettably, many of these models communicate middle-class values of the predominant culture and support a middle-class approach to life. It is unwise to communicate only one model of family life. We have to help people understand that there is a wide range of approaches to getting the job of family life accomplished. Many times a marriage brings together two different cultures and classes. How to connect with and support these differences is the challenge. Education and religious training that favor one approach to family life can undermine the appreciation of these differences.

How Do Developmental Differences Affect Relationship Dynamics?

A number of important studies have been conducted on family and individual development (see Carter and McGoldrick 1988, Erikson 1964, and Levinson 1978). I do not intend to present an in-depth overview of the developmental life cycle in this text; however, it is important to emphasize some of the essential features of how individual development affects the choice of relationships, how we position ourselves in relationships, the type of family we structure, and especially the unfinished business we bring from our family of origin to our family of procreation. For purposes of this text I will present a framework for understanding the developmental influences that significantly shape one's concept of self. The concept of self that one develops from birth has a significant impact on what we project into our adult relationships. This projection process is of vital importance to understanding many of the relationship problems that people complain about when they enter therapy. It is a basic principle that what we have not worked through in our original family will have a profound influence on whom we choose for our primary partner and our basic expectations of what we need from that partner to feel satisfied and safe in that relationship. The degree of emotional deprivation one has experienced in one's family of origin will affect one's ability to separate himself or herself from the reactions and neediness of another.

From Birth to 2 Years

The foundation of personality is laid during the first two years of life. We know now that in these first two years the child is not able to separate out who he or she is from his or her caretakers and the general environment. If the caretakers are rejecting, abusive, and/or inconsistent in their nurturing, the child experiences these behaviors as personal assaults on his or her well-being. The child incorporates messages of general neglect as statements about his or her basic sense of worth. During this period the child is generally fused with his or her environment. The child also feels somewhat omnipotent since he or she can make something happen by crying or fussing. If the child cries loud and long enough, someone will come to hold, change, and/or feed him or her. The child is enraged when this crying and fussing do not bring the necessary results. This rage will in turn increase the crying and fussing; eventually, if there is no positive response, the child begins to withdraw and becomes apathetic. In cases of extreme deprivation the child stops responding to the environment and withdraws inward.

Much of what we learn about ourselves in the first two years of life is unconscious. Many of our basic feelings about ourselves, our general sense of well-being, and comfort within our bodies is set in motion by how well our fundamental physical and emotional needs were met during our first two years. A variable that complicates how well caretakers meet these needs during this period is the child's temperamental style. Temperamental research (Thomas 1968, Thomas and Chess 1977) demonstrates the importance of temperament on the development of the child's personality. Temperamental differences run right through the developmental experiences of a child. The degree of comfort the caretakers have with the child's unique temperamental style will affect the child's development. We know that some children are active, others passive; some are regular in their routines, others are somewhat inconsistent. The parent who is able to adjust to the child's style will greatly enhance the child's feeling of comfort within his or her body and help the child connect with the environment in a safe and comfortable fashion.

The first two years of life set into motion a general way of being in the world. Children who have been deprived, abused, or neglected tend to be tentative personalities who overreact or underreact to environmental stress and demand. Children who have been physically or emotionally abused in their families are restricted in the expression of their needs. They generally respond with less spontaneity and freedom than children whose needs have been consistently met. In contrast, caretakers who are able to meet the emotional and physical needs of their children are able to create an environment in which the child feels safe in moving away from them and exploring the environment.

2 to 5 Years

During the period from age 2 to 5, the child begins to have a more powerful impact on his or her environment. The child is now ambulatory, verbal, and able to take care of many of his or her physical needs. The child can feed and dress himself or herself and fetch things that are needed. He or she learns to say "No" or "I want to do it myself" and begins to act out self-ambivalence actively in the environment. This basic ambivalence is about "I want to be taken care of, yet I want to do it myself!"

During this phase the child moves simultaneously toward and away from the caretaker. Depending on how comfortable the child is within himself or herself and the degree to which the child's emotional and physical needs have been met, the child will begin to move purposefully away from the caretakers into the wider environment. In general, the child becomes more creative about self-fulfillment of needs. Many parents express sadness during this period because they recognize that the child is starting to move away from them. Most parents want to encourage their children to be autonomous yet would like to delay that process and enjoy their dependency a while longer.

The degree of the parents' ambivalence will influence how successful the child will be in moving into the next stage. Erikson (1964) describes this period as the "trust versus mistrust" stage (p. 247). Before the child can trust the environment, he or she must be able to trust himself or herself; the child who is able to develop that sense of confidence, has had parents who have made themselves available to the child in a consistent, loving, nurturing way. Thus, the child's ability to experiment with his or her own confidence in the 2- to 5-year age period is in part determined by how well his or her needs were met during the first two years of life.

It is interesting that a large number of parents present their children to child-guidance clinics during this period. In fact, the two major periods during which parents present their children as "problem children" are (1) the adolescent years, 11 through 19, and (2) the 2- to 5-year period. Parents who present their children to therapists during the 2- to 5-year period generally complain that the child is a behavioral problem, doesn't fit into the family routine, and is uncooperative. Sometimes these complaints are connected with the child's temperamental style, which does not fit comfortably with that of the parents. If there are issues in the parents' own lives that the child's impending autonomy stirs up or reactivates, those issues often get projected onto the child as the problem. How well the parents have sorted out their own issues with their original families will influence their ability to allow the child to find his or her own place in the world without their needing to superimpose their own agendas on the child.

Each child's entry into the family will affect the parents' feelings and reactions to their other children. If the firstborn is an easygoing child who temperamentally fits with the parents' style and is generally able to accommodate to the family's routine, the parents expect that all the other children will be like this. If the second child is not as easy and/or temperamentally suited, that child is likely to be the one who becomes identified as the problem in the family. Siblings have a major impact on how the parents deal with the behavioral style of each child. To understand why a particular child during the 2- to 5-year period is seen as difficult, one needs to understand how the older children were experienced by their parents.

5- to 11-Year-Old Stage

This period is generally a calm one within the family. Considerable time now is spent outside the home. The child is involved in preschool, kindergarten, and then elementary school. If both parents are working, they have minimal contact with their child during the day. It is not unusual for the children and their parents to have just an hour or two together in the evening. Many parents who work full time leave work at about six o'clock, pick up their child from day care or after-school care, have dinner, and see their child briefly before the child goes to bed. The amount of time the parents spend with their children during the evening is minimal. It is important to ask parents how the evening hours are spent. How much time do family members spend together? One major difficulty during this period is that the children are trying to adjust to peer relationships and school pressures. The parents are trying to balance their own career and work responsibilities with family responsibilities. This is a time of heightened stress and potential conflict within the family.

Developmentally, the child in this age group is expending a great deal more energy trying to master extrafamilial expectations. The family is needed more as a cushion and positive support for dealing with the demands and expectations of school, peers, and so forth. Again, the degree to which the parents were able to meet the dependency needs of the child during the first two years of life and the autonomy needs during the next three years will influence how comfortable the child will be in using the family as a positive support system to test new behaviors in the school and community.

11- to 19-Year-Old Stage

This developmental period is probably the most difficult one that families experience. The needs of the parents, who are becoming more realistic about the direction their lives have taken, and the increasing autonomy needs of the teenage child, put child and parents on a collision course. The parents commonly wish to have more family connection and solidarity. They tend to want their child to behave in ways that validate their efforts to be good parents. On the other hand, the child has an increasing need to react against family restrictions, expectations, and values. Adolescents need to experiment with their own sense of identity.

The success with which the parents have been able to meet the child's dependency needs and reinforce his or her basic sense of worth will determine to a great degree the child's ability to test his or her sense of identity without having to go to extremes. When there has been a breakdown of boundaries between parent and child—the parent has demanded too much emotionally, or the parent has withdrawn from and rejected the child because of the child's differentness—the child will express separateness from the parent by exhibiting extreme behaviors of anger, rebellion, and rejection. However, to some degree, most children have to display these behaviors. They need to define themselves in reaction to authority figures. How well the parents respond to this active rebellion by their teenagers determines the extent, duration, and intensity of the child's rebellion. The child needs to experience the parents as being more powerful, less reactive, and more solid in their belief system than the child feels or acts. As the child uses the parents as a sounding board to discover his or her own basic differentness, and as the parents respond with caring, consistency, and general understanding of what the child is going through, the child will begin to make peace with his or her internal conflicts.

This is a crucial period for parents and children. The

parents have to deal with a wide range of losses in their own lives. Their own parents may be in poor health or have recently died. The parents' careers may be winding down, and some of life's dreams given up. The relationship between husband and wife, which may have taken second place to parental responsibilities, has to be renegotiated. These major changes for the parents may be seen either as opportunities to work on self or as major losses. Similarly, the teenager's attempt to move away from the family can either remind the parents of yet another loss or can be seen as an opportunity to rethink the relationship between parent and child. The parents' ability to deal with the child's emerging independence while dealing with their own changes and losses strongly influences the degree of unfinished business the child will take from the family of origin into adult relationships. It is important to know how adults left home. Was it in rebellion, out of anger, or feeling rejected? Were they able to say good-bye to family members knowing their leaving was supported? The more cut off the adolescent feels from his family the more difficulty he or she will have in forming adult relationships after leaving home.

19- to 29-Year-Old Period

During the 19- to 29-year-old stage most young adults have left home and started their own lives somewhat separate from attachments to their family of origin. Young adults may find many different ways to leave home. As mentioned earlier, some leave out of rebellion and anger, others leave to go to school and seek a career. Others form a relationship with the opposite sex and begin to live together or get married as a way to leave home. The major developmental task for the young adult during this period is to begin to feel confident as a self and to move into more intimate adult relationships. During this stage the ability to be intimate increases.

During the earlier developmental stages we relate through play, activity and competition, and generally test skills against those of others. Later, as we develop and feel more solid within ourselves, we begin to feel safe in sharing our feelings, worries, anxieties, and dreams with others. Before we can risk this sort of self-revelation, we have to have worked through our feelings of general competence within the world. This general sense of competence is achieved through experimenting with our abilities through work, play, and the forming of relationships.

Young adults in this age group are concerned with outcome. They tend to base their sense of self-worth on outside measures. How they feel about themselves is disproportionately determined by what they do, how they perform, the feedback they get from others, and their general successes in work and play. It is difficult to know self from inside until self has been validated from the outside. It is usually not until our thirties, that we are able to begin to let go of needing others to tell us how solid we are. During the 19- to 29-year-old period our major preoccupation is in proving our adequacy through our performance. Job, career successes, possessions, relationships, and general approval from others all indicate how solid and how successful we are in the world. We have to go through these experiences before we can begin to let go of needing external measures to prove self-worth.

Our success in connecting in our most important familial relationship provides the basic emotional foundation for being experimental, spontaneous, and creative in the world. The more deprived, neglected, and rejected we felt in our family, the greater will be our need to prove ourselves in the world, and the less satisfied we will feel with our accomplishments.

This period can be a confusing one. Many young adults acquired from their families the basic feeling of safety within themselves to be experimental in the world; however, they still need to succeed in the world to put to rest the question "Can I manage successfully?" But for some, who did not receive enough emotional support from their families, no amount of accomplishment will put to rest their feelings of inadequacy.

The 19- to 29-year-old age group does not place a high priority on connection with family of origin. The young adult needs to know that his or her family is managing satisfactorily and that he or she is free to explore and experiment with the world. The need is not to reconnect with the family in this period but to find a place in the world. The parents, on the other hand, have to let go of needing the adult child to be more involved in their world. The child's successes and gains or failures and losses should not be seen as reflections of the parents' successes or failures but rather as separate issues for the adult child to resolve as the child struggles for personal accomplishments.

29- to 39-Year-Old Period

The 29- to 39-year-old period is dominated by a preoccupation with work and nuclear family matters. Most adults are married before or during this period and their nuclear families are taking shape. Their careers become dominant influences on their decision-making processes. This group tries to actualize its dreams about family and work. For many it is the most productive period of their lives. As these adults begin to move out of their thirties, the reality of what the future will hold becomes more apparent. The needs of their young children and the demands of their career may begin to conflict. In addition, their parents are aging and concerns about their health and relationships with them may be heightened.

In the 1980s significant changes occurred in people's decision making with respect to getting married, having children, and sacrificing for career. Generally people married later, had children later, and became less willing to uproot family for a career. As well, it was common for both partners to work. A significant number of partners were married for the second time. As these adults move into their forties they tend to lower their expectations and attempt to make peace with the fact that their dreams will not be fulfilled as hoped. Reconnecting with their families of origin is one way in which they try to achieve this peace.

39- to 49-Year-Old Period

This time is a major transitional period. Many of us have lost one or both of our parents; if not, our parents may be of increasing concern to us. We face a midlife transition in our careers and our families. Our children are moving away, our careers are winding down and we have to find some new meaning to stay enthusiastic about our future. This period can be exciting and challenging, or frightening and overwhelming. How solid one feels about oneself, how well one has made peace with one's past with a minimum of regrets will determine whether this midlife period is seen as a time of opportunity or a period of loss. During this time we have to renegotiate our relationship with our spouse. No longer is the connection focused primarily on parental concerns. Levinson (1978) expresses it well when he says:

> The mid-life transition is a bridge between early adulthood and middle adulthood. As in all transitions, a man must come to terms with the past and prepare for the future. Three major tasks must be worked on. One task is to terminate the era of early adulthood. He has to review his life in this era and re-appraise what he has done with it. A second task is to take the first steps toward the initiation of middle adulthood. Although he is not yet ready to start building a new life structure, he can begin to modify the negative elements of the present structure and to test new choices. A third task is to deal with the polarities that are sources of deep division in his life. [pp. 191–192]

In many ways these tasks are faced by women as well. Their childbearing years are over and their children are moving away from home. Their role as mother and caretaker is less central. This change is significant for women who have worked outside the home as well as for women who have remained at home. Their vision of what they want as a woman and a partner, rather than as a mother and caretaker, has to be reexamined.

The divorce rate during this period is quite high. Many couples postpone focusing on relationship needs in preference to dealing with parental concerns. Many families are out of balance, having put most of their energies into parenting issues without balancing those issues with spouse concerns. Husbands and wives have to rediscover each other during this phase. Many may feel it is too late. How well they dealt with their differences around childcare concerns will influence how well they will be able to rediscover each other separate from their parenting roles.

49- to 65-Year-Old Period

The period from 49 to 65 years of age is dominated by the need to evaluate one's life choices. A fair number of people choose to start a second career or a second family. Some become depressed and dysfunctional. Others see this time as an opportunity to consolidate gains, feel satisfied with accomplishments, and develop more depth in life activities. The direction a person takes during this period is important. Those who give up in despair have not been able to achieve a sense of satisfaction with their sense of self. No matter what they did or how it turned out, the feeling remained that "Something is wrong," "I'm not good enough," or "In some way life has defeated me." These people, in their fifties and early sixties may still be questioning their life choices, evaluating their life in terms of negative feelings, still trying to prove to their parents that they were good enough and lovable enough, not being able to feel satisfied within themselves and still needing others to prove that they are adequate.

During this period a number of men seek out younger women to start a second family. The dynamic behind this is unclear. We need a lot more research to understand what motivates men to start over again. Some of the men I have interviewed in their late forties or early fifties say they are starting a second family because they have learned much from what they were not able to do earlier in their lives, and they want a second chance. These men also say they were not able to stay connected with their first wives because the wives really did not want them involved in the ways that they now wish to be involved. Some men say they now need to feel intimately connected in a relationship. They want from their mate an emotional connection that earlier in their lives they did not value or feel they needed. On the other hand, the wives in their forties and fifties feel their husbands were not there for them. The cooperation, support, and connection they so desperately wanted but never received from their husbands got diverted from the relationship to children, friends, and career. Now that their husbands are in their fifties and are ready for that type of intimacy and connection, the wives no longer feel a connection to their husbands and have shut their hearts and minds to that relationship. Both people over the course of their adult years have learned a lot about themselves and have worked through a number of different issues but have not been able to communicate and connect on these changes with each other. It is almost as if each has to go into a new relationship to experience that part of themselves.

The fifties and sixties should be a period of integration, of making peace with one's history, and of developing new dreams and challenges. It is a time to say good-bye to one's parents and to make peace with the memory of other family members who have died. The rethinking of what family means is a crucial task of this period. We become grandparents and parentless, and for some of us a spouse has died or left us. How we integrate these losses and use them to connect more deeply in the world is the ultimate challenge.

65 and Beyond

More of us are now living longer than ever before, well into our eighties and even nineties. This phenomenon is relatively new. We do not know too much about successful aging. Traditionally, the general belief was that one had to let go of life to age successfully. Recently, this belief has been challenged. Erikson's most recent book, *Vital Involvement in Old Age*, describes his research into the aging process. Erikson and his colleagues studied the older population to discern their attitudes about the last part of their lives. They discovered that living remains a vital, stimulating, challenging process. Most older adults are not happy with letting go of life. They try to stay involved in meaningful and challenging ways to the end. How life begins determines to some extent how it ends. If our primary caretakers took care of us in the beginning, then we learned how to care for ourselves throughout life and were better able to give back to life what we had received. To quote Erikson and colleagues (1986):

> In old age, time for solitary reviewing of the past is essential to reconciling the psycho-social tensions of a lifetime.

> Part of the old-age process, of reviewing the sense of oneself across the life cycle involves a coming to terms with perceived mistakes, failures, and omissions—with chances missed and opportunities not taken. Now the unescapable fact of life clearly indicates that there will not be time to return to the roads not taken which may all along have remained a part of an underlying sense of identity. Many of our aged informants speak wistfully of aspects of deferred or bypassed roles. They endeavour to integrate, rather than resolutely deny, the mixed feelings that inevitably result from com-

paring the life actually lived with the life anticipated in youthful fantasy and imagined, over decades, as waiting to be claimed at the next opportunity. [p. 141]

There is a general assumption that people entering their late seventies and eighties are experiencing various infirmities and chronic illnesses. This assumption is being questioned. However, even when it is true it does not take away from the fact that there are still many tasks left for the aged during this period.

The aged have an important opportunity to convey to the next generation the wisdom of life. The aged person in the family becomes the senior statesperson, the elder. This person has important stories to tell about the present family and the past generations. It is tremendously helpful for the therapist when working with a family to involve its senior members and to encourage them to tell their stories. This provides an opportunity for an elder to be a storyteller and impart important lessons to the younger generation, which they in turn can use as guides for living. It is a treasure for our young people to have stories. The more stories they have about their history, the more solid their foundation of themselves and their sense of family will be.

The aged person has had to integrate developmental issues successfully throughout the life cycle. One of life's true challenges is how to use one's history to learn about self in the world. The aged person has much to teach the children and grandchildren in this area. Their stories truly become guides for future generations.

Major Concepts for Understanding Relationship Behaviors

This section provides a working definition of a number of concepts that underpin the dynamics in relationships. The developmental framework that has been presented is an essential part of the foundation required to understand what happens in relationships. In addition, a number of important concepts must be defined and understood to complete the theoretical framework for understanding relationship behavior. A number of these concepts have been defined in the author's texts, *Techniques of Family Therapy* and *Multigenerational Family Therapy*. This section reviews some of the more important aspects of these concepts and presents some new ones. However, it may be helpful to the reader to refer to the other texts for a more exhaustive discussion of the family as a structural, functional, and developmental unit.

The Family as an Emotional System

The family is greater than the sum of its parts. It is not possible to understand how the family functions by simply learning about its individual members. The family as a whole acts in unique ways. One has to observe the whole family to appreciate the complex way it functions as a system. It is helpful to understand that the family is comprised of a number of subsystems. In a nuclear two-generational family there are a minimum of four subsystems: (1) parent/child relationship; (2) husband/wife relationship; (3) sibling relationships; and (4) the individual member in his or her own right. When these subsystems are in balance, they are mutually supportive and fulfill both family and individual goals. However, the family is more than a two-generational system. The role the extended family plays in the nuclear family is also important to our understanding of the family. From a community perspective the family should be seen as the middle system that meets individual needs and expectations on the one hand, and societal demands on the other. Usually the most powerful subsystem within the family is the parental unit. The parental unit brings into the family many past experiences that get played out in how the family is organized structurally, functionally, and developmentally.

The family is a multigenerational emotional system. The

parents bring in from their own families important lessons that they try to put into operation in running their own family. A family is comprised of a minimum of three family influences: the husband's family of origin, the wife's family of origin, and the synthesis of those two families in the couple's relationship. How these differences and similarities are brought together by the parents will determine the overall balance of the new family unit.

No matter which subsystem the family therapist works with, he or she needs to appreciate how the family behaves as a unit in its own environment. How it operates as a unit has a direct bearing on how free any individual member is, in the presence of the family group, to be his or her own person. It is quite easy for people to alter their behavior and experiment with being different when away from the family. However, the key to change is acquiring the ability to bring that difference back into the family and allowing the family to experience the change. Usually the family pressures the individual member to conform to familiar behavior. If the individual can maintain the new behavior in the presence of the family, irrespective of the family's counterpressure, the individual and family will undergo significant behavioral change. It is an underlying principle of family behavior that the family repeatedly expresses some habitual behavioral patterns. There is reciprocity in a family in that each member expects certain responses from other family members. These responses are predictable and occur with regularity over time. When one member of the family changes his or her part in the reciprocity it produces strain, stress, and anxiety in other family members. The change that one family member exhibits in the family is not seen positively. This ambivalence about change is one reason it is so hard for individual members to be different in the family's presence. The family as a group will coalesce to pressure the deviant member to go back to old behavior. Emotional systems behave in a predictable way over time. We have mutual expectations and when they are violated other family members feel resentful, confused, and angry. The way family members deal with change in the family is connected with how they have dealt with anxiety historically. There is much to be learned about a family from watching how it deals with one of its members being different.

Unfinished Business

One of the principles underlying the concept of unfinished business is that we learn from our parents how the world is organized. The way our parents dealt with us as children teaches us about ourselves. As young children we do not grasp that our parents' reactions to us have more to do with their own family of origin experiences than with us. We incorporate our parents' values, attitudes, and emotional issues and make them our own. We express many behaviors that we do not question. When we get angry, feel hurt, are needy, or are critical of another, we do not question why we are reacting with such strong emotion. We assume we are right and that the behaviors we express are correct.

Another principle underlying unfinished business is that we cannot give to another emotionally what we have not received. Unfinished business implies a multigenerational process. What parents did not receive from their own parents they are unable to give to their children; in turn, this blocks the children's ability to give in certain ways to their children. Thus one generation projects onto the next generation its own unfinished emotional issues. These issues get acted out by that generation as their own issues, which then become part of the heritage of the following generation. This complicated process affects our decision-making more than most of us realize.

Not all children are equally affected by their parents' unfinished business. One's sibling position, the parents' ages at the child's birth, the parental relationship, the physical well-being of extended family members, job pressures, and the general health of the parents and extended-family members all have an impact on the degree to which any child in the family becomes the center focus of the parent's unfinished business. Only children have greater potential to inherit unfinished business from their parents because their parents are not able to spread their issues among several children. If the parents are successful at dealing with their conflict and neediness in their relationship with each other, then less unfinished business is projected onto the children. If a child temperamentally and by timing of birth reminds a parent of an unresolved issue with his or her own parent, the child will more likely be the focus of the parent's emotional issues.

Unfinished business is present in all families. One cannot come out of a family without a certain degree of unfinished business. What is important is the degree of unfinished business that a person carries from one generation to the next. Built into family life is a certain degree of deprivation; how much deprivation one experiences in the family will strongly influence the degree of unfinished business carried into the next generation. Unfinished business does not go away; it is something we all need to work on and understand, so we do not indulge that part of ourselves in our relationships with others.

The Projection Process

The multigenerational projection process is connected with the concept of unfinished business. Parents have a tendency to project certain characteristics—positive or negative—onto their child. There are children who remind us of special issues in our own life. If these issues make us anxious, we try to change our child's behavior so our anxiety is lessened. If the behavior reminds us of positive things in the family, we are likely to reinforce such behavior because we think this is a positive attribute. It is important for the parent to be as clear as possible about the child's uniqueness apart from the parents' emotional history. How much we need our children to perform in the world is connected in part with our unresolved family of origin issues. Parents should not become overly excited about a child's successes or overly dismayed about a child's failures. Rather, they should understand the child's experiences as learning opportunities. Many children become confused because they do not understand their parents' reactions to their behavior. Some amount of projection occurs between parent and child in all families. This can be very burdensome for the child. Children rarely have enough information to understand what underlies their parents' reactions to them and tend to interpret these reactions as statements about their general ability to perform or to be loved in the world.

The Emotional Triangle

The emotional triangle is the process by which couples stabilize their relationship by externalizing their anxiety into something or somebody outside of themselves or what is going on between themselves and another person. It is difficult to avoid being in an emotional triangle. Use of an emotional triangle is the customary way in which couples avoid intimacy. People appear to be intimate with each other by talking about another person — for example, two people sharing a confidence about a third. Bowen (1978) gives the clearest definition about how a triangle operates:

> The basic building block of any emotional system is the triangle. When emotional tension in a two person system exceeds a certain level, it triangles a third person, permitting the tension to shift about within the triangle. Any two in the original triangle can add a new triangle. An emotional system is composed of a series of interlocking triangles. The emotional tension system can shift to any of the old pre-established circuits. It is a clinical fact that the original two person system will resolve itself automatically when

contained within three person systems, when one of them remains emotionally detached. [p. 306]

One way for an individual to avoid working on self or looking at his or her own part within a relationship is by triangulation. Triangulation provides the opportunity to stabilize one's emotional feelings while talking about a third person. The more anxiety there is in a dyadic relationship, the more likely one or both will move out of the relationship by involvement with another individual, such as friend, therapist or family member, to reduce the tension level.

The more fused the relationship, the more important it is for the individuals to maintain it for emotional survival. If one is holding on to a relationship for emotional survival, then the best way to reduce the anxiety is to avoid talking about the relationship or focusing on anything that might throw the relationship into question. In other words, one can triangle not only by moving out of the relationship to talk about it with someone else; one can also triangle within the relationship by talking about anything but the relationship. In this case, discussions about politics, religion, what is on TV, or other people's problems are all ways to avoid dealing with what is going on with self, other, and the relationship.

Triangles serve as a stabilizing influence by helping to keep the status quo in a relationship. They are a way of maintaining calm; the higher the anxiety, the more likely that people will talk in triangles; the lower the anxiety, the safer it is to talk about self. Triangles are a major block to being intimate. When we are fearful of sharing vulnerable parts of ourselves, we will use the triangle process to make it emotionally safe for self in the relationship by focusing on something outside of ourselves. It is important for the clinician to understand the meaning that self attaches to problems in the other. Usually self will project self's vulnerabilities onto the other to reduce self's anxiety. The problem one projects onto the other is usually symbolic of what self feels most vulnerable about.

Fusion

The concept of fusion is connected with the principle of development. At birth a child is fused with the environment and gradually develops to become a separate emotional identity from those around him or her. We move from a relative state of fusion to one of separateness. Before this process can occur, one's dependency needs have to be met. The greater the deprivation the child has experienced in having his or her dependency needs met, the greater will be the need to fuse with others. We hope that our partner will help us finish off emotionally those unresolved issues from our family-of-origin experience. We fuse with our partner in the hope that he or she will take care of that unfinished part in us. We do not feel we can take care of that part by ourselves. The emotional need is for the other to complete that part of our personality, and make us feel whole in the world. Fused partners have tremendous difficulty in being comfortable with differences. A fused person equates differences with deprivation. The tendency in fused relationships is to work toward agreement, we-ness, togetherness. Any attempt by the partner to take a different position, to express different values, a different view of the world will be experienced emotionally as invalidating the other and undermining the relationship.

As people learn how to let go of needing the other to be a certain way to make it safe for self, the process of fusion becomes less of an issue in a relationship. However, early in most relationships there is a significant degree of fusion. We marry with the hopes that someone will take care of us, meet our needs, and make the world safe for us. As we grow and develop in a relationship, this need should become less of a driving force. For two people to be truly intimate and connected with each other, they have to be able to feel comfortable with each other's differences.

Loyalty and Debts

Most of us feel fiercely loyal to our original family. We show this loyalty in many ways, the most important of which is by adhering to family values. Loyalty has been greatly underestimated as a major dynamic in our decision making. The better one partner understands the other's loyalty ties to his or her family of origin, the better the sense of connection will be between the couple. Honoring debts is another way we show loyalty. We want to honor our mothers and fathers. We want to take care of them if necessary and remain responsible members of our family. We also want to be able to pay back some of what our family has given us. Few people appear to realize how often they make decisions in a certain way to honor family.

When parents divorce and remarry all sorts of loyalty issues are stirred up for the children. Each parent tries to arrange a family with his or her new spouse. The children, however, maintain loyalties to their original family. Meanwhile, the parents in their new relationships are trying to develop family structures that integrate their new partners' needs. This new structure may offend the child's sense of loyalty to the original family. The following example illustrates this dynamic:

A couple came in to see me. It was the second marriage for both. They had been together as a family for approximately one year. They were experiencing difficulties with the wife's 11-year-old son. They had attempted to set up a family that was tightly structured. They had a set bedtime, the child was expected to come home from school on time, there was little flexibility. This boy would come home late from school, stay up beyond the set bedtime, and generally refuse to cooperate with the new structure. The couple became very angry at the boy and began to punish him severely. Over time the family relationships became severely strained, and the couple brought the boy for therapy. Their sense of the boy was that he was very disturbed, refused to cooperate, and did not fit into the new family unit.

The mother reported that prior to her new marriage she had very little difficulty with her son. From the time she left her husband, her son's father, until her remarriage, the boy had behaved adequately. She was quite confused about what had produced this drastic change. She said there was very little contact between the son and his father. She didn't think the father had much influence on him.

After several sessions I suggested that I have a session with the boy's biological father. What I discovered in that session was that the son was visiting his father in secret after school. The boy's fear was that if his mother discovered these visits she would stop them as punishment when he did not cooperate with her. The boy's biological father also kept the secret because he was afraid that his wife would pressure him not to maintain the contact.

Another discovery was that the father's way of conducting his life was quite different from that of his son's stepfather. The boy's biological father was an artist and led a life that was less structured and less predictable. This 11-year-old boy was caught in a loyalty dilemma between fitting into his mother's new family and being disloyal to his biological father or adopting his biological father's life-style and being disloyal to his mother and her new family. When this became clear, the biological father released his son from misguided loyalty toward him and said, "When you are with your mother and her new husband, it is important that you fit into that family. When you are with me, we can do it our own way." After the father released his son from this loyalty issue, the son was better able to integrate the two families.

Loyalty dilemmas are common for children when they have to balance two different family styles. It is important for parents to understand that whenever a new adult is brought into the family or a relationship, there will be issues about honoring the old life-style while at the same time modifying it to integrate the new person.

It is helpful to ask people how they honor their parents. Career choices, the type of wedding, the naming of the children, and so forth, are all potential ways in which we honor our family. It is important that we make peace with our parents. The degree to which debts and loyalty issues influence our decision making for the future is connected with how well we have been able to make peace with and say good-bye to our parents and our old attachment issues. Helping couples understand how their own parents dealt with loyalty and debt issues provides them with a clearer sense of how to honor the family throughout the generations.

Loss and Mourning

Built into family life is a certain degree of loss. How well we have made peace with family losses will determine to some degree how free we are to move on in our own lives. Each family has to deal with separation issues, death, and many different forms of disappointment. As parents get older they have to deal with losses in their lives—their parents' failing health and eventual death, their older siblings' failing health and eventual death, and their own losses in terms of career, relationships, and dreams for the future. Many parents try to hide their sadness from their children. In our society we have made it increasingly difficult for children to learn that death is another part of the life cycle. We generally do not have rituals that allow children to mourn, with their parents, the loss of a loved one. There is a tendency in our culture to hide death from the living. How a family teaches its members about death and dying will better prepare its members for living. Family members mourning together share the experience and feel connected. Observing a parent grieving, expressing sorrow, and later coming out of it gives hope to the children.

Part of the therapeutic process is to help people reflect on how they said good-bye to family members and to help prepare family members to say good-bye to aged relatives. Couples who are able to understand each other's sadness, losses, and disappointments are less likely to misinterpret each other's reactions in these areas. They will understand that a great deal of anxiety and fear is connected with sadness and grieving about losing special people. We also know that the more connected and solid the relationship we have with our parents, the fewer regrets we have when they die and the more at peace we are with the relationship. The more conflictual and cut off the relationship between parent and child, the harder the death is on the surviving child.

Balance

Family balance is an important indication of family health. It is a complex task to keep all the relationships in some sort of order so that they do not seriously compete with each other. Balance is achieved when each subsystem is able to have time to meet its own special needs without taking away from or undermining the needs of other subsystems within the family. Each one needs to be attended to, nourished, and given sufficient time to feel connected and cared for. Some parents put their relationship issues secondary to their parental concerns. There are also parents who seriously interfere with the sibling relationships of their children. In some families the individual feels he or she has to give up autonomy to meet the needs of the family. Some parents are overly involved with a child while the other parent is peripheral. Sometimes over-involvement takes the form of one parent making a child his or her confidant.

All these examples of imbalance can create problems for the healthy development of the individuals in the family. These potential problems will be discussed in the next chapter. However, *husbands and wives should give thought to how they want to keep their family in balance.* They must decide how much time they want to devote to work, to relationship concerns, to parent/child concerns, and to individual needs apart from work and family. Each family has to develop its own formula for successful balance.

One of the demands on the family is balancing its members' needs for individual autonomy with the group's needs for family solidarity and togetherness. Ideally, family members should feel connected with and involved in each other's lives yet also allow individual members to develop a life apart from family concerns. To complicate matters, the developmental needs of the members may conflict. For example, parents with teenage children are aware that within a few years these children will be gone, and they want to maximize togetherness during this period. At the same time, teenagers have a sense of urgency about being able to spend more time away from their family with their peers and friends as a way to discover themselves as entities separate from their family. The family's challenge is to be able to balance these two opposing developmental issues.

Becoming Your Own Hero

One of the major developmental tasks for individuals is to leave their families feeling solid and in control of their lives. The goal is for the individual eventually to become his or her own hero. The prerequisite is to have had proper heroes or mentors in one's life. First and foremost, parents should be heroes to their children. However, as children grow older they become able to find other mentors and heroes as well. A hero or mentor is someone who can serve as a healthy role model for the child. A proper hero believes in the child's ability to come out of difficult situations with new learning and skill. A healthy hero does not need to play this role and often is not even aware that he or she is cast in this way. A healthy hero intuitively believes in the strength, goodness, and ability of the child to overcome problems and learn positively from experiences.

It is not possible to become your own hero unless you have had an earlier history of people believing in you. One of the major difficulties that people bring into relationships is that they do not believe in themselves. Many people marry herolike figures to feel safe and taken care of. Rarely are these feelings sustained. When the herolike figure does not carry out his or her implied role in the relationship, self feels betrayed, deserted, and abandoned. This dynamic disturbs the very foundation of the relationship. However, the basic difficulty is that the individual did not have a sense of being his or her own hero and put the responsibility for feeling safe in someone else's hands.

It is essential, developmentally, for people to have proper mentors in their lives. Osherson (1986) said it well:

> Mentoring is such a fashionable word these days. It is casually dropped into conversation; many young adults assume they have a mentor as if you can't be truly dressed for success without one. Psychology and business texts wax poetic about the mentor's importance. Both parenting and mentoring link the generations — a latch-pin is Erikson's metaphor for this volatile relationship. In the process the old find a way of seeing their ideals and values survive, while the young find sturdy, trustworthy elders to give them a competent view of the future. [p. 76]

The young find in the mentor safety and guidance. Of particular importance is the mentor's belief in them. Armed with this belief the young develop confidence and eventually let go of mentors. They develop a belief in themselves and a solid sense of self.

One of the major tasks of the therapy process is to encourage people to become their own heroes. Part of this process involves going back to lost or forgotten heroes and rediscovering the herolike qualities in them. Our parents, siblings, grandparents, uncles, and aunts all have the potential to provide herolike qualities we can use to discover the herolike potential in us. *If we did not have proper heroes in our young life, we will look for them later.* Unfortunately, many of us will find false heroes — people who need to be heroes to feel good about themselves. This need fosters fused and emotionally undermining relationships. The task of the therapist is not to be a hero to his or her clients but rather to help the clients believe that they have herolike people available to them from their own families, and most importantly, that they have a herolike person within themselves who can be discovered. This process of discovery is the underlying goal of family therapy with couples—to find the herolike qualities within both the family and the individual, and to expand on them during the therapeutic experience.

Reactivity versus Proactivity

The more anxious and needy the person, the more likely he or she is to behave in reactive ways. Unfinished business leads to reactive behavior. When individuals experience anxiety, it is common for them to respond with defensive behavior. There are two major types of defensive behavior: fight or flight. Both are reactive and one-dimensional. The job of the therapist is to help individuals begin to respond to life situations using thought. There are two aspects of brain functioning. One is basically via the feeling brain, where people respond through their emotional thinking, the other is through the thinking brain, where they are "able to take in information, process that information and think through a response based on the situations and current data (Kerr and Bowen 1988, pp. 92–93)." When anxiety is too high, thought is affected. The person's emotional solidity will influence whether he or she can handle anxiety sufficiently to allow for thinking to play a part. During the therapy sessions it is important to keep anxiety down so that the individual feels safe and understood and therefore less likely to become defensive and reactive. Whenever reactivity occurs, it is a sign that the individual is responding to a situation based on some past experience. Usually that response will be inappropriate and will add to the individual's dilemma. The job of the therapist is to encourage the individual to become increasingly proactive.

Proactivity is the ability to take a research-curious stance. It is the wondering and questioning about what is happening in front of a person rather than the reacting and defending against the stimulus (Freeman 1991, p. 39). The therapist staying calm, involved, and curious about what is going on will generally reduce individuals' reactivity, allowing them to become more curious and hopeful about what is happening around them.

Anxiety can be extremely debilitating. When we experience fear, tension, and apprehension our usual response is defensive. The job of the therapist is to help people increase the level of anxiety they can tolerate before a defensive, reactive response occurs. Anxiety is actually a window into unfinished business; how our original families dealt with anxiety will influence the way we deal with it as adults. When a situation goes into high anxiety and we observe how we respond to that anxiety, we have an opportunity to learn how our families dealt with anxiety.

The job of the therapist is to help the individual become more curious and research-minded about anxiety. At times it is necessary to encourage a person to go back to his or her original family during high anxiety periods and have him or her take a research stance. This process offers one of the most effective ways to learn about managing anxiety. By placing ourselves in high-anxiety situations while simultaneously taking a proactive position, we can learn much about ourselves and our ability to embrace others in a positive way.

Need for Comfortable Distance

One of the important lessons we learn from our family is how to deal with closeness and distance. As children we wanted to be loved, held, and nurtured. How well our parents were able to meet these needs and how safe we felt in their embrace has a significant impact on the degree of closeness with which we are comfortable. Many partners require a certain degree of distance to feel safe. When one partner moves too close or demands too much closeness, the other partner will display behaviors guaranteed to create more distance. Fighting, focusing on content issues, conflict, and highlighting differences as negative are all ways in which we maintain comfortable distance. Blaming, triangulation, and feeling hurt and unloved are all ways in which we justify the distance we need to feel safe. One of the tasks of therapy is to help people understand that the distance they experience in a relationship has more to do with what they brought into that relationship emotionally than what the other is doing in the relationship.

One way to determine how much distance or closeness we can handle is to allow ourselves to become more emotionally involved with the other without using old behaviors to justify distancing. Each partner is responsible for putting in an equal amount of effort to make a relationship work. Neither is entitled to more than 50 percent of the credit or 50 percent of the blame. When one person decides to put in full effort irrespective of what the partner is doing, two things become apparent. First, the individual begins to realize how well he or she is able to put in his or her 50 percent emotionally. When self no longer uses a partner's behavior to justify distancing, self begins to understand how capable self is of becoming close in a relationship. It can be difficult to stay involved with the other when the other is behaving in ways that can easily be used to justify distancing. However, when individuals can maintain this involvement they become their own heroes in the relationship. They discover they can behave in ways true to themselves without having their partners' behavior shape them. Second, when we are able to put in our full share of the effort we learn what our partners are able to do emotionally in the relationship. This stance produces a greater degree of clarity. With this clarity we begin to realize what can and, more importantly, what cannot happen in the relationship. Clarity is a mixed blessing. With clarity we have to decide about the relationship. We begin to appreciate what our partners can provide. Clarity cannot be achieved until one is prepared to put 100 percent emotional effort into the relationship. When one accomplishes this task, the need for comfortable distance lessens. One begins to realize emotionally that self can take care of self and no longer needs to use blame, anger, and conflict to justify emotional distance.

Underfunctioner/Overfunctioner Reciprocity and Pursuer/Distancer Dynamic

To understand the relationship dance, we have to comprehend how relationships develop balance through a particular type of reciprocity. It is not possible to understand one person's role in a relationship without comprehending the compensating responses from the other. Most relationships have some balance. If one person is taking care of things, usually the other person is allowing that to happen.

> Relationships have to achieve balance in one way or another. The stronger the sense of self the less a person will require other to provide emotional support. The weaker the self, the greater will be the tendency to enter into fused relationships. Fused relationships operate primarily in emotional triangles and set in motion an overfunction/underfunction reciprocity process. One member is usually perceived as more adequate than the other in a fused relationship. The adequacy of one is balanced by the inadequacy of the other. The understanding of this concept is crucial to work with families and/or couples. If one gets involved with the more inadequate or underfunctioning member of a family without recognizing the underfunctioner is sustained by the other's overfunctioning there is limited possibility for change in the system. [Freeman 1991, p. 47]

A related process is the pursuer/distancer dynamic. Many therapists assume that the partner who talks about wanting closeness is actually prepared and able to handle closeness. In my clinical work I have discovered that the person who presents lack of closeness as an issue actually needs the partner's distancing as a way to stay safe.

> In many couples one member actively pursues the other member for change. The pursuer usually wants the distancer more involved. The more he/she pursues, the more the distancer moves away. Often therapists will collude with the pursuer in pursuing the distancer. In my opinion many therapists are natural pursuers and are not aware how counter-productive it is to join with the pursuer to get the distancer more involved. I have discovered that each partner in the pursuer/distancer relationship has difficulty with closeness and intimacy. At some level the pursuer counts on the distancer to distance in order to make it safe for the pursuer to be involved in the relationship. [Freeman 1991, p. 48]

The task of therapy is not to pursue the distancer but rather to have each person understand how much distance is needed to be comfortable. When each person fully understands the degree of distance that is comfortable, therapy is underway. The task of the therapist is to help each partner understand the role unfinished business plays in their need for distance and closeness and the ways they go about trying to get these needs met. When each person assumes responsibility for his or her sense of self in the relationship and stops blaming other for not being there, the relationship changes fundamentally and the potential for greater connection begins to grow.

3

Understanding Relationship Problems Systemically

What Are the Most Common Types of Relationship Problems?

Couples present a wide range of problems. However, familiar themes underlie most of their concerns. The couple usually perceives the problem as resting in the relationship and/or the other partner. It is unusual for partners to begin therapy by presenting concerns about self. Many couples believe that if the relationship could be improved or if the other could be different in the relationship, it would work. The general themes that people present include such concerns as: (1) my partner is too different; I cannot connect with him or her; (2) we cannot communicate, and I feel too alone and separate; (3) our values are too different, and/or we have different goals; (4) I have fallen out of love, and/or I don't feel enough love to sustain the relationship; (5) we fight over problems with our children, and/or my partner is overly involved with an extended family member; (6) my partner is depressed, has a chronic illness, and/or has a serious addiction; (7) my partner is having an affair; and (8) we have sexual problems and/or have lost interest in sex.

It is important for the therapist to have a framework to help understand what is underlying these complaints. Rather than attempt resolving the problem as presented by the couples, the therapist's task is to help the couple deal with the deeper issues these problems mask.

High Expectations

Most of us enter relationships with high expectations. We have dreams about what we hope will happen. We want to be loved, accepted, appreciated for our uniqueness, and made to feel safe and cherished. Many of us hope that our partner will make up for some of the losses we experienced in our own family of origin. Some of us carry a romantic notion that once we find a loved one we will feel "right in the world." Many equate getting married and starting a family with becoming adult and responsible.

We bring into our relationships certain expectations, values, and goals, and then proceed to try to make these come true. Many of our wishes are not made explicit; we feel that our partners should understand us, know us, and have similar desires and expectations. Feelings of disappointment, resentment, confusion, and rejection occur early in the relationship for many people. We do not understand why our partner behaves in certain ways; he or she doesn't seem to understand our needs to the degree that we had hoped. We want our partner to be more available, more sensitive, and more supportive. Often we find that our partner is preoccupied with his or her own needs and is to some degree critical and judgmental about the way we conduct ourselves in the relationship and in the world.

Once these hurts, resentments, and feelings of rejection surface, we have to find ways to protect ourselves, to become safe emotionally. The individual deals with these general feelings of disappointment and hurt by setting in motion the process of distancing and emotionally shutting down.

It is essential when working with couples to understand how each partner has explained to himself or herself the failure of the other partner to be there emotionally to the degree expected and desired. The beginning of fantasy-making in the relationship occurs almost from the beginning. It is a profoundly powerful process that over time blocks partners' learning about each other. When one partner feels disappointed or hurt by the other, he or she will provide himself or herself with an explanation for the partner's behavior. These explanations set the myth-making process in motion. The degree to which we develop a set of assumptions about our partner to explain why the partner isn't more loving, caring, and available is directly related to the amount of emotional distance and distortion in the relationship.

Mythmaking

We use the stories and explanations we develop about the other to protect ourselves from the hurt and pain we experience in the relationship. When we experience the other as being too distant we rely on explanations developed in our family of origin to deal with pain experienced in that family. We are not likely to ask ourselves, "I wonder what is happening with me that I need my partner to be different?" Our usual response is, "What is wrong with my partner that makes him or her unable to be more loving, caring, sensitive, and available?" It is safer for us to project outward, to blame the other, and then to use that explanation to withdraw from the other.

There are two common types of defensive reactions to hurt: to attack, and/or criticize overtly and to withdraw and shut down emotionally. Both these reactions are used to make it safe emotionally for self when self feels threatened. The individual's particular style of defensive reaction is learned over time as he or she deals with emotional pain. The explanation we give ourselves about why the other is causing us pain is symbolic of the explanations we have given ourselves throughout our lives about why our family was not more loving and accepting of our needs. The ways in which we dealt with emotional loss in the past and how we deal with it in the present are intimately connected. Over time we define our sense of loss in terms of relationship problems. We feel unloved; we stop loving. We feel our partner is not available to us; we stop communicating our needs to the other. We feel alone and frightened in the world; we may develop somatic problems. We shut down sexually or lose interest in making ourselves available sexually to our partner. It is important to understand the presenting problem in terms of how people use issues (problems) to make it safe for self in the relationship.

The Presenting Problem

The therapist needs to understand the historical significance of the presenting problem. The definition of the problem by the couple is not accidental. Rather, it is related to something that has been learned or experienced in the past. This presenting problem usually is used to mask a basic sense of feeling alone, rejected, and unloved in the world. When we feel unloved and uncared for by our partner, we tend to respond in one or more of the following ways: by moving up a generation or across the generation to deal with the loss by getting involved with an extended family member—a parent or a needy sibling—by moving down a generation and becoming overly involved in our children's lives; by turning inward and becoming preoccupied with our own emotional and physical functioning; and/or by moving out of the relationship and trying to find someone else in the world who will meet our needs. The general style people use when feeling rejected in a relationship is to move up or across a generation, down a generation, out of the relationship, or inward.

What Is the Functional Nature of Family Problems?

Assessing Problems

Many families are organized around problems. Several questions must be addressed before we can understand the functional nature of these problems, such as how long has the problem existed in the family? Who is involved in the problem? How much time and energy do family members expend to deal with the problem? How has the problem influenced the way the family behaves, both structurally and functionally? Who else has the family involved in its attempts to understand and deal with the problem? What meaning have various family members given to the problem? What would be the loss to the family if the problem did not exist?

It is naive to assume that elimination of the problem will improve family functioning. Problems have useful purposes. They give meaning to the family. They help organize family members in a way that allows connections between members around the problem. And they make certain relationships safe by providing a focus to the relationship apart from individual issues, that is, the problem becomes the safe element in the triangle.

Symbolic Meaning of the Problem

The symbolic meaning of the problem refers to the purpose the problem serves for the family. The problem must be understood in a multifaceted way. We need to consider such issues as whether there was a similar problem in the extended family of either or both parents, how the parents developed their particular understanding of the problem, whether they sought help from other professionals and/or family and friends, how their perception of the problem was different from the perception of others, whether there was general agreement between husband and wife about the nature of the problem, where the family placed the problem in terms of the various subsystems, and whether the family was organized around the problem with an extended family member. The therapist must have an in-depth understanding of the above issue before he or she can help the family reframe the problem.

The problems that family members describe can be placed in one of the subsystems of the family: between siblings, between parent and child, within the husband/wife relationship, with an individual member within the family, or with an extended family member. Regardless of where the family places the problem, how they define it for themselves determines their approach to resolving it. Unless they are able to redefine the problem, they will not be able to develop alternative strategies and approaches to resolve it.

The first step to approaching a problem differently is to understand its nature. The major areas the therapist has to explore are:

1. What does the problem represent symbolically?
2. How has this family learned to deal with the problem?
3. Who has the most invested in maintaining the problem?
4. What would be the loss to various members of the family if the problem were not available as a focus for them?

Reciprocal Nature of the Problem

Family problems are reciprocal in nature. If one family member is experiencing a problem other family members will be trying to do something about it. One should not conceptualize family functioning in terms of healthy, sick, functional, and/or dysfunctional family members. There is a reciprocity in which certain members perform certain tasks for other members. Once one member of the family refuses to play his or her part in the family dance, other family members have to change their way of dancing as well.

Family process is a tightly interconnected series of relationship behaviors. Family members are quite tuned in to each other's way and style of functioning. If one member begins to change the way he or she operates within the family, other members will experience that change as a loss and will try to correct the imbalance. Family members find it difficult to learn new ways of behaving with each other. When a family has had a history of problems with an individual member it is hard for the other family members to perceive him or her as other than incompetent and dysfunctional, even when the community at large may see this same individual as quite adequate and competent. To change one's perception of a family member is probably one of the most difficult things to do. If we change how we perceive another in the family, then we somehow have to change how we perceive ourselves in relationship to the other. The following case example illustrates this dynamic:

I had been working with a middle-aged couple for over a year. During the course of the therapy the husband mentioned that his brother was coming into town and he was very anxious about the visit. His brother was his only sibling and was three years his senior. The brother had recently separated from his wife of twenty-five years and to this point had never visited alone. My client explained that the reason for his brother's visit was that he was very upset about the separation and was worried that his decision to divorce his wife might change his role and relationship in the extended family. I asked my client more questions about his anxiety over his brother's visit. He responded by saying that he was comfortable with the way the relationship had been historically because his brother had always maintained a certain degree of distance.

He explained further that he had always wanted to be closer to his brother but that his brother had difficulty with intimacy. He went on to give several reasons for his belief that his brother was the one who maintained the emotional distance in their relationship. We spent several sessions discussing how and if my client wanted to change the relationship. He felt it would be impossible to be different with his brother because his brother consistently emotionally distanced from him.

Prior to the visit I coached my client on how he could begin to respond to his brother differently and change the old sibling relationship structure. After the brother's visit my client reported that he had discovered some interesting, although disturbing, facts about himself. He said that for the first time his brother was much more willing to be intimate with him. He wanted to spend a lot of time alone with him and talk about his own ambivalence and struggles in his marriage and his role in the family. My client related how anxious this made him and acknowledged that he was the one who then began to emotionally distance in the relationship. He said he had never realized before how much he had played into the emotional distance that existed between him and his brother. When his brother tried to talk to him about important family issues my client found himself avoiding these discussions or changing the subject. By the end of the visit he had gained some important but unsettling insights about himself. He had to come to terms with the fact that he could no longer project his need for distance onto his brother. His brother was now ready for more closeness and he had to examine his own reasons for needing the emotional distance. If my client's brother hadn't changed his emotional position, my client would have gone on believing that the reason for the emotional distance rested solely with his brother.

Understanding the part one plays in maintaining distance can be quite upsetting. Once a person understands that the reason for distance rests with himself or herself, it becomes more difficult to project out emotional issues onto others, and consequently one has to confront one's own need for distancing. Once this breakthrough occurs, there is increased potential for self to reevaluate other significant relationships.

We develop certain attitudes and feelings toward various family members as a way to remain emotionally safe in our relationships with them. As long as we can perceive the other as having the problem, then we can use our understanding of the problem and our way of dealing with the other around the problem as a way to keep the relationship safe for ourselves. In other words, the definition of a problem allows us to behave in a certain way. To tinker with the story we have constructed to explain the problem challenges our way of positioning ourselves in our most important relationships. We need to look at what someone loses in giving up his or her own definition of the problem. If an individual has to let go of perceiving the other in a certain way, how would he or she then have to be different in the relationship with the other? The following case example provides another illustration of how we hold on to stories we have developed out of fear that we will have to be different if we let go of them.

A couple entered therapy because they were feeling quite distant from each other and were thinking about separating. The wife said she wanted more closeness with her husband, but he continually backed away from her. The husband complained of being overwhelmed by what he perceived as his wife's neediness. This was a first marriage for both. The husband was a second-generation Holocaust survivor, and the wife had converted to Judaism. The wife reported that she was somewhat distant from her own family. On the other hand, the husband was in a reactive, ambivalent relationship with his mother. His father had died several years previously. The husband immediately reported that he was overwhelmed by his mother's neediness. He reported that both of his parents were damaged by their war experiences. When he was a child his parents were unable to care for him emotionally, and even at times physically. He was the older of two siblings, having a sister three years his junior. He said that from an early age he had to distance from his family emotionally. He got married in his early twenties and very quickly had three children. He then started feeling overwhelmed by family obligations. In listening to his description of relationships within his nuclear family it became clear he had difficulty separating out his emotional needs from those of his family. He said he never did learn this lesson from his parents. When his father died he felt a lot of guilt for not being more involved with him. His current relationship with his mother was conflictual. He felt her needs were excessive, and he needed a lot of distance to feel safe from her intrusiveness.

In the course of therapy I encouraged him to bring his mother in so that I could begin to work with the two of them around some of his ambivalent feelings. He said his mother was ready to come in, but he wasn't sure if he was ready to handle the sessions. Over time he grew more comfortable with this idea and agreed to bring her in. A session was scheduled, but when the time arrived he came without his mother. When I asked him why his mother was not there, he said he couldn't bring his mother in because he was afraid I would encourage him to get closer to her. I asked him what he felt would be the loss for him if the story that he carried about his mother changed. He replied, "I spent a lifetime developing a story about my mother that allows me to keep safe distance from her. If you challenge that story then I will have to change how I am with my mother and that would be too overwhelming and scary." He said it was safer for him to keep the story that he had in his head about his mother than to take the chance of changing it.

This example shows how risky it is to move too quickly in challenging people's definitions of their world. The way we define the world involves constructing a series of assumptions about the important people in our world. We use these assumptions to maintain a comfortable distance. Therapists try to move people in direction of more contact, better understanding, and less anger toward important people in their lives. However, therapists need to recognize that maintaining the anger allows for the distance that helps keep safety in the relationship.

The Functional Nature of Relationship Problems

Why Relationship Problems Work

In the previous section the focus was on family problems and the functional nature of those problems to the family as a system. It is also important to understand the functional nature of relationship problems. One important principle about families is that the husband/wife relationship will determine the functioning level of the entire family. If the parental unit is able to maintain a balanced relationship, the children will be positive recipients of this balance. However, if the parents are not able to work through their self and relationship issues without involving the children, the children will develop significant unfinished business in their lives. The therapist needs to understand the basic dynamics of relationship problems and why it can be safer for some couples to have relationship problems than to be intimate and connected with each other. A basic assumption of this text is that it is safer emotionally for some people to stay angry and hurt than to risk change. Relationship problems are predictable and safe; they help stabilize relationships.

There are two major relationship complaints: "You don't love me enough" and "I am not good enough." These complaints are interrelated. "You don't love me enough" is connected with "I am not good enough" because if I felt good enough, you would probably love me. Many of us have to hide from the emotional fear that we are not good enough. By projecting this fear onto other and staying angry and hurt by the other's behavior, we don't have to deal with the fundamental question "Are we good enough?" If our parents were our proper heroes and made us feel we were basically lovable and special, then we do not enter relationships with the defensive stance of not being good enough. For many of us, when we carry this issue into our adult relationships, no matter what we get from the other, it never quite makes up for our feelings of inadequacy. When people enter therapy complaining about the other not being there for them, it is important to ask these questions:

1. What gets stirred up in self when other is not there for you?
2. What losses does this behavior remind self of?
3. How does self protect self from that feeling of not being good enough?

Relationship Dance

Reactive couples are predictable in their relationships. A very tight reciprocity process gets played out. Ordinarily one person pursues, the other distances. One overfunctions, the other underfunctions. The pursuer/distancer dynamic is extremely common. An emotional pursuer wants more from the other, and the other uses the emotional pursuing as a reason for emotional distancing. The emotional pursuer is usually viewed as the overfunctioner in the family, and the emotional distancer as the underfunctioner. The emotional pursuer believes he or she can handle intimacy better than the distancer and often has confidants or other family members who support that belief. It is crucial for the therapist to remember that pursuers and distancers operate at the same emotional level. As soon as the pursuer stops pursuing the distancer, the distancer becomes the pursuer and the previous pursuer the distancer. This dynamic is played out consistently in relationships. For example, a distancing wife may change her stance and say she wants more connection with her husband. It is not uncommon for the previously pursuing husband to then say, "It is too late. I can't trust you anymore. I'm afraid that if I open myself up to the relationship you will reject me again." The wife is now the pursuer trying to convince the husband that she really wants the relationship to work. The husband now needs to distance from the relationship for fear he will be hurt again.

In many relationships both people need emotional distance. The pursuer counts on the distancer to make it emotionally safe for the pursuer to be in the relationship. As soon as the distancer changes the balance, the pursuer becomes more anxious and will contribute something to the relationship that will restore the comfortable balance. There is nothing creative or spontaneous about this type of relationship. The therapist needs to understand that both partners bring into their relationship fears of being hurt by the other. They have to find some way to protect themselves from being too vulnerable. They are sensitive to picking up in the other flaws and shortcomings to which they can attach meaning that will allow them to distance emotionally.

Another principle to understand when working with couples is that both people are emotionally at the same level. Each person provides the other with a behavior to which the partner can attach meaning to justify emotional distance. For example, if I am not available to you to the degree you need, you will use my lack of availability to justify distancing. This stance allows you to be safe and comfortable in the relationship, even though you say you want to be closer and more involved. If I then change the contract and consistently stay more involved and connected with you regardless of your stance, then you will become more anxious about my availability. Usually, when one person in the relationship changes his or her part in the reciprocity and no longer responds in kind to maintain the emotional distance, the other person will become increasingly uncomfortable and show this discomfort by becoming more critical, negative, and distant. If the person who is changing his or her role in the relationship is able to sustain increased involvement even in the face of the partner's critical, distant behavior, and avoids using this increased criticism and distance to justify returning to the old behavior, then a profoundly different relationship develops. This process will be discussed in more detail in the therapy section of the text. The main point to understand here is that *partners provide each other with behaviors that allow for a certain degree of mutual distance to occur.*

It is a basic premise of this text that the functional nature of relationship problems allows partners in relationships to maintain comfortable distance by projecting the problems onto the other. When the therapist begins to tinker with the stories that each person carries about the other, there will initially be increased anxiety and acting out. The partners will try to present more evidence in support of the "rightness" of their stories to correct the balance. For change to occur the therapist must stay neutral but involved and avoid colluding on content issues. The therapist must repeatedly ask each partner what he or she would lose by giving up the old conflict issues. The therapist must also coach one partner on how to stay progressively more positive and less reactive in the relationship over the long term. When this has been accomplished, there will be a relationship shift, as evidenced by the fact that the couple will no longer need an issue to keep them feeling safe.

What Part Does Family of Origin Play in Relationship Problems?

The Loss of Self

Self seeks emotionally from the other what self most lacked in his or her family of origin. However, it is not possible for one partner to make up emotionally for the losses of the other partner. Usually what we find most attractive about the other is what we feel we are lacking in ourselves. Paradoxically, what partners initially find most attractive in the other's personality is, in the long run, what they find the most infuriating and disappointing. In assessing what self issues each partner is struggling with we should ask the following questions, which are directly related to family of origin issues.

1. What do you want from your partner emotionally that you feel you did not get from your own family?
2. When did you first discover that your partner does not give you what you want emotionally?
3. What have you done to minimize the loss?

In order truly to be intimate in a relationship, we have to make peace with our original losses from family of origin. How well we have dealt with our initial attachment and separation issues from our parents will have a powerful influence on how well we are able to connect with our partner's differences.

Another underlying principle of this text is that self cannot give to the other what self has not received emotionally from the family of origin. Often one partner will feel that the reason he or she is unhappy in the relationship is because the other doesn't love him or her enough or make enough of a commitment to him or her. However, *what we don't get from the other has little to do with loving, caring, or being committed and more to do with unfinished business from the past.* It is important to remember that we are attracted to people who are emotionally like ourselves. Many of us marry people who have similar types of unfinished business. If we need someone to take care of us, then we will find someone who needs to be a caretaker. Being able to take care of someone makes one feel good; being taken care of makes one feel safe. When the caretaker is not able to take care of the partner to the degree that the partner requires, then a sense of loss and betrayal sets in. Self then has to protect himself or herself from the overwhelming sadness of not feeling taken care of. How self goes about doing that can mark the onset of serious problems in the relationship. When we experience loss, most of us begin to shut down emotionally and construct a story about other that makes it safe for us. We tend to experience the same hurt, disappointment, and disillusionment that we felt in our family of origin. The significance of this pattern is that the story we constructed to explain why our original family did not take better care of us is what keeps us stuck in our adult relationships. Developmentally, we took on our parents' losses as our own and felt that the reason they did not love us more was because of some lack in us. If we had been more lovable, more desirable, then our parents would have taken better care of us. We hope that in our adult relationships we will feel more loved and desired. When our partners do not fulfill these hopes we feel great pain, sadness, and hurt. We are reminded at some level that once again we are not really lovable or desirable and we have to protect ourselves from our overwhelming sense of loss and grief. The best way we know to do this is by using the same defense mechanisms we used as children. We get angry, withdraw, project, punish, and shut down.

Reconstructing the Emotional Story

Basically, for us to be different in our adult relationships we have to reconstruct the emotional stories we have developed earlier in our lives. The stories we carry about ourselves and our families are part of the problems we bring into our adult relationships. One of the most profound therapeutic interventions is the gentle challenging of these emotional stories. It is not possible for an individual to come out of his or her family experience with an accurate emotional memory of the family. Although there is a factual reality, the emotional meanings we give to those facts and events are colored. One family member's memory of an early event, be it positive or negative, is likely to be different from any other family member's memory of the same event.

Usually we construct emotional events in a certain way to deal with various losses in the family. As we become stronger within ourselves our need to hold on to those memories in the same old way is lessened. We become more open to other people's interpretations of those events, and gradually we are able to let go of old hurts and resentments. Over time this process also allows us to become less reactive and more curious about our partner and consequently, more intimately involved. This process is facilitated when the therapist intervenes by:

1. Encouraging adults in the family to begin to make peace with their own family histories.
2. Helping family members to let go of their old emotional stories and to be able to look at their partners and their children separate from their own emotional issues.
3. Encouraging family members to allow important people to re-enter their lives in a more positive way.

To put this therapeutic model into operation, we have to be alert to the part history plays in the present dynamics of people's lives. Whom we involve, the questions we ask, the therapeutic positions we take regarding people's problems, and how we expand the therapeutic field are all crucial factors in how we make this model come alive.

4

Beginning the Therapy Process with Couples

Beginning the Therapy Process

Beginning the First Interview

One of the first and most important decisions a therapist must make is deciding who should be seen in the first session. The family member who makes the initial call to the therapist will define the problem over the telephone. The caller, on the basis of how he or she views the problem, will usually have some ideas about who he or she thinks should be seen. If the caller sees the problem as resting with one of the children, the caller is likely to suggest that the child come for therapy. If the caller sees the problem as involving the relationship, then he or she usually suggests that the couple be seen.

It is important that the therapist ask the caller some general questions before deciding whom to involve in the first session. *How we define the problem influences how we try to resolve the problem.* The therapist's decision about whom to invite to the first session begins the process of challenging and redefining the family's definition of the problem. If the caller's definition is accepted by the therapist at face value, then the therapist will likely agree with the caller about whom to invite to the initial session. This approach is risky. It is essential that the most powerful, key members of the family come to the first session. Connecting with them and developing a solid relationship with them provides the therapist with the opportunity to expand the therapeutic field and lay the groundwork for involving other important family members at a later date.

When the therapist begins with the entire family, there is a tendency to focus on the children, and it is more difficult to gain an understanding of the parents' emotional systems. The parents may use the children in various ways to camouflage their self issues. The children in turn will act to keep the focus on them. In this way the family therapy session will replicate the home behavior.

Starting with the adults automatically and gently begins to redefine the problem apart from the children. This approach also allows the therapist to form a solid relationship with the parents. It is crucial that the parents trust and feel connected with the therapist. If not, they will continually struggle to maintain their definition of the problem. If the therapist continues to behave in ways that the parents feel undermines them, they will eventually terminate the therapy and look for a more compliant, accepting therapist.

Engaging the parental couple, then, is the first step in the therapeutic enterprise. By developing a strong, positive relationship with the parental couple, the therapist sets the stage for helping the entire family redefine and restructure itself as a system. During the therapist's initial telephone contact with a parent the therapist should try to convey to the parent the wisdom of meeting without the children to discuss their concerns. The therapist should use the initial session to help the parents understand that he or she will support their position about how they want the family to operate, while using therapeutic influence to redefine the family as a behavioral unit.

The following telephone conversation provides an example of what areas to cover with the caller prior to setting up the first interview:

Negotiating the Telephone Call

Caller (Husband): I am having a problem with my wife and our relationship with the children, especially our 16-year-old daughter.

Therapist: Can you tell me a little bit more about your concerns?

Caller: Well, she feels I am not involved enough with the children, especially our daughter. Sue, who just turned 16, has run away from home twice. My wife and I have been fighting a lot about her. My wife thinks that I'm not involved enough with her and continually criticizes how I deal with Sue's behavior. Things have gotten so bad that I am thinking of leaving, too.

Therapist: Can you tell me who else is in the family?

Caller: We have one other child besides Sue, Daniel.

Therapist: What is Daniel's age, and how does he get involved?

Caller: He is our younger child, and is 9 and doing well. No problem with him whatsoever. Our daughter is the problem and my wife's reactions to her. Unfortunately, I get in the middle and probably make it worse. No matter what I try to do, it doesn't seem to work. In the last year things have gotten really out of hand.

Therapist: Have you discussed this call with your wife?

Caller: She is so upset about what's going on in the family that whenever I try to deal with her she just screams. The reason I'm calling you is I'm so distraught about the family thing I don't know what to do anymore.

Therapist: Have you ever seen anyone else about the problems you are having? Is there anyone else currently working with the family?

Caller: We did get involved with a psychiatrist for Sue, but she refused to go. My wife went to see the school counselor once or twice. I haven't seen anyone except I've talked with my brother about my family problems. He is the one who suggested I call you.

Therapist: Have you and your wife seen someone together about your concerns?

Caller: No, never. No one has ever suggested that. We've always thought that our problem was more about our daughter, but since we are fighting so much between ourselves maybe that's not such a bad idea.

Therapist: Well, for the first session why don't you and your wife come in together and meet me. This will give me a chance to talk to both of you about what you see happening within the family. After this session we can decide who should be involved. How would that be?

Caller: I think that would be a good idea. However, my wife has been so upset and pessimistic that it may be hard to get her to come in.

Therapist: Well, I can understand that. However, you should mention to her that it would be helpful to me if she shared with me some of her experiences and concerns. And if both of you fill me in on the experiences of the family, we can then decide together about how to proceed.

Caller: That sounds like a good idea.

This conversation illustrates a situation in which one family member is concerned about, and trying to get help for, another family member. If the therapist handles the call well and makes the correct decision regarding who should attend the first interview, he or she has begun to help the caller redefine the problem. The therapist could have suggested that the entire family attend the first interview, but instead decided that the parents should first be given an opportunity to feel comfortable with the therapist before exposing their children to a stranger. In the long run, the therapist will be able to provide more support to the entire family if he or she has gained the confidence of the family organizers, the parents. Once this comfort is developed between therapist and parents, the parents will be more likely to allow the therapist to see the entire family when appropriate.

The parental couple usually experiences considerable anxiety about the family problem, whether it is about a relationship concern or about one of the children. There is usually a great deal of anger, hurt, and conflict around the problem. When the problem is focused on the child, it often leads to a relationship conflict between husband and wife. When the problem is focused primarily on marital concerns, the children are likely to exhibit behavioral problems in relation to the conflicts they observe between their parents. In any case, when there is a problem in one of the family subsystems—that is, between husband and wife, parent and child, or the siblings—it usually affects the whole family, and everyone plays a part in it. Eventually the family therapist must sit down with the whole family to understand how all its members interact around the family concerns. However, it is important for the therapist to start with the parental unit. When the therapist suggests this approach it stirs up the parents' anxiety about being held responsible for the difficulties. In addition, they may fear that in the end therapy will undermine their efforts and confirm their worst fears. It is important for the therapist to recognize these fears and help the parents feel heard and understood. In this way, their fears can be allayed and they will usually become more willing to allow the therapist entry into the family.

In the telephone call example, the therapist elicited information about family composition and the caller's perception of the involvement of various family members in previous treatment encounters. If the caller had indicated that one or more family members were currently in therapy, the therapist may have declined to get involved.

In summary, the therapist should obtain basic family information before deciding whom to invite to a first interview, or, in some cases, before deciding whether to become involved at all. The following checklist outlines the information that it is helpful to obtain during the first telephone call.

1. Who are the family members (determine the age and sex of all family members and all others living in the home)?
2. Have any members of the family experienced previous therapy? What type? When?
3. Which family member is most anxious or involved in the expressed problem?
4. Which other family members are peripherally involved?
5. How long has the problem existed?
6. Who is willing to attend therapy sessions?
7. Have certain members of the family left home? If so, when? Where do they live now?
8. Are both parents working? What are their schedules and availability for sessions?
9. Have there recently been any changes in family structure, such as birth, separation, remarriage, death?
10. If there has been a remarriage, or divorce, what is the nature of the involvement of the absent parent, stepparent, or both with the rest of the family?
11. Has the caller discussed coming with his or her partner and other family members?
12. Who suggested that the family initiate therapy?

Many times a referral will come to the therapist from an agency or a family doctor. The referral source will reflect a certain view of the problem and may also suggest who should be involved in the therapy process. Sometimes therapists take a referral at face value and proceed to work with the family on the basis of the given information. However, the usual referral information does not reflect the strengths and resources of the family. The referring agency may have been involved with just one family member or have accepted the family's definition of the problem. It is unusual for the referring agent to understand how the family operates as a system. It is essential for the therapist to make his or her own decision about who should come to the first session.

During the assessment period the therapist should be examining the following areas: (1) the spousal relationship, (2) the parent/child relationship, (3) the sibling relationships, and (4) the parent as a individual unit. In assessing the individual parents, the therapist observes what each parent has brought into the family of procreation from the family of origin. The therapist will be paying particular attention to the individual's value system, personal expectations, and expectations of others in the family. These expectations influence how each spouse behaves in the family. The assessment should provide a multi-generational perspective of the family as well as a subsystem analysis. The subsystem analysis gives the therapist a general idea of how the family operates as a system. During the assessment period, the therapist develops a relationship with the parents that will serve well when involving the children. When the parents experience the therapist as a supportive, accepting individual who understands their struggles and will not undermine their authority, they will allow the therapist to see other family members when appropriate.

Conducting the First Session

Regardless of how the caller has defined the problem, it is important for the therapist to begin the first interview with a neutral question. General questions such as, "I'd like to get a sense from each of you about your understanding of why you are here today," are nonthreatening and productive. When the therapist has arranged the first session personally, he or she has already developed a beginning hypothesis about what is going on in the family. If the caller, who is usually the overanxious one, seems overly involved with family issues, the therapist will avoid allowing that person to dominate the initial part of the interview with his or her anxiety. Instead, he or she will make the therapeutic maneuver of starting with the noncaller. In this way the therapist brings the underinvolved person into center stage.

When the therapist starts with a general question he or she does not define the problem for the couple. Although it is essential for the therapist to begin to reframe the problem, the couple must be allowed to explain how they see the problem. It is never wise for the therapist to overtly challenge the couple's definition of the problem. How they define the problem will help the therapist develop some hypothesis about where the couple may be stuck emotionally in their own families.

There are two types of questions that the therapist can ask with respect to the problem. The first type is direct questions that elicit more content information about the problem. The second type addresses the meaning that each person gives to the problem, and inquires into how the problem has shaped, affected, and dominated his or her life. The second type of question is far more fruitful. It allows the therapist and the couple to begin to understand the functional nature of the problem, how the problem has actually produced a structure in the family around which various family members stay connected. If the therapist simply asks for more content information about the problem, then the problem serves as a corner of the emotional triangle and the couple focuses on the content as a way to distance from their own pain, anxiety, and sadness.

Taking a developmental history of the family helps to

reframe the problem. It is important to put the problem in some sort of historical perspective. The therapist will be interested in learning what was different about the family prior to the development of this particular problem. It is necessary to understand the parents as individuals before they became a couple. It is also important to understand how each adult in the family experienced his or her family history.

Genogram

One of the best methods of conducting a developmental survey of the family is to construct a genogram, a technique that allows for a therapist to structurally, functionally, and developmentally survey the family field. The genogram helps the therapist quickly develop a multigenerational perspective of the family. It allows for understanding the problem that the parents are presenting in a historical perspective. As the therapist constructs the genogram with the couple, each member of the couple has a chance to review his or her history in a neutral, nonjudgmental setting and may learn something new about himself or herself and his or her partner. McGoldrick and Gerson's (1985) *Genograms in Family Assessment* is a helpful text that provides instructions on how to construct a genogram. Figure 4–1 provides an example of a multigenerational genogram.

The genogram allows a therapist to survey the family's emotional field. It helps the therapist understand the nuclear family both structurally and functionally. The genogram presents a dynamic picture of the family. A therapist never completes a genogram with the family; it changes over time. As the couple becomes more comfortable with the therapist and feels less threatened, they begin to expand their definition of family. Whom the couple presents as family in the first session is quite different from later in therapy. Many couples are quite guarded and defensive about their family. The more anxious the couple is, the more protective they are about their stories concerning their own family. An example of this dynamic follows:

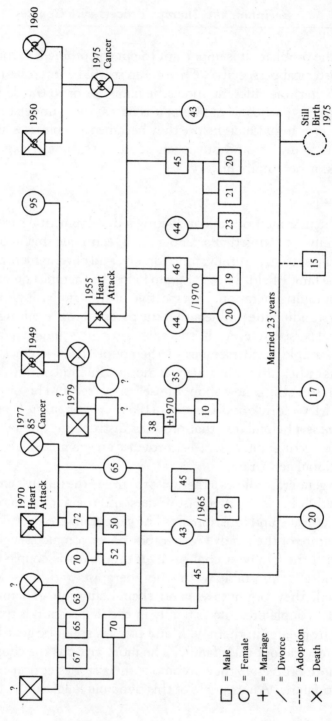

FIGURE 4-1: Example of a Multigenerational Genogram. From David S. Freeman, *Techniques of Family Therapy* (Northvale, NJ: Jason Aronson, 1991), p. 77.

□ = Male
○ = Female
+ = Marriage
/ = Divorce
--- = Adoption
X = Death

A couple came to therapy after living in a common-law relationship for over 14 years. They had two children together. The husband had been married before and initially said he had no other children. The wife had been married before and had one child from her first marriage. One of the major problems that the couple presented was that the wife now wanted to have a formal marriage and also wanted all the children to have the same last name. Two of the children had their father's name, while one child had the mother's maiden name.

In the first few sessions the couple indicated that basically they were very happy together. Their difficulty was the confusion about whether they should marry and allow all members of the family to carry the same name. As the sessions continued, it became obvious that there were a number of secrets in this family. For example, the husband's mother had never met her granddaughters. Later in the therapy the husband revealed that he actually had two additional children from previous relationships. One daughter, who was 21 now, had recently gotten in touch with him and wanted to reinvolve herself in his life. The wife in this relationship also revealed that, in fact, her first daughter's biological father was not from her marriage but from a brief relationship she had when she was a young woman. These secrets emerged only after the couple began to become comfortable in the therapy sessions. Initially they presented as a straightforward family, three children, two parents. But as the therapy continued, these important secrets were revealed.

This case example illustrates that the genogram provides a changing, dynamic portrait of the family. As the family members become more trusting and more comfortable they will provide more information. The therapist continually needs to go back to the genogram and expand on the family story.

When one begins to construct the genogram, it is necessary to obtain a history of developmental changes within the family: births, deaths, accidents, moves, children leaving home, major illnesses, and so on. Every significant developmental event has an impact on each member of the family. Developmental shifts often create the sort of stress that leads to more unfinished business. The genogram, by identifying these developmental events, helps the therapist develop hypotheses about when unfinished business began to develop.

The experiences people have in their family of origin influence their expectations for their own children and how they structure the sibling roles of their children. Family-of-origin experiences provide the individual with memories about sibling relationships and the roles siblings play in the family. A parent will either try to duplicate the structure he or she experienced as a child or to improve on it in his or her own family. To understand fully how a family has organized itself structurally, it is necessary to understand how its members deal with the various sibling positions in the family—for example, such matters as the role the oldest plays compared to the youngest.

By going back at least three generations, the therapist can gain a better sense about why certain problems are emerging in the family of procreation. The more problems there were in the family of origin, the more likely there will be unfinished business passed on to the family of procreation. Of course, the extent to which problems were passed on depends on which members of the family of origin were central to the difficulties in the family. Where there is one child who was the center of concern in the family of origin, the other children are often not as emotionally involved and may have been able to develop with minimal stress. By taking at least a three-generational reading, the therapist can learn a great deal about who was of central concern in the family of origin.

A multigenerational perspective provides the family therapist with a clearer sense of the emotional level at which the parents operated within their own families and also helps the therapist to understand why certain problems concern various family members. It is not uncommon to find that the father and mother have quite different concerns regarding family behavior. Many of these concerns are based not on what is going on in the present family but rather on issues stemming from their families of origin. The genogram helps the therapist gain an understanding of these issues in a systematic way.

The genogram is usually constructed during the first interview. After the parents have defined their view of the problem, the therapist may suggest that it would be helpful for the parents to put the problem into historical perspective. The therapist uses this opening to begin to redefine the problem. This approach also helps the therapist begin to connect with the parents as individuals in their own right rather than solely as parents in the family. Constructing a genogram accomplishes several tasks for the therapist:

1. It helps the therapist to understand who the parents are as emotional beings.
2. It shows how the parents' history has played into their view of themselves in the world.
3. It helps the therapist develop some hypotheses about why this problem is affecting this family at this time.
4. It helps identify multigenerational themes that are being played out in the present.
5. It allows the therapist to form a solid connection with each parent by helping the parent feel understood and accepted for his or her unique history.

Goals of the First Session

During the first session the therapist should be developing some hypotheses about the family struggles. These hypotheses will influence the types of questions the therapist asks and the direction to take with the couple. Quite often the adults recognize that their own family-of-origin themes are the bases of the family struggles. After the first session it is not unusual for the adults to say that they would prefer to work on their own themes and issues. The following case vignette illustrates this process.

A couple entered therapy after being married for less than a year. In the first several months of marriage they had a lot of conflict. One of their major issues had to do with responsibility and honoring commitments. The husband complained that his wife never followed through on her commitments. She would always come late to engagements and/or not follow through on her promises. The wife, on the other hand, felt that her husband overreacted to her tardiness and expected her to be more accountable than she thought she needed to be. In their short marriage they were already experiencing criticism and disappointment.

As the husband began to describe some of his early family experiences, it became clear that he had experienced a lot of abandonment. He was the first born in his family. His parents separated when he was in his early adolescence. He had a younger brother and sister whom he had to take care of. Basically he felt that there was no one there just for him. At one point in his adolescence he became very ill and was hospitalized for six months. This illness coincided with the time that his parents were going through their divorce. He felt that they were so caught up with their anger toward each other that they abandoned him. He reported he had gotten married because he wanted to be loved and taken care of. During the courtship he experienced his wife as very loving and supportive. It was a bitter disappointment to discover in the first year of marriage she was not as loving, considerate, and available as he wished.

On the other hand, the wife came from a family of eleven children. She had an identical twin, and the two of them were in the middle of the sibling group. She talked about feeling invisible in her family except for being a twin. She did not feel she had a separate identity from her twin sister. She was usually referred to as "the twin"; she was rarely called by name. She was convinced that her father was unable to tell her apart from her twin sister. When she was 14 she finally pointed out to her father that she had a mole and she believed that this helped him differentiate her from her sister.

She went on to say that being compliant and available in her family meant being invisible. Her way of getting attention was to do something outrageous. It had never occurred to her before talking about it during a session that one way she tried to be special was either by becoming overly available to someone and/or by doing something outrageous.

As the husband and wife listened to each other's story, they began to realize that what they needed and were reacting to was not about the marriage but what they were bringing into the marriage. Both of them had experienced some profound feelings of abandonment in their families of origin and hoped that in the marriage they could finally feeled loved, safe, and accepted. When one or the other did not react in a way that fostered these important feelings, they felt abandoned, lost, and betrayed.

Whether couples present with relationship problems or concerns about a child, the therapist takes the same approach. The focus is on developing an understanding about self and what self brings into the relationship rather than on the relationship itself.

The goals of a first session are to:

1. develop a positive relationship with the adults in the family,
2. understand their problems in an historical developmental context,
3. begin to reframe the problem from either a relationship problem, a problem with a child, or a dysfunctional adult to a family systems concern that in some way affects all members of the family,
4. help the adults to begin to identify the family of origin themes that are getting played out in the way they define the problem and deal with the problem,
5. construct a genogram that allows the couple and the therapist to identify the key family members who are

involved in the problem and others who may be involved in therapy at a later date, and

6. develop hypotheses about the symbolism behind the problem.

How to Structure the Interview to Make It Safe for Both Partners

Content Issues

There are several procedures the therapist should follow to help make the first session a positive, safe, and profound experience for the couple. The therapist must stay in control of the process at all times. It is important for the therapist to remember that the stories and content issues that couples bring into therapy reflect where they are stuck. The reality of the stories is not so important. The therapist who tries to figure out the rightness or wrongness of a story will quickly discover the futility of this endeavor. No amount of persuasion has ever convinced anyone in a relationship to agree to another person's version of events. Basically, the importance of a person's story lies in the way it reflects the need to maintain a safe distance from his or her partner. *When the content of a person's story focuses on something happening between self and the other, the intensity increases.* The therapist can defuse this intensity by shifting the content, either down a generation to focus on the child or up a generation to focus on an extended family member. The therapist should always remember that the issues that people project onto each other, their children, or extended family members are actually about their own pain, sadness, and anxiety. To try to sort out the content issue is pointless. However, if the therapist can understand the content issue as a metaphor for the loss the individual carries, he or she will have made a start toward helping the individual deal with his or her vulnerability, anxiety, and sadness.

Family members hold on to their content issues to stay emotionally safe. How they use that content, what meaning they place on it, and how they develop that particular content issue all help the therapist understand the unfinished business of the parties involved. The therapist needs to float above the content. Most people have friends, confidants, or colleagues who have bought into their content stories, and taken sides and positions. This offers comfort but produces no change. Family members need people who can stay detached from the content and ask questions not previously considered. When a wife says, "My husband is never available to me. He does not seem to care for me. He does not seem to be around for me," the therapist, rather than asking the wife more about the husband's behavior, should ask her questions such as, "What do you need? How do you know when you get what you need? How do you protect yourself when you feel you are not getting what you need? What is different about you when those needs are met?" If the therapist becomes bogged down with content issues and asks the wife more questions about what the husband did or didn't do for her, the therapist becomes part of a dysfunctional triangle, two people talking about a third.

The therapist must be careful to avoid alliances or collusions with members of the family. It is essential that the therapist avoid becoming part of family secrets. It is also important that the therapist avoid becoming involved in a relationship with one member of the family to the exclusion of another. The therapist needs to maintain a balanced relationship with both adults in the family. Therapy with just one adult can undermine the solidarity and the basic foundation of the couple's relationship. It is crucial for the couple to feel that the therapist is connected with both of them, understands the struggles of each of them, and will not take sides with either of them.

Often partners will try to get the therapist to take sides. They will approach the therapist in the same ways that they approach others in the world and will try to get the therapist to play a more familiar role with them, a role that is consistent with the roles played by other adults in their lives. The therapist must meet the challenge of avoiding these types of collusions and alliances, while at the same time communicating to the adults that he or she is connected to both of them and is trying to understand their struggles.

The Therapist as "Detached I"

The therapist has to stay detached, yet involved. It may be helpful to conceptualize the therapist as floating above the emotional system of the family. Part of the therapist's mind must be outside the emotional processes in the session. The therapist has to be able to watch himself or herself work with the couple and cannot become so involved in their emotional issues that detachment is lost. Once the therapist gets stirred up, takes sides, feels angry, feels overly elated about the progress of the couple, needs to make things different for the couple, or takes responsibility for the outcome, he or she has lost detachment and usually effectiveness with the couple. It is important for the therapist to know where his or her responsibilities stop and the couple's responsibilities begin. The therapist should not use the success of a couple as a measure of his or her own competence. Similarly, a therapist should not become overly concerned about a couple not being able to do things differently or overly pleased by their ability to change things in their lives.

A therapist should be curious about the meaning each person in the family attaches to the attempt the therapist makes to change things. When a couple complains that things are not going well, the therapist should ask questions such as, "What have you learned from that experience? What has each of you tried to do to make it different? What would be the loss for each of you if you were able to make something different?" When a couple reports that things are better, similar questions must be asked. It is important that the adults own their changes; they should not change for the therapist. For a more in-depth discussion on the importance of the therapist's staying detached from the outcome see Freeman (1991, pp. 57–68).

The Importance of Self Questions

A skilled therapist has developed the ability to ask "self questions." A self question allows a person to describe what is happening for self rather than talk about wanting something different from other. The challenge to the therapist is to avoid entering into a dysfunctional triangle with the couple. Individuals enter therapy talking about the problem with the other. The therapist needs to shift the focus by asking questions about self rather than the other or the relationship.

The therapist must understand that clients are ambivalent, not resistant. The ambivalence is between the part of self that wants things to be different and the part that is frightened of change. We have all developed certain ideas or stories to make sense out of our world. We hold on to these stories to feel safe. Although we wish things to be different, often we are unsure whether we want to give up our stories about the other. When the therapist begins to challenge people's stories, they will react in ways that allow them to hold on to them. The therapist must ask family members what they lose by giving up their stories. The therapist should not try to convince the family members to give up their stories. As people talk more about what they could lose, rather than gain, by making things different they become better able to deal with their basic ambivalence about change. The case examples in this text illustrate how to deal with clients' ambivalence positively.

Process of the First Session

Before ending the first session, it is important that the therapist help the couple connect the past with the present. The session should not end in the past. If the developmental history of the partners is not connected to the present life, the couple may leave with the impression they are just providing information to the therapist for him or her to analyze apart from them. On their own, the couple will not understand how their history is connected to their present dilemma. Chapter 5 provides an example of a first interview in which the therapist demonstrates how to connect the past with the present to encourage the couple to confront the future creatively.

5 ────────────

The First Interview

Conducting the First Interview

This chapter focuses on the stages of the first interview. It is important for the therapist to start with the couple. The presenting problem may be about a child, the marital relationship, or difficulties one of the adults is having in his or her own life. Regardless of how the couple defines the problem, the therapist should encourage the couple to attend the first session together. There are some exceptions to this rule, which will be discussed in Chapter 10, on therapeutic dilemmas. There are three distinct stages in the first interview. The therapist should be aware of these stages and have a strategy for successfully negotiating them. These stages are:

1. the reactive stage: presenting the problem
2. the reframing stage: focusing on self-issues
3. the ending stage: contracting for ongoing therapy.

The Reactive Stage: Presenting the Problem

Couples enter therapy with definite ideas about their problems. The therapist needs to listen closely to how they describe their concerns. Commonly, each partner sees the problem somewhat differently. As discussed previously, the problem is usually a metaphor for something more significant. Beginning to develop hypotheses about the symbolic nature of the problem is the major objective of the therapist at this stage. The therapist needs to understand the problem in terms of the following:

1. What is its functional nature?
2. How has the problem stabilized the family?
3. Who has the most invested in the problem?
4. How does the problem allow each person in the relationship to stay safe?
5. How long has the problem gone on?
6. Who else has been brought in to help stabilize the problem?

It is important that the couple feels understood by the therapist. If the therapist challenges the couple's definition of the problem too quickly, he or she will increase their anxiety and sense of vulnerability. Each member of the couple should be given the opportunity to explain in some detail his or her thinking and feeling about the problem. However, at the same time, the therapist must gently begin to shift the couple away from their preoccupation with the content of the problem to a deeper, more systemic understanding of how the problem has influenced their lives.

During the reactive stage of the first interview there is a covert struggle around defining the problem. Both partners carry their personal mythologies about themselves. It is important to them that the therapist understand how these mythologies keeps them safe. However, the partners also want to experience something new in the session. They need to feel that the therapist, in some sense, is wiser than they are about their struggles. The therapist's initial task is to help the partners feel understood while at the same time challenged to rethink their personal explanations for why this problem at this time is affecting their family in this way. The timing and sensitivity of the therapist are crucial. The therapist should communicate understanding of the partners' needs to hold on to their personal definitions of problem while at the same time challenge them to go beyond their thinking and feeling about the problem. How quickly the therapist can nudge the couple into the reframing stage is determined by the degree of reactivity the couple brings into the session. Several diagnostic indicators of how quickly the therapist can move partners into rethinking their definition of the problem are:

1. the ability to listen to each other talk without needing to jump in and correct
2. the ability to reflect on one's history without feeling criticized and defensive
3. the ability to process self-questions without feeling defensive.

The couple's problem gives the therapist permission to enter the family. It legitimizes the need for therapy and opens the door for therapeutic intervention. The therapist needs to understand how to use the couple's problem to position himself or herself in the family in a way that will expand the couple's worldview. It is helpful to begin therapy with general questions along the lines of the following:

1. What would you like to have happen today?
2. What is your definition of your concerns?
3. How have you tried to resolve this problem?

4. What do you hope will happen in this session to give you a sense that things could be different?
5. What other therapies have you been involved in? How useful have they been?

These initial questions begin the slow process of moving the couple away from their preoccupation with the problem. The therapist should avoid responses in which one partner builds on the story of the other. Regardless of how one partner answers a question, the other partner should be asked the same question. The therapist should encourage each partner to direct his or her answers to the therapist. This approach purposely discourages interaction between the partners. One way couples try to achieve safety in therapy is by attempting to duplicate in the therapist's office the experiences they have with each other at home. If the couple manages to do this during the initial reactive phase, they will feel safe but stuck. The goal of the therapist is to offer the couple an experience they have not had before, such as being able to talk about self in ways in which they have not been able to do previously with each other. A powerful way to accomplish this is to encourage the partners to talk through the therapist to each other. When one partner is answering questions, the other assumes a passive, observant role. The challenge is to give one partner an opportunity to think about a question, reflect on it, and answer it while the other partner hears the question, listens to the answer, and reflects on his or her own thinking about the question without feeling the need to assume a defensive stance. When the therapist can provide this type of structure at the beginning of the first session, there is greater likelihood that the couple will be able to move into the second stage of the first session, the reframing stage.

The Reframing Stage: Focus on Self Issues

If each partner has been able to explain his or her reasons for seeking therapy and has felt understood by the therapist, the couple is then ready to move into the middle stage of the first session. The middle stage is evident when the partners begin to talk more about self issues than the presenting problem. During the reframing stage the focus is on how the individual has developed into a self over his or her life span. The emphasis is on broadening the concept of family. The process of constructing the genogram begins in the reframing stage. During this stage the therapist will devote several minutes to each partner's story about his or her family-of-origin experiences. This focus provides the partners with a chance to reflect on their history in a safe, neutral environment. It is quite common for the partners to begin to acquire new information about each other just by listening to each other's stories about their early years. The type of new learning that can occur is illustrated in the following case example:

A couple presented with severe marital problems. They were considering divorce because each felt the other was more preoccupied with his or her career than with the marriage. When I asked the wife to tell me her story about her family she explained that her father was never there for her. He died when she was 11 years old. Basically she was raised by an older sister as her mother had to return to work. After the father died, she felt alone and abandoned. When she was 15 her mother remarried, and she never got along with her stepfather. At age 16 she left home to live with her sister, never to return to her family home. As she told this story she cried about the father she had hardly known. She felt that if her father had lived she might have felt better about herself, more loved and wanted. When she finished, her husband remarked that he had never realized she had lost her father at such an early age, that she had left home when she was 16 and didn't get along with her stepfather. She had never told him this sad story. The knowledge he gained truly gave him a different sense of his wife's struggles and why she felt safer in her career than in the relationship.

During the reframing stage the therapist encourages the partners to reflect on their family-of-origin experiences and how their current problems are related to some of their early losses. As this process unfolds there is generally a softening of the issues and the beginning of a deeper connection between the partners.

The task of the therapist during the reframing stage is to stimulate the couple to think in new ways about their problems. A therapist should not offer quick answers to or explanations about the problems.

During the reframing stage the therapist lays the groundwork for the ongoing therapy. If the therapist has taken each member methodically through his or her family history and identified themes that help explain why the person is emotionally stuck, then the therapist can build on those themes in future sessions. There are several common themes arising out of family-of-origin experiences, such as abandonment, death, loss, shame, isolation, intimacy, and safety. Once the therapist has been able to identify the major themes he or she can begin to contract with the couple about ongoing therapy.

The Ending Stage: Contracting for Ongoing Therapy

The ending stage of the first session builds on all that has been accomplished thus far. The therapist should ensure that approximately 5 minutes are available at the end of the session for contracting.

By the end of the session the therapist should be in a position to convey to the partners that their problems are symbolic of family-of-origin issues. The therapist should make it clear that for ongoing therapy to be successful, the partners will have to be prepared to work on their own personal themes. It will be difficult for the couple to understand this principle if the therapist hasn't brought out their powerful family themes earlier in the session.

The case example that follows illustrates how the therapist, through questioning, brings out the important themes in the life of each member of the couple, so that by the conclusion of the session they are prepared to think about family-of-origin work rather than focus on their relationship problems.

In concluding the first session the therapist should explain to the couple the theoretical bases for the therapy. The explanation the therapist offers will be consistent with and reinforce what the couple has already experienced in the session. The therapist will want the couple to leave the session feeling understood, curious, challenged, hopeful, a bit confused, yet connected, both individually and as a couple, with the therapist.

To accomplish these tasks, the therapist must employ several specific strategies.

Practice Strategies for the Beginning Stage of Family Therapy with Couples

There are a number of practice strategies to employ in the beginning stage of family therapy with couples. In fact, these strategies are employed during the entire therapeutic process but are most evident during the reactive stage of therapy.

Staying in Control of the Process to Influence Content

The family therapist must always be in control of the process. People bring well-established stories to therapy and use their stories to stay emotionally safe. They are comfortable with them intact. The challenge for the therapist is to be able to understand how people use these stories to distance emotionally. The therapist will encourage the individual to begin to talk about the meaning of the story for self rather than focusing on the content. For example, an individual may tell a story about how angry and upset he or she is with his or her partner. The individual will accuse the partner of a number of hurtful behaviors and generally put pressure on the therapist to agree with his or her perception of the other. The therapist should respond by asking such individuals how they have learned to respond to the other in their particular way. Focusing on self in the story rather than on the other is a way of controlling the content. The emphasis is on what is stirred up in self rather than on what is going on with the other. The therapist must proceed with caution and sensitivity as some individuals become more anxious and defensive when asked self-questions. Certain individuals are so used to projecting out their anxiety onto the other and the world at large that when the therapist focuses on self, the individual feels criticized and blamed. The therapist must know when to stay with self-questions and when to allow the individual the safety of projecting out.

Avoiding Collusions

A major challenge for the therapist is to avoid colluding with people's stories. Each partner will try to get the therapist to join with him or her around that person's point of view about what is wrong with the family and/or the relationship. The therapist's commitment to both individuals in the relationship always has to be balanced. The therapist needs to remain neutral and avoid being drawn into content issues, secrets, conspiracies, privileged information, or becoming a party to a special relationship with one family member at the expense of other family members.

The therapist must make it clear to the couple that his or her involvement is with the entire family. He or she should discourage any one family member from developing a special relationship with him or her. It is wise for the therapist to see the couple together on an ongoing basis unless something unusual is happening. When there is a reason to see an individual alone, it is important for the therapist to explain to the couple that whatever is discussed by individual members will be brought up when appropriate at family or couple sessions. When the therapist is able to remain evenhanded and join with all important members of the family, he or she can become a powerful, positive force for helping the family members find their way with each other.

The Therapist Stays Detached, Curious, and Involved

The therapist takes a "detached I" therapeutic stance. He or she does not become overinvolved with the family. The therapist is curious about the couple's stories, asks questions that allow each partner to define self-issues better, and avoids taking responsibility for the therapy's outcome. The therapist allows each member to present issues in a safe, nonjudgmental atmosphere. Rather than become preoccupied with outcome, the therapist should remain curious about what impact a change has had on any member of the family. If a couple complains about how things have gone since the previous session, the therapist should ask them about how they understand that experience. Similarly, if a couple reports that they have had a successful week, the therapist should be curious about how they managed to make this happen. The therapist should put the responsibility for change on the couple and should ask them questions that allow them to understand their part in that experience. The therapist must remain detached from the family members' emotional systems. If the therapist becomes anxious, reactive, or needs certain changes to occur, he or she will lose this detachment and can potentially become a negative force in the lives of the family members.

Self Questions

The therapist must ask the couple questions no one else has asked. Ordinarily, clients' answers are not as important as their thinking about the questions. There is a difference between the verbal answer and the thoughts the question stirs up. The therapist should not ask questions that make a client defensive.

Once an individual becomes defensive, he or she stops thinking about the question and puts energy into defending a position. The therapeutic benefit of the session is reflected in the individual's private thoughts about the questions. A therapist's questions can:

1. plant a new idea into the thoughts of the person,
2. elicit more data, and
3. enable the client, through responses to the questions, to share something new with other family members.

Planting new ideas by asking questions is an intriguing way to teach clients about themselves. The client is aware of the discrepancy between what he or she says publicly and is thinking privately. If the therapist can remain sufficiently detached to ask the client good questions without stirring up reactivity and defensiveness, the client will begin to rethink the story, sometimes without acknowledging it outwardly. Often when the client is answering a question he or she is privately reevaluating the answer and taking a different position regarding the issue. *The therapist should not interfere with this process by trying to make something happen for the client that is based more on the therapist's need to have it happen than the client's.* I have often had clients report that they were struck by a certain question and mulled it over for many weeks afterward. In many cases I wasn't aware that the question had had such an impact. In talking more about this dynamic, clients have reported that they have watched themselves answer a question and realized as they were talking that the answer did not really reflect what they were thinking. As they considered the question later at home and further pondered its meaning they found they began to change their position about the emotional issues with which they were struggling.

In asking clients questions that encourage them to tell their stories, the therapist learns more about the clients' lives. This knowledge helps the therapist develop hypotheses that lead to further questions. *The therapist should not become committed to his or her hypotheses.* Basically, a hypothesis helps one formulate questions. When a client's story or response to a question challenges a hypothesis, the therapist should give up that hypothesis and formulate new ones. If the therapist tries to prove a hypothesis, he or she is no longer sufficiently detached. He or she is reacting to the client's story instead of being proactive and curious about how the client's story is shaping the client's life.

When the therapist asks a question that allows the client to share something intimate with other family members, a positive connection occurs. One of the major tasks of the therapist is to provide the client with a safe milieu in which to tell a story in a way that allows other family members to learn something. The client has an opportunity to share a part of self in a way that is impossible to replicate in the family setting. When the therapist blocks other family members' usual responses to the client's story, thereby giving the client the chance to be heard, both the client and other family members learn about themselves.

As the therapist observes how a client responds to self-questions, the therapist begins to develop a sense of how solid the individual is emotionally. Three major indicators of unfinished business are reflected in how a client responds to self-questions. A solid self can:

1. reflect on his or her family history,
2. listen to the partner's story without interrupting and needing to defend, and
3. talk about self issues without blaming or criticizing.

When an individual can respond as a solid self to questions, therapy is likely to move rapidly. In contrast, when an individual is cut off from his or her history, is quick to react to the partner's story, and frequently blames and criticizes, the therapist will have to slow down the process.

As therapy progresses the therapist is able to ask an increasing number of self-questions. A self-question is structured to allow the individual to reflect on his or her own part in an interaction rather than to project out. Examples of self-questions are:

1. What have you learned about your concerns in the relationship?
2. In the past, what worked for you in the relationship?
3. What part have you played in your current dilemma?
4. What would you lose if you did not react to the other in this way?
5. What themes of yours are being played out in this issue?
6. What can you do to respond differently to this situation?

The degree to which a person is able to reflect on these types of questions gives an indication of how quickly he or she will be able to move from the reactive stage of therapy to the proactive, reframing stage.

Using Expressions of Clients' Ambivalence as Positive Openings

An important systems principle is to "go with the energy." Most clients are ambivalent when they enter therapy. They both want to change and dread changing. They want a therapist who is able to show them a better way of living, yet are terrified about having to take responsibility for their part in the problems. Ambivalence is healthy and normal. The therapist's challenge is to connect with the healthy parts of the ambivalence. *Ambivalence* is a more positive term than *resistance*. Generally, people are not resistant to therapy but are anxious about experimenting with new ways of being different. The therapist should ask questions that help people to gain awareness of their basic ambivalence and find creative ways to experiment with being different without becoming anxious to the point of being debilitated. Going with the energy involves encouraging clients to talk about what makes it better for them to stay the same. Asking a question such as "How have you learned over your life what works for you?" helps clients understand how their problems actually keep them safe in the world.

Connecting Past Issues with Present Concerns

Clients' problems usually have some connection with past issues. The therapist should ask clients about what have they learned in the past that has given meaning to their present concerns. Many lessons from the past serve as guides for the present. The legacy of our family-of-origin experiences is played out in the present. When an individual assumes a strong emotional stance, it is helpful to ask about how he or she learned to take that stance. Two questions that help couples connect the past with the present are "How do you honor your parents' relationship in your own marriage?" and "How do you honor your original family in your new family?" These types of questions help the individual reflect on the choices he or she has made for dealing with the present in a different way. Many of us don't realize how bound we are to our past experiences. When we become anxious, our tendency is to react as we did in the past. When the therapist questions how individuals have learned to respond, they are encouraged to reevaluate their ways of dealing with current dilemmas.

Placing the Problem in Historical Perspective

It is important for family members to understand that their problems have a historical connection—the timing of the problem is often linked with some major event in the multigenerational family history. The construction of the genogram—surveying the family field—often reveals the link between major family events and the onset of certain symptoms. Often a problem with a child commences around the time of a significant loss in the extended family. A marital relationship problem may coincide with the death of a parent or the breakup of a sibling's marriage. The timing of family events is critical. Developmental losses, changes, marriages, divorces, and illnesses are all potentially high-stress events. The death of a parent can throw a family into disarray. At one time I saw a couple in which the husband's family had experienced eight deaths within a two-year period. The couple married during this period and were soon having serious marital problems. The husband never connected the deaths in his family with his withdrawal from his bride. The wife almost immediately felt rejected by her husband. She was not aware that his having to deal with all the losses in his extended family affected his ability to give her what she needed emotionally. When family members can understand the impact of major life events they begin to develop a different appreciation of what each family member struggles with to feel secure and cared for.

Understanding the Presenting Problem as a Metaphor for Unfinished Business

Throughout the therapeutic process the therapist will be attempting to help various family members understand that their focus on the other is basically about some fundamental loss, vulnerability, or anxiety within self. The need to have the other be different for self to feel safe actually erodes the sense of connection and intimacy in a relationship. When individuals begin to understand what they emotionally bring to a marriage, they become better able to deal with their self issues without resorting to blame, projection, and criticism. The therapist should try to develop hypotheses about what the problem represents symbolically in terms of self issues. The therapist can then help the individuals rethink how they use the problem to maintain safe emotional distance.

It is important to understand the concept of blame. If an individual blames and projects, he or she will be unable to learn something new or be creative about how to solve life dilemmas. When an individual realizes his or her need for the other to be different is really about self, the individual can begin to slow down the process of projection and defense and become more curious about what that issue about *the* other really represents in terms of self. The importance of understanding presenting problems as metaphors for loss, vulnerability, and anxiety is discussed in detail in Chapter 8.

Balancing Problems with Successes

The therapist must not get lost in people's problems. There isn't much therapeutic value in devoting the entire session to the clients' problems and losses. It is more productive to give balance to a session. Balance involves giving clients an opportunity to talk about their successes as well as their problems. It is helpful to encourage clients to talk about the heroes, guides, and mentors they have had in their lives, the mentors and guides who served as role models and positive influences on the development of their sense of self in the world. The therapist should bring out clients' sense of competence, health, and positive vision about how they can be different in the world. The essential goal of the therapist is to make each client his or her own hero. Each client will have had some successful experiences but the memories of those experiences may have gotten lost in life's anxieties. The challenge for the therapist is to reduce the anxiety within individuals to a level that allows them to reflect on their own ideas of how they wish to get the job of living done. To discover people's wisdom, the therapist has to believe there is wisdom in each individual, that throughout people's lives they have had some successes and have encountered people who have offered them positive lessons about how to be in the world.

The therapist should ensure that a part of each session is

devoted to giving the client the opportunity to talk about experiences that have resulted in his or her feeling successful, competent, or hopeful. If an individual can reflect on something positive in his or her life, then that person has a foothold into health. By focusing on health and competence, the client can expand self-vision in the world; over time this will become more and more the client's own reality. *The therapist should not be the "wise one."* The therapist is a guide who allows the individual to find his or her personal wisdom.

The following interview illustrates many of the already described practice principles. This interview was for the purposes of a consultation, and not ongoing therapy. For this reason, the session takes on a slightly different dimension. Nevertheless, it is representative of a first session with a couple who is experiencing both marital and family problems. The couple had separated; however, they had continued together in therapy with another therapist. One of their goals was to reintegrate as a couple and family. In preparation for the consultation, they were told only that a consultant would be seeing them and that they would have an opportunity to discuss what they had been working on in therapy to that point.

First Session with a Couple and Commentary

When beginning a first session it is important for the therapist to connect quickly with each partner. He or she should begin by asking each partner what he or she anticipates will happen in the session. Even in a consultation, the couple should be asked about how they understand their coming to the session. These questions help the therapist understand the clients' assumptions about and expectations for the session. The session commences:

Dr. F.: I think it might be wise for me to ask each of you what you were told was going to happen this afternoon, what your expectations are.

Peter: We were told that you would know very little and would add more light to the subject. Other than that, that's about it.

Dr. F.: Wendy, you?

Wendy: Just about the same.

Dr. F.: Maybe you could tell me, then, what did you think about doing this?

Wendy: Besides being camera-shy . . .

Dr. F.: What did you hope would happen when you agreed to the interview?

Peter: No expectations; it couldn't do any damage, so we might as well give it a shot.

Dr. F.: And for you, Wendy?

Wendy: It might be helpful. Nervous about doing it.

Dr. F.: Well, then, let's start. Tell me what you've been working on.

Peter: You go ahead, Wendy.

Dr. F.: Catch me up on the work you've been doing.

Wendy: Lately?

Dr. F.: Say, over the past six months or so.

Wendy: Okay. I'm very busy right now. I went from doing absolutely nothing, I didn't leave the house, didn't go anywhere. I've been taking different courses, going different places, and meeting different people.

Commentary

The partners have each had a chance to communicate their general understanding about what the experience is going to be.

Now Dr. F. encourages the husband and wife to define the problem as they each see it for themselves. The therapist tries to tease out their personal theories about the family concerns. It quickly becomes clear that the wife takes the major responsibility for the relationship and family difficulties. She puts herself in the center of the problem and in some ways blames herself for the couple's struggles.

The job of the therapist is gently to challenge the wife's definition of herself as the family problem. If he colludes with her thinking, then he becomes part of the couple's stuckness. If the couple is left with the belief that the wife needs to change for the relationship to work, then the therapist has colluded with the couple's definition of the problem.

Dr. F.: Wendy, maybe you could tell me how you define the problems that have been happening. What do you tell yourself?

Wendy: Oh, boy that's a difficult one because there are lots of little things, I think.

Dr. F.: But I imagine you have an understanding that you carry in your head about what's been happening . . .

Wendy: Okay. Well, I think a lot of it has to do with me. That I got to the point that I was doing absolutely nothing and wanting so much out of him . . .

Dr. F.: Out of Peter?

Wendy: Yeah, to provide things for me, or entertainment for me that it just got to be overwhelming, just too much.

Commentary

The therapist will now begin to shift away from the wife's defining herself as the problem by expanding on whom she defines as family.

Dr. F.: You've been married how long?

Wendy: Fourteen years now.

Dr. F.: Fourteen?

Wendy: Or 13, I've lost track of it.

Dr. F.: Thirteen years, and you are 33?

Wendy: Yeah.

Dr. F.: And you have how many children?

Wendy: Two.

Dr. F.: Two children and how many pregnancies?

Wendy: One.

Dr. F.: You have two children and one other pregnancy? Three pregnancies altogether?

Wendy: Nope. Two, oh just a minute now, our oldest was mine, the younger one is adopted.

Dr. F.: That's John?

Wendy: Yeah.

Dr. F.: At what age did you adopt him?

Wendy: He was a newborn.

Dr. F.: The oldest one?

Wendy: The oldest one is 12.

Dr. F.: Any other pregnancies?

Wendy: Yeah, one other pregnancy. I was 17, 18.

Dr. F.: What year was that?

Peter: '74, '75.

Wendy: No, we were married in '73. It's got to be '72, '71.

Dr. F.: '71, '72. Kind of vague now. Tell me when you first said to yourself something isn't working here in this family.

Wendy: When he said he was leaving.

Dr. F.: I don't understand. Give me a date.

Wendy: November thirteenth; it's my lucky number.

Dr. F.: What year?

Wendy: '88

Commentary

The therapist now asks the wife her thoughts about what was not working for her in the family. This shift in questioning reframes the concerns toward what the wife needed to have different in the family. It encourages the wife to talk about her own needs for things to be different rather than focus on her feeling responsible for the family concerns. The therapist plants the thought that she has needs, too.

Dr. F.: Until then, were you concerned about anything for yourself?

Wendy: Well, I knew we had a few, I knew I had a few problems. I never could figure an answer to them. There were a few things wrong but it wasn't all that bad. It was a shock to me.

Dr. F.: You weren't expecting it.

Wendy: Nope.

Dr. F.: No other separations in 13 years?

Wendy: No.

Dr. F.: Then you had to give yourself an explanation as to why Peter said he was leaving.

Wendy: Yeah.

Dr. F.: What did you tell yourself?

Wendy: It was me.

Dr. F.: What about you did you think he was leaving about?

Wendy: That I just expected too much, that I did absolutely nothing, I mean literally nothing. I always was mad at one thing or another, not from anything that was happening, I always seemed to be mad.

Dr. F.: That's what you said to yourself. Did you get anywhere close to a separation before that day?

Wendy: I don't think so.

Dr. F.: Just as you remember it.

Wendy: No.

Commentary

The therapist now shifts to the husband and asks him similar questions. He tries to tease out the husband's theories and assumptions about what went wrong in the family and marriage.

The therapist does not build on the wife's theory. He attempts to ask the husband neutral questions about where he places the problem. This approach is important. If the therapist simply asked the husband to respond to the wife's story, then it would be difficult to determine whether the husband had developed a separate story for himself. The therapist now has an opportunity to learn about the differences between the people in this marriage. Asking each to define the problem separately helps determine who is the more reactive in the relationship, who needs more distance, and who has more ability to stay curious and objective about the family situation.

Dr. F.: Well, you tell me, Peter, what story you carry about what has been happening.

Peter: Basically the same story, only I discovered the problem over eight years ago or better. I realized that we weren't getting along and weren't creating a life, just existing. So at that time I tried to talk Wendy into going to counseling and doing something so we could cure the problem. . . .

Dr. F.: This is eight years ago?

Peter: It was eight, seven, somewhere around then. Anyway Wendy wasn't interested at that time and I couldn't convince her so I tucked myself into a job and went to work, seven days a week, twelve hours a day until I guess last year I realized that it was still not really curing anything on my end. And Wendy still didn't seem to have any interest in—

Wendy: I just went on in my head.

Peter: And we had the same constant fights and the same constant battles over the same very small things so I just threw my hands up in the air in November and moved out.

Commentary

The therapist attempts to define a time in the relationship when the problems first occurred. By fixing this date he can go back to a time when things were better and begin to build on a history of positives. This maneuver is necessary to show that the family concerns did not always exist. If the couple can identify a time when things were better, this knowledge can serve as a beachhead for the couple to build upon. When couples say there was never a good time in the relationship, that the marriage started on a downturn, it is considerably more difficult for the therapist to reframe the relationship problems. However, most couples are able to identify a period in the relationship when they felt more connected and worked better together as a family. This period becomes an important one to focus on in ongoing therapy.

Dr. F.: So your concerns go back at least eight years.

Peter: Yeah, seven, eight years.

Dr. F.: Peter, tell me what you said to yourself, what was the explanation you gave yourself back then about what wasn't working?

Peter: I wrote an awful lot of it off as Wendy being very ill for a period of time before that, and when you're in the hospital a long time and you come out of the hospital, you're housebound. So I think that accounted for a couple of years, anyway. After the houseboundness didn't go away I realized that things were getting pretty boring. Uninteresting. That's when I thought we should go see a counselor or do something like that but Wendy didn't think we had a problem. . . .

Wendy: I thought he said to me at that time *I* should see a counselor or something. I didn't realize that he wanted *us* to see one, that there was a problem with *us*, I thought it was just *me*. I figured there was something wrong with me.

Peter: We had a terrible communication problem for a lot of years.

Commentary

The therapist does not permit the couple to fight or react to each other. At this point, if the therapist did not stay in control of the process, the couple might carry out a familiar fight, one of blaming each other for the family difficulties. The tendency during the reactive stage of the first session is for the partners to try to reinforce their own definitions of the problem. The therapist must discourage the couple from reacting to each other by asking each partner questions and directing the partner's answers to the therapist, not the other partner.

Dr. F.: Let's go back then even farther. Tell me, Peter, when was the best period for the relationship, when things were working the best?

Peter: Oh, really we had a very good first five or six years. It was really good.

Dr. F.: From '73 to '78, '79.

Peter: Yeah, somewhere around there, '77, '78.

Dr. F.: What was good about it? What was working then?

Peter: Well, communication was a lot better. We were doing things. Out and about, I guess. Not a continuous high, you know, but at least there was the good with the bad.

Commentary

The therapist takes the husband back to the beginning of the relationship. He tries to get him to talk about his hopes and dreams, and what he needed from the marriage to feel safe. He is connecting with the husband on the positive history. He also begins to discover unfinished business as he hears stories about how the partners found each other, what they needed from each other, and how they started their family.

Dr. F.: How long had you known Wendy before you got married?

Peter: Six, nine months. Somewhere in there, I think, six months or three months.

Dr. F.: How old were you then?

Peter: 20.

Dr. F.: So you were both 20.

Wendy: How about 19?

Dr. F.: Had you been close to getting married before, engaged to anyone?

Wendy: Actually, it would have been six months. My dad talked us into it earlier for taxes at that time.

Dr. F.: It was a short courtship.

Wendy: Very.

Dr. F.: Tell me what was it, go back in your memory, what was it about Wendy that made you say to yourself, "This is the one for me"?

Peter: I think that one I would need about four hours to come up with an answer for. . . .

Dr. F.: Well, take your time.

Peter: It was enjoyable. We were compatible at the time in what we were doing. It worked. We really didn't plan on getting married in three months. As I say we planned on getting married in the spring and for tax purposes rushed it ahead a little, I guess.

Commentary

The therapist now begins to ask questions that focus directly on unfinished business. He asks the husband what he needed from his wife to feel safe in the world. Questions such as these can elicit information about the parts of self the individual feels most vulnerable about. It is helpful to ask couples at the beginning of therapy what each needed from the other to feel safe in the world. This question also shifts the focus away from the relationship struggle to what self needed in the relationship to feel safe and connected.

Dr. F.: Well, let me ask you this question, then, and it's kind of an odd one. What did you think Wendy could give you when you first met her?

Peter: I think it was just the companionship.

Dr. F.: That you needed from her that you couldn't give yourself.

Peter: Yeah.

Dr. F.: And the companionship looked like what? The type of companionship that you needed?

Peter: Companionship only means one thing to me, being together, having someone to do something with on a regular basis.

Commentary

As the session proceeds, the therapist mentions to the husband that he was informed by the couple's therapist that the husband was an only child. By focusing on the husband's family-of-origin experiences the therapist begins to move into the middle stage of the first interview. The therapist has been able to move away from the couple's reactivity about the relationship problem to a beginning discussion of what each has brought into the relationship. The therapist now becomes more direct about asking the husband questions about his own extended-family experiences. The therapist begins with the husband because he senses that the husband is a bit of a distancer. The therapist wants, as quickly as possible, to connect with the husband around his sense of family.

Dr. F.: Well, Bob told me you are an only child. So your parents had no other pregnancies as far as you know?

Peter: As far as I know.

Dr. F.: Any other children brought into the home?

Peter: No.

Dr. F.: No cousins?

Peter: No.

Dr. F.: And you grew up where?

Peter: In Vancouver.

Dr. F.: What part did you play as the only child in the relationship between your mother and your father?

Peter: My dad passed away when I was 6, so being that young I really don't have any recollection.

Commentary

The therapist begins to learn about some significant losses in the early life of the husband. First there was the death of his father. A little later, the therapist learns that the husband stayed with an aunt after his father's death, resulting in a year's separation from his mother. The therapist's view that the husband is a distancer becomes more understandable.

The therapist hypothesizes that part of the attraction to the marriage for the husband was his hope that his wife's family would be a replacement family. This hypothesis is confirmed later in the interview, when the therapist discovers that the husband had been very involved with his wife's father, and had deeply mourned his death. The theme of loss of father and a sense of family abandonment is played out in this relationship. The husband shows a beginning recognition of this dynamic when the therapist begins to ask specific questions about family-of-origin losses.

Dr. F.: Any sense of your father?

Peter: Yeah.

Dr. F.: What memories do you carry about your father?

Peter: Just the standard issue trip. I remember us going to a hockey game.

Dr. F.: Do you have pictures of your dad, you and your father?

Peter: Oh, yeah.

Dr. F.: What did he die of?

Peter: Brain hemorrhage.

Dr. F.: And then what happened to your mother after your father died?

Peter: I went and lived with my aunt for I guess about a year.

Dr. F.: Did she have children?

Peter: Yeah. As far as I knew I thought my mother got along quite well, but you know as you get older you realize that she probably had quite a bit of difficulty for the first few years. None of it was ever relayed to me at that time. When I moved back from my aunt's it seems my mum had sold the house and moved around and things seemed quite normal.

Dr. F.: You were 7 by then?

Peter: Yeah.

Dr. F.: And your mother remarried?

Peter: No, not until just about—

Wendy: We were already married.

Peter: Yeah, about maybe nine years ago.

Dr. F.: Outside of that one year with your aunt, you and your mother were together in a household. What happened to your father's family after your father died?

Peter: We were still close.

Dr. F.: You stayed involved with them?

Peter: Oh, yeah. My grandmother lived with us for a short period of time. My dad's brother and all the girls were quite close.

Commentary

The therapist now attempts two things. One, he tries to help the husband identify important family members. The therapist may wish to involve some of these important family members in therapy at a later date. The father's uncles and aunts, grand-mother, mother, and other extended family members may have important information that it would benefit the husband to hear about later. Laying the groundwork for this involvement begins in the first session. The second objective is to obtain a sense of the family model the husband carries in his head. Making the private, personal definition of family public allows the husband, through the therapist, to explain his need for family to the wife without its becoming a battleground. When each partner talks about his or her private model of family and relationship new learning often occurs. Many times our personal definitions of family stay private and are fought out around content issues. Many couples do not realize that they try to make certain things happen in their family as a way of making up for earlier losses in their original families or try to replicate powerful positive experiences they had in their original families.

Dr. F.: I'll tell you why I was asking you that question because I want to ask you a similar question from your experience in family. I was wondering what picture you carried in your head about how a family should look, how a relationship should look.

Peter: Yeah, I've always considered a family to be a group. I like to go places with the kids, I really like to take them everywhere we go.

Dr. F.: That's a high priority for you. Well, tell me about that. How did you know that? Where did that come from? It's important.

Peter: I never really thought of it before because I never tried to picture what I thought a family should be in those terms.

Dr. F.: I'll tell you what I've learned: I've learned that we have a picture of how a family should be from what we've experienced and from what we haven't experienced. So that's what I'm wondering, which one it was.

Peter: I don't know, my mother never left me behind. It didn't matter where she went, I usually could go if I wanted to go, so I don't think it is from being left behind. I had a relatively free rein for what I wanted to do with my own free time from about 9 years old on.

Commentary

The therapist now asks questions that are directed toward learning more about Peter's connection with his original family. How did he involve important extended family members in his decision making? The therapist tries to discover the husband's degree of involvement, both positive and negative, in important extended family relationships.

Dr. F.: How did you prepare your mother for your getting married?

Peter: Told her. Nothing much, just went down one weekend and saw her.

Wendy: And said, "Hey, we're getting married!"

Peter: This is going to be my wife, we're going down to buy a ring, and we're going to get married.

Dr. F.: And you were 19. What did she say?

Peter: Fine.

Dr. F.: How soon after you got married did your mother get married?

Peter: It was five years. John was a couple of years old, it was quite a while.

Dr. F.: What were you worried might happen to your mother when you got married and started your own family?

Peter: My mother is relatively strong. I had no concerns

about her ability because I had already moved out at that time. I hadn't lived at home for a year and a half.

Dr. F.: So you didn't have anxieties about her feeling alone, then. What size family do you think would be ideal for you? How many children?

Peter: At one time I thought an awful lot would be good, but then—

Wendy: Just after we got married he said he wanted twelve kids. I'm going NO!

Peter: See, I've got great patience. They don't bother me at all, but after being married to Wendy for a couple of years I knew that would have been a very big mistake.

Commentary

The husband has commented on two important matters, his disappointment in his wife and a personal dream. The therapist ignores the negative comment about the wife and focuses on the husband's comment about the personal dream. The husband's comments reveal his ambivalence. It is safer for him to focus on how his wife has defeated his dreams than to talk about the reasons for his hopes and desires. As the therapist sidesteps the negative comment and focuses on the sense of loss that the husband has experienced about not being able to fulfill his dreams, the wife becomes more connected with the husband and begins to understand at a deeper level how his losses originated in his family of origin.

It is essential for the therapist to understand this process. For healing to occur in a family, the therapist must be able to bring out the dreams and hopes of its individual members, always recognizing they may frame these in negative terms based on their perception that other family members and/or the world has prevented them from attaining these goals. By sidestepping the focus on the other, which is a form of a triangle, and staying focused on the origin of the dreams, desires, and hopes, the therapist can begin the healing process of allowing the individual to talk about a part of himself or herself in a safe, connecting way.

Dr. F.: But that was a bit of a dream, having a large family?

Peter: Oh yeah, kids.

Dr. F.: And have you asked yourself why that would be nice for you?

Peter: You can make a baseball team up without a problem. Obviously what you miss in your own childhood I guess you look for, and being an only child you think that brothers and sisters can be an asset rather than a hindrance. Then you watch your own two children fight and you think it might be easier if one lived in one house and one lived in the other.

Dr. F.: Your kids are six years apart. It is almost like you have two only children there, eh?

Peter: Yeah.

Dr. F.: In some ways. How did that spacing happen?

Peter: Basically because of the adoption, the way the time periods work. We applied quite early but it took oh, three years before anything, four years.

Wendy: Yeah, we were adopting a 3-year-old boy which they said there were lots of and somehow we ended up with a newborn kid. It was a mix-up in our paperwork.

Peter: After waiting that long, when they finally decide that you can have a child, you don't really quibble at the age of them.

Wendy: Otherwise they would have been only a year apart, really. When we first started.

Commentary

The therapist has asked the husband about several important developmental issues. He has gently moved the husband away from focusing on the relationship problems to looking at self issues. The task now is to go through a similar procedure with the wife. He will then have moved the couple into the middle of the reframing stage of the first interview, both partners having spent a fair amount of time sharing important self issues without resulting in conflict and blame.

Dr. F.: Well, Wendy, you come out of a family quite different from Peter's, I gather from the little bit that Bob shared with me. Four siblings?

Wendy: One brother, two sisters.

Dr. F.: What did you learn about family that you've brought into this family, into your new family?

Wendy: Well, I actually think I learned quite the wrong things.

Dr. F.: Tell me what comes to mind.

Wendy: Well . . .

Commentary

The wife begins her discussion about family on a negative note. The therapist is attempting to encourage the wife to talk about some positive lessons she brought into her new family but discovers that the wife is somewhat down on herself. Rather than encouraging this sort of discussion, he stops her. He encourages her to think about the question but does not allow her to answer it at that time because of the likelihood that it would result in her feeling more negative about herself. The therapist takes a different tack and asks the wife about what she needed from her husband that she felt she didn't get enough of in her family of origin. The therapist is now trying to discover the degree of unfinished business each has brought into the marriage.

Dr. F.: Let me ask you another question first because your mind will work on that. You heard me ask Peter what he saw in you that made him think you were the woman for him. Were you close to marrying anyone else, or engaged?

Wendy: Oh, somebody had once asked me but I had no thoughts or questions about it, it just wasn't going to be. You know, for myself, no.

Dr. F.: So this was the first guy where you said to yourself, "This is the guy for me." You were 19 years old?

Wendy: Yeah.

Dr. F.: What was it about him that made you think this would be right for you?

Wendy: Companionship.

Dr. F.: Same thing.

Wendy: Yeah, we were able to talk for hours and hours on end. We got along very, very well. It seemed to be a great friendship. Things just seemed to blend and to work quite well.

Dr. F.: What did you think Peter could give you that you thought you didn't get enough of or didn't give yourself?

Wendy: Friendship.

Dr. F.: Friendship. Now, here's a tough question: How do you remember your father making you feel special, different from the other three kids?

Wendy: He used to say I had a great temper on me, very stubborn person but in some ways even though it doesn't sound very nice it made me quite different from the other kids in the family because that part of me made me very strong. He always knew that I could get what I wanted or you know, I was always going to be able to do what I really wanted to. I could just go out and get it whereas the rest of the kids really wouldn't. They would talk about it but they wouldn't do it.

Dr. F.: He admired that.

Wendy: Yeah.

Dr. F.: And that allowed you to do what? His admiring helped you to do what?

Wendy: I think it gave me the strength to go through all the sickness that I did and still come out of it. And now I think, right now in my life it has given me the opportunity to be able to stand on my feet, which at first I wasn't sure that I could, but I think that I can now. I think that is probably what he gave me.

Dr. F.: So when you think of my question about family, you have a model in your head for how it should be. What you hoped would be between you and Peter?

Wendy: Well, I always hoped that everybody would get along really, really good. That they would have fun together and nobody would always be saying, "The other one is getting more," you know, "I'm not getting enough." Our family isn't quite like that, but that's what I would like. Everybody would be doing their own thing and getting along really good. Like a bunch of friends instead of rivalry between kids.

Dr. F.: So describe how it worked in your family, in the family you grew up in.

Wendy: I don't know, because I felt quite separated from the rest of the family.

Dr. F.: More so than your sisters and brother?

Wendy: Yeah. I always felt I was quite different from the rest of them. I was called the black sheep, you know, and I didn't get any emotional support out of my family. . . .

Dr. F.: When you say your family, you mean your mother?

Wendy: My mum and my dad.

Dr. F.: Your brother and your sisters?

Wendy: No. No. So I mean I wouldn't want to model my family after that but yet things seemed to be all right as we were growing up. It's only now that I can take a look at it and say, "I don't like it." But yet that's what I did with my family. I did it the same way as my parents did.

Dr. F.: Well, you must have a theory about why you felt separate. You used the black-sheep reference. What is your theory on that?

Wendy: Well, I don't know. The others seemed to be quite smart all the time. They seemed to be able to whiz by their schoolwork. They always had thousands of kids around the house playing with them. I seemed to struggle with my school-work and I never seemed to have anyone to play with. Those are the two main things. They always just seemed to be able to go out of the house and talk to people and I seemed to have to work so hard at it.

Dr. F.: Well, Wendy, tell me which of the kids, which one was closest to your father?

Wendy: Closest to my father?

Dr. F.: Got along with him the best, was the most con-nected?

Wendy: I don't know, I would almost say me.

Dr. F.: That's kind of different from what you were saying a minute ago. Was it a negative connection more than a positive connection?

Wendy: There wasn't any real connection, like he didn't really get involved in this because he was always working or doing something, you know, but like my older sister, all I ever remember is they were always fighting. My brother, well, actually, he's four years older, so they seemed to do a lot for a while until he got older. There was nothing then.

Dr. F.: How about your mother? Who was the most connected with your mum?

Wendy: The most connected?

Dr. F.: Yeah, out of the four of you?

Wendy: Well, I'd say my sister Sarah.

Dr. F.: Is this sister younger than you or older?

Wendy: Older.

Dr. F.: What was the connection that they had?

Wendy: I don't know. It's kind of a strange family because I didn't actually ever really see. The only thing I ever remember is them making sure we had things done and we did things. You know, for work. For anything else it wasn't there. We just came home and we did our own thing. I mean, they used to talk but they used to also fight a lot, too, so that is a very difficult one to answer.

Dr. F.: Have you talked to your siblings about that, your sisters and your brother, about any of these questions I'm asking you?

Wendy: Yeah, lately we have.

Dr. F.: You're just starting to do that.

Wendy: Yeah, and we've all come to the same thing. That there was no emotional support in our house whatsoever. We've actually all said that. I haven't talked to my brother, but . . .

Commentary

The therapist has taken the wife through a brief but important discussion about her relationships with her extended family. The wife has revealed her mythology about her parents and siblings. The therapist stayed curious and open to the wife's set of assumptions about her mother, father, and siblings. He tried to ask questions that did not produce defensive responses. The therapist was looking for degrees of reactivity in all of the relationships in the family. He discovered that the wife has ambivalent feelings about many of the members of her family. The father/daughter relationship is usually important in terms of unfinished business brought into a marriage. When daughters have felt special, approved of, and safe with their fathers, they are usually less needy in their relationships with their husbands. Father/daughter relationships and mother/son relationships are important areas to explore. These relationships seem to provide the training ground for the emotional expectations we carry into a marriage.

Now that the therapist has surveyed the wife's extended family, he moves into a more tender area in her early experience: the abortion she had as a teenager. The therapist's objective is to learn how the wife used her family in deciding not to have that child. Did she discuss it with her mother, her father, her siblings? Did she feel alone with her decision? How supportive did she experience her family as being? It becomes obvious that the wife felt alone in her family. She expected her parents to be more supportive and basically felt that her father did not care enough about her. The wife carries pain arising from a sense of abandonment and betrayal by her family. However, when she begins to discuss how she dealt with her father's cancer and death, she reveals a part of herself that is herolike. The task of the therapist is not to build on the failures of the family but to look for the strengths and connections and to try to make them come to life in a clearer way.

Dr. F.: Wendy, is it okay if I ask you a bit about your first pregnancy?

Wendy: I was 17 years old.

Dr. F.: Can I ask you a few questions about that? Because what I want to ask you is how you involved your family in that decision.

Wendy: It happened and it was forgotten about all at the same time. There was no talking about it. There was no support. No nothing.

Dr. F.: You told your father and your mother?

Wendy: I told my mother. My mother told my father. My father never talked to me about it, never brought it up, never acknowledged it.

Dr. F.: Still?

Wendy: He's now dead. Never even brought it up, no. It was just forgotten about.

Dr. F.: Your father died what year?

Wendy: He died just this past November.

Dr. F.: What did he die of?

Wendy: Cancer.

Dr. F.: How long did he have cancer?

Wendy: Well, he had it eight years ago, and it was the last year that he was sick.

Dr. F.: So you never dealt with your father on this one?

Wendy: No, never again with my mother.

Dr. F.: You still haven't dealt with your mother?

Wendy: No, no.

Dr. F.: Your sisters, how were they with this one?

Wendy: I didn't tell anyone.

Dr. F.: You didn't tell anyone. How did you tell Peter about that?

Wendy: I just told him. He was actually the only person I ever told.

Commentary

It is clear that the abortion stirred up a great deal of resentment for the wife. The therapist asked her how she informed her husband about it to learn whether she used her family experience of feeling alone with the issue as a guide for how to deal with it with her husband. Her revelation that she decided at the beginning of the relationship to tell her husband about the abortion is quite encouraging. Her ability to trust herself enough to tell her husband about this important loss in her life indicates that there is more strength in this woman than first meets the eye.

Dr. F.: How soon into the relationship did you tell Peter about that?

Peter: April.

Wendy: Yeah.

Dr. F.: That must have been a pretty big decision on your part to tell Peter about that.

Wendy: Oh, yeah, because I didn't know how he was going to react but, you know, he even dropped it. You know, I mentioned it and he never said, really, he never said nothing about it either, so it was just like everything else.

Dr. F.: But you made the decision anyway to tell him.

Wendy: Yes.

Dr. F.: Can you go back in your memory, if it's possible to go back, to how you decided, how you made the decision to tell him?

Wendy: Oh, well, that's an easy one, because I figured if a marriage was going to work people had to be really honest. I figured, I don't know. . . . No one else had ever said anything else about it so I thought, oh, well, I'll tell him, because that was the only thing about my past that I didn't like.

Commentary

The therapist asks the wife how she would like to have been able to deal with her father around the pregnancy and abortion. This question is an attempt to get the wife to explain, through the therapist to the husband, what she needs in a relationship to feel safe and understood. The hypothesis is that what she needed, but did not get from her father, is an unresolved issue that she has brought into her marriage.

Dr. F.: What would you like to have been able to do with your father about that pregnancy, that abortion?

Wendy: I guess I just wanted them to come up and tell me it was okay, that they didn't hate me for it. That they never would.

Dr. F.: And what did you want from Peter when you told him?

Wendy: I don't know. Maybe I was looking for an answer from him that I never got from my father or my mother.

Dr. F.: Maybe. I was wondering if you learned from your family that you have to be cautious with what you talk about. Is that one of the lessons that you learned?

Wendy: Oh, yeah, very.

Dr. F.: How much of that lesson do you think you brought into the relationship with Peter, the caution?

Wendy: I think to begin with actually quite a bit and then I learned to tell him what I was thinking.

Dr. F.: Starting when?

Wendy: Quite early, because we always seemed to be able to talk. That part never seemed to be very hard to do, but there are always lots of things that go on in your head that you just don't say, that you can't tell.

Dr. F.: How do you decide now what to talk about and what not to talk about with Peter?

Wendy: If I feel nervous about it, I don't say it. I mean, most things, people don't always give you the answer that you're looking for. You know, no matter how hard they try doing it, most of the time it's really hard, and even if it's the right answer you can't do anything about it anyway, so a lot of times it's better just to drop it.

Dr. F.: How did you make the decision not to sit down with your father to tell him about this very important experience? How do you think you decided not to share that with your father, not to talk to him about that?

Wendy: Well, if I didn't talk about it and didn't bring it up then, and forgot about it, then everybody was going to forget about it. There won't be anything heard or anything else about it.

Dr. F.: It was a way of making it safe.

Wendy: Yeah. You do what they say. They don't bring it up if you don't bring it up.

Dr. F.: But you chose to go to your mother. I guess you went to your mother with the hopes that she would tell your father, and your father would come and talk to you.

Wendy: Yeah, or both of them. It didn't quite work that

way. She usually ran the house anyway. If there was anything to be asked you asked her first. It wasn't until, you know, after his first bout of cancer that he actually started talking to us, which from what I understand he wanted all along but he didn't know how to do that.

Dr. F.: When did you learn that, that he wanted that all along?

Wendy: After his cancer, after his first cancer.

Commentary

The therapist shifts away from the discussion around the abortion to focusing on the father's cancer and death. This event is a very significant one in the family's life. The way in which the wife dealt with her father's death is revealing. Her herolike qualities are evident as she discusses being with her father during his last year. Questions about how she approached her father about his cancer, and her own guidelines for dealing with his dying reveal a great deal about her sense of herself, her commitment to her family, and her ability to stay with sadness and loss without needing to distance.

Dr. F.: So that's only about eight years ago. Well, who told you about your father's cancer?

Wendy: The first time? I think my brother did. I think I got a call from my brother. You see, because they were supposed to be on holidays. They came back because he wasn't feeling good.

Dr. F.: What did your brother say?

Wendy: That Poppy had cancer and they weren't sure how it was, whether he would be hospitalized. . . .

Dr. F.: And how do you remember approaching your father about his cancer?

Wendy: Well, I remember going up to the hospital the first time he was in there and telling him that it was going to be okay, not to worry, that it was all right, that he was going to come out of there just fine.

Dr. F.: Over the eight years that he had cancer —

Wendy: Well, he had it and then they said they got it all. Said he had a five-year period, if he got over that everything was just great. . . .

Dr. F.: Then it came back?

Wendy: He made it eight years and then it came back.

Dr. F.: How long did he live after it came back?

Wendy: It was about a year.

Peter: It was about six, seven months.

Dr. F.: Six, seven months before he died.

Wendy: Yeah.

Dr. F.: How were you told about it that time? Who told you?

Peter: Your mother told you.

Wendy: Yes.

Dr. F.: Together? They sat you down —

Wendy: No, because it sort of happened a little bit at a time. He had not been feeling good and he had been coughing a lot. We were trying to get him to his doctor and they were saying there was nothing wrong with him. So it kind of like happened over a period of time. Then they said he had diabetes and then, you know . . . We found out that, you know, he got sicker and so we knew, he told us. He waited a very long time to tell us, I think he knew 'way before he told us.

Dr. F.: Who is the us?

Wendy: Our family.

Dr. F.: Your sisters, your brother, you?

Wendy: Yeah. All of us. I think he waited until he couldn't fight it any more.

Dr. F.: When were you told he was going to die?

Wendy: I think it was last spring.

Dr. F.: Who told you?

Wendy: Oh, it was summertime. He went in for an operation. They said they would be able to remove the tumor and then they said no. I think my mother did because my father was still in the hospital.

Dr. F.: So I still don't have a sense of how you were told?

Peter: I think it drags on so long that you almost know it before someone tells you.

Dr. F.: You felt it—

Wendy: Oh, yeah, you definitely felt there was something seriously wrong.

Dr. F.: So you knew your father was going to die and you only had so much time with him.

Wendy: Well, I hadn't quite thought of him dying, but I knew that he was sick enough and that he was really sick. I really didn't want to say that he was going to die because, you know, my father, that's just not going to happen.

Commentary

The therapist inquires how the wife involved her husband in the process of her father's dying. These questions are more prescriptions than true questions. A prescription is a question designed to influence a piece of behavior. Asking the wife about how she involved her husband in her father's dying and how she connected with her husband around the sadness of losing her father provides suggestions about how she might have handled these matters. It is not really important how she answers the question. The goal is to stimulate her to think about how she might do things differently in the future.

Dr. F.: Did you talk to Peter about it, the fact that your father was going to die? Did the two of you acknowledge it with each other?

Wendy: We knew it, I don't think . . . We talked about it. . . .

Dr. F.: The thing I'm asking Wendy is: How did you use Peter? How did you use Peter to help you deal with saying good-bye to your father, your father's eventual death?

Wendy: Saying good-bye to him?

Dr. F.: How did you bring Peter in on this potential loss that you were going to experience?

Wendy: The only thing I asked him, every so often I asked him to hold me. That's it.

Peter: Wendy had a really weird concept. When my grandmother died I made great efforts to go to the funeral and she thought I was nuts. You know, to drive for twelve hours to go to the funeral and drive eight hours back the same day, but I think after going through with your father—

Wendy: See, at that time I always figured if a person died there isn't anything you can do for them. That's just the way life is to me. So to go to a funeral really wasn't something I was ever going to do. I had never been to one. I wasn't going to go to one.

Commentary

The therapist is trying to coax out of the wife the lessons she learned about how to deal with important developmental issues such as death. The husband interjects a criticism about how the wife avoided funerals. The therapist avoids the negative message. Rather than defending the wife or supporting the husband, he asks the wife a question about how she learned to deal with death. He discovers that in the wife's early years she felt alone with death and abandoned by her family. Her decision about funerals was one of the ways in which she tried to protect herself from that sense of abandonment. It is important for her to be able to teach her husband about this in a caring and safe way. The husband will have his own ways of dealing with death and honoring his family. The therapist should also question the husband so he can teach his wife about his way of honoring the dead.

Dr. F.: How did you learn that principle, about death?

Wendy: I don't know.

Dr. F.: Who taught you that?

Wendy: Me.

Dr. F.: You watched how your mother or your father dealt with their own parents?

Wendy: When my father's parents died. . . . I remember there was a lot, it was very traumatic in the house. I remember him. He was very, very upset. That wasn't shared with me.

Dr. F.: How old were you then?

Wendy: I was about 11, 12. When I asked to go to the funeral at that time they said, "No, you are too young!" I remember crying to myself for many nights, and thinking, well, everybody else is and not once did anybody ever talk to me about it.

Dr. F.: You were alone with your grief and your sadness.

Wendy: Usually I was, I dealt with things on my own.

Dr. F.: So it's hard to bring people in. It would be hard for you, I imagine, to bring Peter in on your sadness. It wouldn't be natural from your experiences.

Wendy: At times I've figured it was something I should handle but he was always there. He was, I knew that. You know, he would help. We would talk a little bit. Mostly he would just hold me.

Dr. F.: Did you find it hard to take care of Wendy in her sadness?

Peter: No, no.

Dr. F.: I mean, does she make it easy for you, or do you have to work at it with her?

Peter: I don't—

Wendy: He was very much a part of the family.

Peter: I mean, you know, I didn't work at it.

Dr. F.: Well, tell me about your grandmother. Your grandmother died, when was that?

Peter: Well, that would be a year and a bit ago now.

Wendy: Yeah, it was actually not that long, maybe three or four months before my father died.

Peter: Yeah, it is only about a year ago now.

Wendy: My grandmother died one week before your grandmother died. It was a week after.

Dr. F.: So your grandmother died first?

Wendy: Yeah, and then his grandmother died.

Dr. F.: This would be your mother's mother?

Wendy: Yeah, my mum's mum.

Dr. F.: And then your grandmother died and then soon after that your father died?

Wendy: Yeah.

Commentary

The therapist highlights an important developmental year in the couple's life. During a single year there was a series of deaths. The therapist speculates that these deaths created a degree of stress not fully appreciated by the couple. It also set in motion their unique ways of dealing with loss. These ways may have added to their sense of distance and separateness from each other. It is important for the therapist to explore how these major developmental losses may have affected the couple and their own family.

Dr. F.: Pretty tough year.

Wendy: Very.

Peter: My grandmother was very old.

Dr. F.: How old was your grandmother?

Peter: 93.

Wendy: Oh, 93, yeah.

Peter: She was well prepared, too.

Dr. F.: She was an important part of your life, your growing-up years?

Peter: Oh, yeah, my grandmother was.

Wendy: She was there, I think, more than your mother was there.

Peter: Well, we were really close.

Wendy: I mean, I remember, this too, she talked no end about him. I mean, it didn't matter who was coming over, she had to talk about Peter and all the things he used to do.

Dr. F.: The apple of her eye.

Wendy: Oh, yeah. Very much so, spoiled him rotten.

Peter: Yes.

Dr. F.: Let me ask you a question, then, about a very important loss for you. How did you say good-bye to your grandmother?

Peter: Oh, I saw her about six months before she passed away. She was not really coherent any more. She was drifting in and out quite badly, so it was kind of a blessing to see her go.

Dr. F.: But you knew for a while that she was—

Peter: Oh, yeah.

Dr. F.: So you probably said good-bye to her before she died, a long time before she died.

Peter: Oh, I knew it was quite close. She'd had a stroke, and there were complications, and she had an enlarged heart, so she just . . . She was always talking about dying for the last fifteen years, you know.

Commentary

The therapist introduces another prescription. He highlights the fact that the couple experienced a number of losses over a short period of time. He introduces the notion of teaching about self to the other. Partners usually don't realize that at times of high anxiety the tendencies are to revert to old problem-solving methods with greater intensity. If one uses distancing to feel safe around anxiety-producing situations, one is likely to distance more. If one feels alone around certain losses, one will feel even more alone if there are a great number of losses and may withdraw or shut down emotionally. The interview is drawing to a close and the therapist wants to begin to connect the past with the present. The therapist prepares to end the interview by bringing the couple's stories together in a systematic way. It is crucial that the therapist connect the history to the present situation to give the couple a sense of how they can be different in the future.

Dr. F.: Listening to you talk about the losses you've experienced over the last year or so has set me wondering about how each of you teaches the other about what you need when you get sad, or you've experienced a loss. Wendy, how do you tell him what you need so he doesn't have to do a lot of guesswork?

Wendy: I didn't think there was anything he could really do. There was nothing he could do. The only thing I wanted was him to hold me, that was it. I would ask him, I would tell him.

Dr. F.: Now tell me why that was important to you, to be held.

Wendy: Security, it felt safe.

Dr. F.: You felt someone was there just for you. Peter, how would you answer that question? How would you try to teach Wendy what you needed around these losses?

Peter: Well, my grandmother's loss was quite expected. I didn't really have any difficulty with that. She was so senile for the last couple of years, you almost begin to hope that she can pass away quietly rather than going on the way she was. I found Wendy's father's death a lot more difficult than the other one.

Commentary

The therapist emphasizes that the death of the husband's father-in-law was an important loss for him. The therapist begins to express his hypothesis that the wife's father's death rekindled the husband's loss of his father at age 6. How the couple understands this and comes together around this profound loss will have a strong impact on their sense of connection in the future.

Dr. F.: You were really involved with him.

Peter: Oh, yeah, we got along very well. Once again, grief, I kind of think there is nothing anybody can do for you, it is something you have to handle, or at least I have to handle on my own.

Dr. F.: Why? How did you learn that?

Peter: Well, it's a personal thing. You have personal memories and you have personal bonds, or whatever you want. I didn't feel I needed any help with either of the deaths, emotionally. Frank's was harder, much harder to take because he was—

Wendy: They were very close.

Peter: Yeah, a lot closer. Also, he was fairly active.

Dr. F.: Did he become like a father?

Peter: Oh, I think so, yeah, in a lot of ways. I don't know, I don't think I really needed any help to handle it, or I didn't look for any help to handle it.

Commentary

The therapist attempts to put the couple in a reflective mode. By asking the husband how the death of his wife's father changed their relationship, he attempts to stimulate the couple's thinking about how this loss affects their life together. It is interesting that the husband hears the question as one about negative change. The therapist reminds him that the question was about change in general, not good change or bad change. The question produces some interesting observations on the part of both the husband and the wife about how the death of the wife's father and the husband's grandmother had a profound impact on their sense of connection with each other.

Dr. F.: Peter, what do you think about this question? How did your father-in-law's death change your relationship with Wendy?

Peter: It didn't really because our relationship had already come to pieces completely before it had happened. I don't know if it really had any great effect on—

Wendy: I don't know. I often wondered, when you told me it was only a couple of weeks after my father died that you were leaving. I almost thought that maybe that was part of the reason because it was very hard on all of us and you know, everyone. And you didn't talk about it very much. You kept saying it didn't matter, but then it seemed to me—

Peter: I don't know. It's just that there really doesn't seem to be an awful lot to discuss in the death of somebody to be precise.

Dr. F.: Did you notice the wording of my question? I didn't say your father-in-law's death made the relationship worse. I asked, "How did it change your relationship?"

Peter: Oh, okay, I automatically look for the worst.

Dr. F.: I'll tell you the reason I asked you that question. It's because I think that after a parent dies, we are never the same. Never again.

Peter: I think quite honestly it probably did improve it.

Dr. F.: I hear that. How do you think it changed it, and how do you think it will continue to change it?

Peter: Continually I'm not sure. I think Wendy seemed to mature a little bit with the death of her father in that even before the death of your father, the couple of months when he was quite ill, you were going home and trying to lend a hand, which is something you have never done before.

Wendy: No, because it was the only time in his life he ever said that I was the only one who could help him because nobody else could get close enough to talk to him and he just wanted to talk to someone. He said, "I don't care if you cry," and I said, "I'm going to cry all the way through this," and he said, "Everybody else just tells me not to say anything and not to talk." He said I was the only one who could, he could sit there and talk to me and—

Dr. F.: That was a special connection for the two of you.

Wendy: Yeah. My brother wouldn't have nothing to do with him. Talking to him, you know, he just fell apart.

Dr. F.: You were able to give that to your father?

Wendy: Yes. I was strong enough to do that.

Dr. F.: Answer the question that I asked Peter. How do you think your father's death has changed the relationship, or changed you in the relationship? That would be an even better question.

Wendy: I guess the death of a relative makes you realize that you are the one—

Dr. F.: Not a relative, a father!

Wendy: A father . . .

Dr. F.: Right.

Wendy: The death of your father makes you feel like, I mean, they are still alive. It's like you are still their little kid, you know, you know that you are still his daughter and when he's gone you know that you are no longer able to be considered that. So I guess in that way it changed me because now I knew that that was it, you know. Now for me it was to make sure that my mother was okay and I think things like that changed. . . .

Dr. F.: How about the change for you with Peter?

Wendy: I don't know. I guess I don't quite feel like a little kid anymore. That you know, I am an adult and I can do what I want. I don't need anybody's permission. I think it just made me realize that I wasn't 17, I am 33. Somehow in there I've missed 17 years.

Dr. F.: That's very interesting. Peter, I'd really like to ask you this question about your own dad because you lost your father at age 6. I was wondering what your thinking has been about how it has changed you not having a father for most of your life.

Peter: Oh, I'm sure that it makes lots of changes.

Dr. F.: I'm sure that you have thought about that a lot.

Peter: Oh, yeah. You go through the embarrassment when it first happens because you are the only kid in school or at least end up in that situation, that doesn't have a father. You even find yourself making excuses for him, you know. I think it makes you probably a little more headstrong than not, there is nobody to clean up your messes, either, you end up in some situations. Or you even probably miss a certain amount of the things fathers do with sons. When you are 6 I think you adjust to it quite quickly. I don't think you can relate to it.

Dr. F.: I don't know if you experienced this or not but it seems to me that when people lose a close relative or friend, or special person as an adult and they have lost a parent as a child, the loss of that person as an adult is like grieving that lost parent again. Have you felt that at all?

Peter: Yeah, I think that is close to the same feeling, when you are exceptionally close to somebody.

Dr. F.: Because you really wouldn't have the chance when you were 6 to understand what that was. . . .

Peter: No.

Commentary

The therapist brings the theme of loss and death home in a more direct way. By asking the husband if he ever connected the two deaths, that of his father and his father-in-law, he is trying to encourage both partners to understand how this loss has strained their marriage. He discovers that the wife has already considered the connection. She has even tried to help the husband understand how her father's death affected both him and their marriage.

Dr. F.: It is like you were mourning two parents when you lost her father, your own father. . . .

Peter: Oh, yeah, quite possibly.

Dr. F.: Did you talk to Wendy about that one?

Peter: No.

Dr. F.: Wendy, do you understand what I'm asking Peter?

Wendy: Yeah.

Dr. F.: Had you thought about it that way?

Wendy: Yes, I did, but—

Dr. F.: You did?

Wendy: I often wondered if he connected the two together.

Dr. F.: What did you ask him about that?

Wendy: I don't know. I think maybe I might have brought it up once and he shuffled it off like he is trying right now and uh—

Dr. F.: You noticed that.

Wendy: It was never brought up. Yes, I noticed it.

Dr. F.: That's very impressive that you made that connection.

Wendy: You know, but it was kind of sloughed off. But I wondered, but then I of course thought I could be off base, you know.

Dr. F.: Do you think you are off base?

Wendy: No.

Commentary

The therapist prepares to end the session. He has moved the couple out of the reactive stage, where each blamed the other for their relationship problems and/or they thought that their major concerns somehow rested within the relationship. He then gave each partner an opportunity to talk about self issues and how these issues played into the relationship difficulties.

The goal at the end of the session is to focus on the future. The therapist will ask each partner what he or she would like to accomplish in the future. If the partners have begun to reevaluate their parts in the relationship struggle, their answers to these questions will be a bit different from what they would have been at the beginning of the interview. The therapist begins with the wife, primarily because she seems a little less reactive and more capable of dealing with intimacy and connections.

Dr. F.: Before we stop today, tell me how you would like your future to unfold.

Wendy: I'd like us to be a family again in a very different way. My perception of what a family should be like is what I would try for. I just won't let things be the way I was making them anymore. I mean, there are always going to be fights and there are always going to be bad times but in general I would like everybody to get along and have just a really good time. Enjoy it while we've got it.

Dr. F.: You are not the same person Peter married.

Wendy: No.

Dr. F.: How are you going to teach him about the new person?

Wendy: I think the separation, of course, I'm just learning myself.

Dr. F.: You can be a learner and a teacher at the same time.

Wendy: Yes. There are a lot of things about myself that I'm not sure about right now. I mean, this is all new. I'm not sure if tomorrow I'm going to go back to the old me or if this is going to stay here. I'd like it to stay but I don't know if it will. So I don't know, but I think with the separation we'll get a chance to . . . it's like a chance to meet, as if we were just starting over again. Whether he likes it or not, I don't know if he will like the new me. I don't know, you know, he might decide he doesn't.

Dr. F.: Would that be enough to discourage you? Give that part of yourself up?

Wendy: I don't know. I don't think about it right now. I hope not.

Dr. F.: Peter, I'd like to ask you exactly the same question. What is your vision? How do you want the future to unfold?

Peter: Oh, family life is nice, but everybody has to have a little bit of room and a bit of balance. That's what I want to see back if I was to move back in with Wendy and the kids. There would have to be some room.

Dr. F.: What would that look like. What would that room look like. What is that balance?

Peter: It is not just necessarily room for me to do something but to have everybody also doing something on their own. Not waiting to have something done for them or waiting for someone to go out and do something and create things, entertain them. I need a little personal time and things like that.

Dr. F.: What are you most anxious about happening if you were back together as a family? Biggest worry?

Peter: Biggest worry that it would solve?

Dr. F.: No, biggest worry that keeps you cautious.

Peter: Oh, I see, it's the going backward.

Dr. F.: Going backward.

Peter: Ending up back where we were. When you are in a situation like that and looking for improvement for a long period of time and it doesn't show up, to jump back in again is something you are very hesitant to do.

Dr. F.: How much effort do you put in to teaching Wendy about the changes in you that have come about over the course of the years you have been together?

Peter: Well, I was a little bit naive because I thought I had stayed pretty well the same for thirteen years. I think Bob is the one that pointed out that I've probably changed quite a bit. In the last couple of months, it is one of my favorite pastimes.

Dr. F.: It is a good pastime.

Peter: As soon as I get it exactly figured out how I've changed I'll let her know. Right now I guess I've come up with lots of things that are changing and are different slightly. I'm more stubborn, more set in my ways than I was before, but we've discussed that quite a bit lately.

Dr. F.: Do you want to ask any questions before we stop?

What was it like for you having a stranger ask you all these questions?

Peter: After all, we volunteered last week.

Wendy: I just came along for the ride.

Dr. F.: For an hour of it, what was it like to go through this?

Peter: Fine, not quite as nerve-racking as I thought it was going to be.

Dr. F.: Any surprises?

Peter: Well, only the one about relating my father's death to Frank's death. I hadn't thought about that.

Dr. F.: Wendy, for you, what was it like for you having a stranger ask all these questions?

Wendy: Actually, it was a lot easier than I figured. I wouldn't have said that a few months ago.

Dr. F.: What surprises did you have in this hour?

Wendy: None. You know, I often thought about how the deaths might have been related to what has happened. I don't think that is what caused us to break up. I think it just added tremendously, too much of an overload to what was happening, and if they hadn't come about then I think we might have been able to do something.

Commentary

The therapist has given each partner an opportunity to talk about how he or she would like the relationship to be different. The therapist emphasized the need for each to teach the other about the changes in their lives over the course of the marriage. Many people assume that their partners will automatically know about these changes and will act accordingly. It is important for the therapist to highlight some of the major changes in each person's life and offer him or her a chance to teach the other about these changes. To summarize the interview the therapist emphasizes the importance of teaching the other about self and not leaving that to chance.

Dr. F.: Well, I'll leave you with a thought. I think that your one big challenge is for each of you to teach the other person that you are not the same. You are not the same people who you've constructed these stories about over the years, stories about why certain things happened or didn't happen. This business about taking responsibility for teaching the other person about the changes rather than hoping they get discovered is worth setting your minds to.

Wendy: Yeah, but how do you get somebody to recognize that?

Dr. F.: It's risky business to recognize change. There is always a downside to recognizing the change.

Wendy: You see, you can tell somebody about it, you can tell them what you are doing, but you can't make them believe it.

Dr. F.: That's right. You can't make them believe it. All you can do is say it. But you can't make them believe it. Even more importantly, you don't need to have them believe it to sustain it. Anyway, I really enjoyed meeting the two of you. Thanks so much for doing it.

Commentary

This session was for the purposes of consultation. The therapist will meet with the couple's ongoing therapist to discuss what he learned about the family so that the themes evident in the session can be focused on during ongoing therapy. If it had been the first session of ongoing therapy, the therapist would have highlighted the importance of each partner working on his or her own themes in the presence of the other. He would have explained to the couple, at the end of the session, that each has brought into the marriage a certain degree of loss, sadness and anxiety, which get projected onto their relationship. The therapist would also have pointed out that as each worked on individual themes a better sense of connection and understanding would develop between them.

6 _____

Beginning of the Middle Phase: Rethinking the Family Story

Introduction

At what point in the therapy do you move into the middle phase? How do you know when you are in the middle phase? What is different about the middle phase of therapy from the beginning phase?

There is no predetermined time for commencing the middle phase. Some couples move rapidly in therapy. Others take longer to move out of their reactivity. As discussed in Chapter 5, there are some reliable indicators of the length of time it will take a couple to move into the middle phase of therapy. When individuals begin therapy with an ability to reflect on their histories, become intrigued and curious about the partner's way of behaving in the world, and avoid resorting to blame and projection, they will move fairly quickly into the middle phase of work. However, when individuals are cut off from their histories and/or have assumed an angry, distant stance toward their extended families, it takes considerably longer to shift them into curiosity and detachment, both about their partners and themselves.

The indicators that a couple has moved into the middle phase are quite clear. When partners are no longer preoccupied with relationship problems, are more willing to talk about self issues, and are less reactive to the way the partner is behaving in the world, the therapy has shifted into the beginning of the middle phase.

The therapist usually begins a session with general questions such as, "What have you been working on since the last time you were here? How has your theory changed over the last little while? What have you experimented with? What have you been working on as a self?" When individuals are in the middle phase they begin to talk about their experimentation with being different in the world.

During the middle phase of therapy each partner has stories to tell about how he or she has been repositioning in various relationships. They seldom focus on the other or the relationship. They are able to talk about a crisis in terms of how self responded rather than what the other did. The general focus of the session is on how self is beginning to use life experiences to learn more about emotional functioning. Although these couples are in the middle phase, at times of high anxiety or family crisis they will revert to old ways of behaving; however, they are able to shift out of this reactivity much faster. Couples who have entered the middle phase of therapy can refocus their anxiety fairly quickly away from the other and the world into self and their own themes.

During the beginning of the middle phase partners will continue to use part of the session to focus on relationship concerns or upset about the other. However, they shift away from that preoccupation more easily and stay focused on self issues for most of the session. With each passing session more time is spent on self issues and less on preoccupation with the other.

Major Indications that the Couple Is in the Beginning of the Middle Phase of Therapy

The Focus of the Problem Has Shifted from the Relationship to the Self

Initially individuals enter therapy with the belief that the problem rests within the relationship and/or the other. Over the course of a number of sessions a gradual shift occurs. Each partner begins to recognize themes from his or her family of origin and begins to focus on these rather than the other's behavior. The questions about self stimulate each partner to become more curious about what he or she brings into the relationship and less reactive about what the other is doing in the relationship. The central focus of the sessions is on discovering how family losses, abandonment issues, separation concerns, developmental issues, and so forth, have shaped each person emotionally and led to pockets of anxiety that have, at times, been acted out in the relationship through conflict, blame, and general distancing behavior.

Anxiety Is Down

During this phase of therapy the partners are less controlled by their anxiety and more able to talk about how to deal with it. The partners begin to embrace each other's differences rather than strive toward accommodation, appeasement, and general "good behavior." The therapist encourages stories in which partners have experienced difficulties that they have used as opportunities to learn about self. The therapist will at times crank up the anxiety and listen to how each partner is able to use anxiety-producing experiences to learn more about self.

The principle of "change without cooperation" is introduced in the middle phase of therapy. This principle refers to an individual's ability to take new positions in the relationship without needing the partner's cooperation, support, and validation. During this phase there is a focus on how each partner deals with life dilemmas in his or her unique way without a preoccupation with how the other experiences his or her choices. Curiosity, rather than judgment, about one's partner is stimulated.

Reflective Thinking

As they enter this phase the couple has become considerably more reflective. On their own initiative the partners offer examples of situations in which they have overreacted, shifted into blame, or indulged their anxiety. They are better able to observe themselves in these situations, are less judgmental about themselves and the other, and are more curious about what got stirred up inside them to trigger the old reactions. The ability to be observational about self during high anxiety-producing situations is a true indication that the individual is in the middle phase of therapy. The therapist should continue to ask questions that help the individuals learn from their anxiety. Sometimes the therapist has to introduce a scenario that stirs up anxiety in the individuals and then ask them how they would deal with the situation differently. The therapist should encourage each partner in the relationship to become more observational about himself or herself in highly charged situations. The therapist does not want the tension and anxiety to be so low that individuals no longer think about self issues in new ways. Conversely, the anxiety should not be so high that people lose their observational ability and get lost in their old reactivity. However, if this does occur, the therapist should use the situation as an opportunity for new learning rather than view it as an indication of failure or a setback.

Absence of Blame

The couple can now relate stories about highly conflictual situations without blaming each other. The partners are now focused on learning about self rather than on blaming and projecting onto other. For example, a reactive husband may say, when his wife is behaving in a certain way, "Why is she doing this to me?" In this phase he is more likely to ask, "Why is her behavior stirring me up in this particular way?"

The therapist should encourage individuals to introduce their full range of behaviors as a way for self and the other to learn about self. When the other reacts in unwelcome ways to one's choice of behaviors, those responses should be seen as opportunities to learn about self and about the other, rather than as reasons to feel defeated, controlled, or undermined emotionally.

Increased Curiosity about Self and the Other

Increased curiosity is another indication that couples have shifted into the middle phase of therapy. Couples present stories about what they are learning about self and the other. When the other reacts unusually, self becomes curious about that behavior rather than defensive and reactive. Partners begin to talk about how they are trying to teach each other about self rather than defending against the other. The importance of the shift to curiosity should not be underestimated. Individuals have to become more curious about themselves and their family of origin before they can become truly curious about their partner. It is difficult to remain curious about one's partner when one is in rebellion and generally cut off from one's original family. The therapist should encourage the partners to become more curious about their extended families by asking them questions about their extended families that they cannot answer. This process heightens their willingness to go back to their original families and ask questions for new learning. In this phase individuals often come to sessions excited about a new discovery about an extended-family member.

One client told a story about growing up feeling unloved by her father. Her father never spent time with her alone, sought her out, asked her questions, or seemed interested in her life. She was convinced that she was a disappointment to him. When she went back to question her father, she discovered that he had been quite involved in her life, but from a distance. He had observed all her achievements but shared his sense of pride with his wife rather than with her. When the daughter asked him about this he explained that he had grown up in a predominantly male family. He had never had a sister and was orphaned by his mother at a young age. Because of this he felt he did not know how to relate to girls and females in general. He had felt quite awkward and ill at ease around his daughter and thought that the most caring, safe thing he could do was allow her her own space. This client was quite touched by her father's story and finally understood that his lack of involvement was a reflection of his anxiety, not a lack of caring. After gaining this understanding, she was able to shift into curiosity about her husband. At the beginning of therapy she had complained that her husband ignored her, failed to make her feel special, and was critical of her. She now began to wonder if some of his behavior stemmed from his own anxiety about being intimate and affectionate. As coincidence would have it, the husband was struggling with issues very similar to these. When he felt anxious and unsure he became critical and withdrew.

Increased Interest in Family-of-Origin Issues

When couples have shifted into the middle phase of therapy, they are more willing to stay focused on family-of-origin issues. During the beginning phase of family therapy the primary focus is on relationship issues. The therapist gradually spends more time each session shifting the focus away from the other and the relationship to self and family-of-origin issues. When the couple has finally shifted into the middle phase, with the accompanying decrease in anxiety and reactivity, most of the session is spent on family-of-origin issues. The therapist concentrates on certain themes and encourages each partner to do some research on his or her family. The major task in the middle phase of therapy is to encourage individuals to return home to attempt some significant repositioning with important family members.

A secondary goal is eventually to involve the parents of the partners in one or more sessions to allow them to begin to tell their own stories, which can be used as positive legacies for the adult child and his or her children. During the beginning phase of therapy there is often a negative reaction to the suggestion of involving one's parents. Many adult children who are still reactive toward their parents hear such a suggestion as a rejection of their own stories, or as a way to put them into a childlike role in relation to their parents. Since their customary way of dealing with their parents is through distance, the suggestion to involve them runs counter to their usual way of getting safe. However, during this middle phase the adult child becomes quite motivated to bring in the parents and has become curious about how the parents will tell their stories. There is a noticeable shift away from worrying about what will happen to them and/or their parents to anticipating the pleasure of hearing the parents' stories in a positive, creative way.

Family of Origin Revisited

When the couple is in the beginning of the middle phase of therapy, the therapist's major task is to encourage each partner to reposition self emotionally with his or her family of origin. The major objectives of this repositioning work are:

1. to discover new stories about the family
2. to be able to embrace positively the family's sameness in a new and different way
3. to develop person-to-person relationships with key family members
4. to avoid using distance and to get emotionally safe.

The therapist must nudge each partner to be more willing to risk being different with his or her extended family. During each session in this phase the therapist will question individuals about work with the extended family. The adult child must seriously question his or her old stories about family. He should make time to ask individual members of the family about their own stories. The therapist must help the adult child do this, by gently challenging the original stories and mythologies he or she carries. The interview in this chapter illustrates how the therapist begins the process of challenging the adult child's story about his or her original family.

Another part of the process of reinvolving oneself with family is to plan family visits around special occasions. Special days such as Christmas, anniversaries, funerals, and graduation parties are present opportunities for adult children to learn more about their extended families. Special family occasions heighten a family's anxiety. The best way to learn about how a family conducts its business is to observe the family during a special occasion. Traditionally, family members get together at Christmas. There are high expectations that Christmas will be special but the reality is that family members often experience the most intense disappointments around this holiday. Christmas presents a unique opportunity for an adult child to visit his or her family, observe the family behaving in a certain way and avoid responding to this behavior in the same old way. This process constitutes a profound learning experience for the adult child.

One of the gifts we receive from our extended family is their tendency to be the same with us. Our job is to be different alongside their sameness. The individual who is able to maintain his or her differences in the face of the family's sameness, has learned how to create a shift in a system. The shift does not necessarily result in the family's being different, but does allow the individual to be the way he or she needs to be with the family. The job is not to manipulate the family but to assume a neutral, observational role and to observe how family anxiety gets communicated among family members and how family members take on certain positions in the family and act out each other's anxiety. It is a great learning opportunity for therapists. If a therapist can stay in the midst of his or her own family's anxiety without being influenced unduly by it and/or needing to leave to get safe, then he or she will be able to work with other people's families without taking on their anxiety and defending against it and/or needing to control it.

It is important for individuals to learn how to develop person-to-person relationships with important key family members. The therapist helps the adult child identify important family members with whom he or she would like to reposition. The therapist then encourages the adult child to spend time alone with these individuals. The goal is for the adult child to be able to spend time alone with these family members and learn how to be open to their stories, their history, their way of conducting their own business without needing to judge, control, or help in any way.

In the process of revisiting the family the adult child also learns that one does not need to distance emotionally or physically to get safe. The adult child learns how to listen to the family's sadness, hurt, and disappointment without needing to take it on or run from it. He or she is able to stay involved without needing to distance by becoming angry or withdrawing or trying to "fix" something. As the individual becomes better able to embrace the family in these new, creative ways, the learning generalizes into current relationships with his or her partner and children.

Therapist as Consultant

In this phase of therapy the therapist moves from being the expert to being the consultant. The partners now become their own experts. They use their own wisdom and family resources to learn more about themselves and their way of being in the world. The therapist helps the couple formulate the questions they can ask extended family members. He or she schedules less frequent sessions with the couple and begins to reposition from being the central player to being more of a devil's advocate. When the couple presents their stories, the therapist introduces an element of doubt and challenges the stories for their validity. The therapist is now trying to encourage the partners to own their stories and to develop their own reasons for wanting to expand on their discoveries. The therapist does not want the couple to do the work to please him or her but to develop greater ownership about their own positions in their families.

During this phase of therapy the therapist teaches systems principles to the couple. The couple has to learn more effective ways to ask questions, develop hypotheses, stay out of triangles, avoid buying into secrets, develop person-to-person relationships with all important members of the family, and so forth. When couples present family dilemmas, the therapist's task is to teach them a principle that will help them become more experimental with their family. The therapist encourages repositioning of the adult child in important key relationships. When the adult child talks about having difficulty in a relationship, the therapist identifies that relationship as an important one and encourages the adult child to find ways to connect in a more intimate way with that person.

The therapist should help family members become their own heroes, to learn how to use each other and their own wisdom as their guides. One of the major shifts that occurs during this phase of the therapy is that partners stop taking positions about each other's stories. This change is significant as partners tend to buy into each other's stories about family. When couples have shifted into this phase of the therapy the partners are able to remain on the sidelines of each other's stories and give positive support to the other's work on repositioning.

Case Illustration: Beginning of Middle Phase and Commentary

The following case is illustrative of beginning middle phase work. The couple presented with serious marital problems. It was the first marriage for both and they had been married for five years. They had one young son. They presented with ambivalence about the marriage. Although both stated that they wanted the relationship to work, their difficulties had led them to have grave doubts about whether it was sustainable. The husband was from eastern Canada, the wife from the United States. The wife's background was Jewish, with a strong Holocaust theme. The husband's background was Catholic; however, during the course of therapy he discovered that his mother was Jewish, and there was also a Holocaust theme on her side. Both parties told stories about feeling abandoned and overwhelmed by their parents' divorces and general neediness.

During the first few sessions the therapy had focused primarily on the husband's family and his themes of abandonment and loss. The session that follows focuses on the wife's family. She tells a powerful story about feeling overwhelmed by her father's emotional needs and the history of the suicide of her paternal grandfather. This session was the first in which the primary focus shifted from the relationship to family-of-origin themes. There had been a breakthrough in the previous session when the couple began to understand how a conflictual issue was a metaphor for their own fears of abandonment. This session begins with a discussion of what they learned in the previous session.

Dr. F.: It is helpful to get a sense of what happens to people when they leave here after the session.

Jane: One thing I guess that I definitely want to say which I didn't express directly last time was that you were reframing your interpretation and it made a lot of sense. I mean it made sense at the time, a lot of stuff felt right. I came in very numbed out and exhausted too, because I hadn't slept and stuff like that. I stayed really numbed out even though everything made sense here and it didn't draw me to feel close to Allan. I mean, I just felt really numbed out, and so we rode home quite silent, although not angry, like it had been, just quite silent. Remember I said, because then I had to get to the lab right when we got home, I said, "I just feel so vulnerable or something. I just don't feel like I can let go of that." But by that evening already things were I guess loosening up in me. I guess it is a bad sign because we had a relatively good week. I mean, between us it actually felt like a lot of warmth. And there are other things going on in our families. I have a lot of worries about my father and that is something I do want to talk about because I have to deal with it right now.

But certainly on and off during the time since we saw you last, we have looked at things in light of abandonment and all of that, and it has made a lot of sense and it has certainly helped us, I think.

Dr. F.: Allan, for you what happened?

Allan: I really grappled with that word "abandonment" and turned it around and tried to really give it a meaning in terms of our experience, both individually and with each other, and it really illuminated a lot of things. I made the comment to Jane, "You notice how over the past four years or so that we have been together, when we have had a particular kind of a crisis our reaction has been, well, our relationship is being threatened and we are going to split up if we don't resolve this issue." There have been times when we have both felt that and there have been times when I've felt that and not Jane, and vice versa. I said, "Isn't that an example of that abandonment that he was talking about?" and I see how that works. We feel so threatened by whatever it is that the other person is doing that we pull ourselves off. As Jane said and I can agree with that, my best defense is just to say, "I can do it on my own. I don't need you, and if we split up that's okay because I can handle this." And I say, "Look, those are examples of how we have done it so much."

So for me there has been a certain clarity. I don't know, I think for both of us it put some light on the relationship. I felt immediately after the session both a lot of relief and for me it felt like it had resolved all of the questions we had had of the dispute that we just had. In fact, I felt a lot of really warm feelings toward Jane and a lot of loving feelings that I hadn't felt for a while and it was, I guess, a realization seeing how Jane is so worried about her father and other things but that I had treated Jane in a way that really pushed her out. I wasn't there supporting her in the way that I could and I could feel how she could feel abandoned. I could really see that, so a lot of good feelings came. When Jane didn't respond feeling numbed out, then I said, well, I'll just wait and see what comes up, but I felt okay.

Commentary

The therapist learns at the beginning of the session that there has been a significant decrease in the reactivity of the couple. The wife talked about her anxiety and reactivity settling down. She made reference to the fact that they had had a good week and with a little laugh commented, "I guess it is a bad sign." This comment was a reference to the therapist's observation in previous sessions that it wasn't necessarily a good sign when things just went well, that, in fact, one could learn more about the connections in a relationship and about self when something went wrong and new learning was stimulated. The more significant statement by the wife was that she was able to stay with her own issues around abandonment rather than shift into her preoccupation about her partner. This statement indicated that a shift was taking place in her thinking, and it might be a good time for the therapist to move her gently into focusing more on her extended-family losses.

Another positive sign that a shift had taken place was that the husband also identified his abandonment theme. He talks about how thinking somewhat differently has affected his behavior in the relationship. Both partners were more reflective. In previous sessions they often began by talking about being upset, angry, and hurt by the other's behavior. In this session they start by talking more about what they are learning about self and how their worries about abandonment stir up their anxiety, which then gets acted out in their relationship. This shift is a sign that they are moving into the beginning of the middle phase.

The therapist asks the husband certain questions to see if he can respond to anxiety in a different way. For example, he asks him how he understands his reactions when his wife distances in response to his attempts to reach out and support her. In posing this question the therapist is trying to get the husband to think more about his own anxiety and reactivity than about what his wife is doing. He is attempting to help the husband become more detached, curious, and observational about his own needs, and less preoccupied with his wife's behavior.

Dr. F.: Well, that's interesting. I wanted to ask you about that. What gets stirred up in you when you are ready to embrace her and she still needs some distance to get safe?

Allan: I kind of wait until Jane gets there or I know that when I'm in a good space, when I have sort of resolved an issue in my mind then I'm ready to do it. And if it is waiting, then that is what I will do, but I will take my cue from Jane basically. You want to talk about something, then I will sit down and be ready, but I know that when I will be talking I will be in a much more positive mood. I won't be defensive, and that's the sort of mix that is required to make the thing resolved. That's how I go about it.

Commentary

The therapist pushes the husband into thinking more about his own themes when he becomes reactive. It is especially important at this point that the husband be able to reflect on his own family background.

The therapist theorizes that the husband has shifted into the beginning of the middle phase because of his ability to reflect with some comfort, on his own family rather than remain focused on his wife's behavior. The therapist can now build on some of the family themes and stay focused on family-of-origin issues. If the husband had shifted to a preoccupation with the other, the therapist would have known that the middle phase had not been reached yet. However, in this portion of the interview it is clear that the husband has become much more thoughtful about the earlier forces that shaped his life.

Dr. F.: What is your understanding about when you lose it, when you find it hard to maintain that sort of involved detachment?

Allan: Well, from experience, Jane has pointed out a lot that I get terribly defensive. Mind you, two or three days later I sort of turn around and see the point that Jane was making but at that particular time I just can't. And yet, just recently we had a bit of a dispute where Jane was saying, "I want to get pregnant and we're not making love," and there was a lot of defensiveness and I really tried to help hold it at bay. What it meant was that I could acknowledge some of the things that I was bringing into it that on previous occasions I just wouldn't have. I just have a really hard time. Right away in my mind comes an experience from when I was a teenager that is certainly pertinent to that. See, there was a lot of competition in Betty's household, I hope you don't mind my—

Jane: No, no, no, go ahead.

Allan: In Betty's household when I moved in there . . . that's my stepmother and stepbrother and stepsister. A lot of competition for having the final word, for being right. And there was a sort of verbal jousting going on where you couldn't expose any weakness and you had to know everything. And if you didn't, you had to bullshit to look like you knew it. It felt awful in a lot of ways, from the inside it felt awful. Particularly an awful lot of the time I talked about stuff that I knew and it was clear to me that they didn't but they just persisted and I thought like, "Come on, let go!" And that would never happen. And conversely then, I started talking about stuff that I did not know but wouldn't let on to it. And that is so striking in my mind that whole period, there is a good two or three years.

Dr. F.: What age would you be?

Allan: 15, 16, 17, 18?

Dr. F.: What do you think the emotional lessons were? The emotional lessons that you learned from that sort of exposure?

Allan: You don't give up an inch of yourself. No way. And it's been a sore point between us because it's so opposite to Jane's style of being forthright and the best way to deal with a situation is to own up, acknowledge your own weaknesses so that you can resolve the issue at last. Like I learned a different style. I'm not saying that I didn't experience that before when I was younger but at least there it was so clear and obvious.

Dr. F.: If you gave up an inch what would you fear would happen?

Allan: That's interesting. I'm not really sure I've thought about it, because it didn't happen.

Dr. F.: What would happen to you emotionally if you gave up an inch?

Allan: I guess you would be clobbered verbally. You're no

good. You don't know what you're talking about, ha! All that stuff.

Dr. F.: The reason I ask that question, Allan, is because I remember you mentioning this thing about the fear of not being good enough whenever Jane makes a demand and you begin to feel vulnerable.

Allan: Yeah, yeah, it's a lot of that.

Dr. F.: That's not what her intention is, that is what you emotionally hear.

Allan: And that's a longer theme for me.

Dr. F.: That's right because the most powerful story you've told me is about your mum and basically feeling she turned her back on you. That you tried so hard to make it right and you weren't successful. Because that's your cross to bear.

Allan: And it's a lot in flux right now. I'm working an awful lot on that.

Commentary

The therapist now introduces two important principles: (1) change without cooperation, and (2) the importance of rethinking one's family story or the mythology we have constructed about our family. This is a crucial part of the interview. Although the therapist is talking to the husband, he is also encouraging the wife to rethink her own stories. One partner can learn powerful principles by listening to the therapist discuss them with the other partner. The silent partner has an opportunity to be a little bit more detached and thoughtful about what is being said.

The therapist introduces the concept that for solid change to occur one has to be able to introduce new behaviors without needing cooperation, support, or validation. He suggests that our difficulty in accomplishing this is related to our emotional stories about our families. The therapist puts forth the idea that the way to begin the process of working on self is not so much by repositioning in the relationship but by beginning to understand our original family stories differently. The therapist is attempting to challenge, and to confuse the couple slightly. He is challenging them by encouraging them not to play down their differences or become too preoccupied with the other's reaction to those differences. He is confusing them by challenging their stories about their original families. In the beginning of the middle phase the therapist should gently provoke each partner to begin the process of rethinking his or her family story and to develop some theories about how the story is brought into the couple's relationship.

At this point the therapist should be very careful not to stir up defensive behavior. If the couple responds defensively, then the therapist should back off, move into the questioning stance, and allow the anxiety to subside.

Dr. F.: Because that's what I mean about losing it. You see, you will never really know how far you have come until the other person behaves in a way where traditionally you protected yourself in an old way and you now respond differently, or pull yourself out of it quicker, or you watch yourself and react differently to it. Because the theme is not going to go away. Those themes can't go away because there will always be behaviors that will stir that up. Something will happen. To really get a handle on this we need to go back to our family and rework our ways of responding and begin to change our story about our original family.

Allan: What do you mean?

Dr. F.: Well, Jane can avoid saying certain things, or you can try really hard not to react but that is situational. It is not actually your core self. I think the core self gets free by going back to something more fundamental that shaped us. It's necessary to understand the family story differently.

Allan: Although my feeling of it in terms of how you tackle it is you put your feet on solid ground here and now, and then you can deal with the past.

Dr. F.: Well, that's the beachhead. You're exactly right about that.

Allan: Yeah, that's exactly it. It needs to be between us and within.

Dr. F.: I agree with you on that one.

Jane: That's actually another way of saying a thought that I had at the same time which is that somehow rather than the effort or something contrived or I try not to trigger, or he tries not to respond, it feels at least like it's moving in the direction. There is a kind of trust that's developing between us. It's a real trust, so that when we feel, I mean, I should speak for myself, when I feel myself going into that "Forget it. I don't need you, blah, blah, blah," I can remind myself, "Look, okay, we can talk about this"; it's a real trust level.

Allan: And having gone through it a number of times and seeing that we still are here together, that's a real part of the experience because I guess we haven't experienced that a whole lot.

Jane: Well, I have definitely not with my family ever felt like I could trust that they could be there. And I guess I mean that both literally, physically, and also emotionally. So I never could do that.

Allan: You know it was much the same with me, much the same.

Dr. F.: It's good that you are now aware of these themes and you are working on not indulging them.

Allan: There is so much of those comments I was telling you, Jane, you are so critical, you point out all the negative things and this and that. That just doesn't work for me. You know it is the whole dynamic.

Jane: Right, right.

Commentary

The therapist now has a pretty good indication that the couple can think about these principles without getting reactive or defensive. This knowledge encourages the therapist to introduce a few more principles about systems behavior. He begins by introducing the concept of themes. It is important during this phase of therapy for each partner to understand how family themes get played out in their marriage. He has two objectives for introducing this principle: to help the individual become more observant about how his or her themes interfere with the ability to avoid reacting to the partner's behavior, and to help the individual become more curious about what went on in his or her family to give these themes such a powerful hold on self. The therapist explains that when partners have similar themes it is difficult for each to become curious and objective about the other's anxiety. But for intimacy truly to be achieved, that is exactly what must happen. When one partner becomes anxious and overreacts, the other partner ideally should shift into curiosity and nonreactivity. However, this cannot be achieved when someone feels unsafe or vulnerable in a relationship. When the partners' themes are similar, they may feel unsafe at the same time, with the result that neither one is able to get on the emotional sidelines and allow the other the space to work through anxiety, fear, or a sense of vulnerability.

It is important for the therapist to pay attention to the couple's reaction to this principle. If either partner is upset by this principle and justifies his or her position, the therapist knows it is a bit too soon to introduce this complicated concept. If the therapist continues teaching a principle when the indicators are that the couple is not emotionally prepared to understand it, then the therapist is acting out of personal anxiety or need to make something happen. The therapist must not have a predetermined agenda for the couple. It may happen that one partner is more ready than the other. When this happens, the therapist can speak to the more functional or less anxious member, hoping that the other will be able to put the ideas into operation later.

Dr. F.: People have themes. You don't really think about this when you get together. I have found that if your themes are so different, your historical themes of loss and anxiety are so different from each other's, you can be curious about a reaction. There is an ability to want to know more about it but you don't take it on. But if the themes are close, if they dovetail, they are deadly. That is what I was saying last time. Your themes really do dovetail. So you have to be more alert. And what you said, Allan, is so true. If you get so caught up in relationship issues, it prevents you from looking at self. You get bogged down in the conflict or the preoccupation or the hurt. But it also keeps you safe. That's the other side of it. You can then use blame and anger to justify the distance you need to feel emotionally safe.

Allan: Well, we're both familiar with that.

Dr. F.: It's difficult making a relationship safe enough to look at self and those vulnerabilities because when you get anxious you will look at your partner so you can get refocused on the safer thing, which is blame. So I say to people, "Blame is always about self. Blame about the other is a way self gets safe." Now, if we can understand that, the other can always ask "What is this really about?" and not take the blame on and get angry. Or self can say, "Isn't it interesting how I'm using my partner to get safe," and stop oneself more quickly. One or the other or a combination of the two is wonderful. Think of blame as a way of getting safe. It's really not about the other.

Allan: Sorry, go ahead.

Jane: Is it my turn? Okay, it's interesting because two things are going on. One is I'm feeling almost a little sick right now, I'm not sure why. I think it's emotional. There is stuff going on. And when we were driving up here I said to Allan, "I feel a little bit defensive going into this." I'm not sure exactly what's going on. When you're using the word "blame" and that it's really something that one is doing as a way of making oneself safe, not looking at one's own thing. That is one thing that I also left here feeling last week is how very blameful I had been to Allan. In fact, when you told us the story about the father having dinner with his children and so on and how his wife had pointed out how his back was to his son and how he embraced that as a way of growing and recognizing it rather than getting angry and so on, and I heard that and I really responded to it and yet my response was but look, I tell Allan, "When you criticize me I say give me more but when I criticize you look what you do," and it was "It's you, it's you." But I really felt wronged and I felt hurt and I felt vulnerable. I felt all of those things but I also saw myself making it all Allan's doing somehow. I was the victim. There is something very wrong with that.

I don't want to hog all the time, but there is one more thing I need to say because I think it's part of what is going on here but this is a messy one or whatever. I think I have a feeling for what I want to say. I don't know how well I will be able to articulate it. This feels very bad. I'm quite sure that part of my making things safe for myself in our relationship, and this is very conflicted, but it has to do with Allan not feeling like he is good enough. I don't know if this makes sense to you, but we have talked about it. I remember one talk we had on a beach last summer and it has to do with I think, at least this is my level of understanding at this point, with my relationship with my sister or something. I have a very disturbed sister, a very depressed and unfunctional sister, and in our family I was always the golden child, or whatever you want to say, and she was always really unwell. And I know at some point when I was in my late teens I suddenly had some feeling for the fact that there was, although everything I did on the surface was to help her, I was always being good to her, I was always rescuing her, but there was really a part of me that needed her down because if she wasn't down I wasn't up or something like that. And I know that I have had flickerings of feelings sometimes, you know, more or less, that Allan's insecurity, which we all have, but somehow that is important for me to know that he is not feeling 100 percent in order for me to feel all right. It's something I hate about myself.

Allan: That you need me to be down in the same way you needed your sister to be down.

Jane: In some way.

Allan: I've taken her place in that.

Jane: In some way, yeah, in some way.

Commentary

The therapist now challenges an old story of the wife, who introduces the issue of her sister being the sick one in the family. If the therapist leaves this one untouched, in some subtle way he colludes with the old family story that the sister is the identified problem in the family. It is important for the therapist to find a gentle, noncritical way to introduce some doubt into that old story. The therapist decides to raise the issue of how siblings take care of each other. This approach is a major reframe. When the therapist talks about how important it is for siblings to be able to learn about themselves by observing each other, he is beginning to challenge the old story. The therapist takes it one step further by telling a story of his own. The process of storytelling is an intriguing one. When the therapist thinks that a direct challenge to a story will stir up defensiveness, then a safer way to challenge the story is by telling a story about another family. The couple will listen to the story and think about its symbolic meaning without having to defend their personal stories. The therapist should not collude with the couple's stories about their families, or stir up defensiveness, which reinforces the stories. The therapist also should not challenge the stories so that the couple feels they have to justify them.

One of the major tasks in the middle phase of family therapy with couples is to encourage individual members to work on family connections. Colluding with a negative image of a family member undermines this process. As partners feel better connected with their original families they become less needy in their relationships with each other and their children. With this couple, opening up the possibility that the sister is a functional person who in her own way tried to take care of their family paves the road for greater positive connections in the future.

Dr. F.: Think about how sibling problems shape us. We know how good we are by how bad they have been, how healthy we are by how sick they have been.

Jane: You think that's generally the case?

Dr. F.: How else do we know how good we are unless we have something to compare ourselves to? Hopefully we work that out, but it's hard for only children. They have no one to compare themselves to. They get very anxious because they don't know if they're good enough. Because siblings do that for each other.

Jane: Are you describing something that you see as healthy? I mean, just sort of the way things are?

Dr. F.: Just natural. But I think it can become a problem, depending on its intensity. How it shapes the other siblings without their knowing it.

Jane: Well also isn't it how dysfunctional the family is?

Dr. F.: You are talking about degrees of intensity because I think normally it goes on.

Allan: And may I add parenthetically it is my observation, right or wrong, that equally your sister needs you to be great to make herself feel safe where she is.

Dr. F.: I've got to tell you a little story about a couple I have been seeing for a while. He was going on and on about how dysfunctional his sister is in the family. His sister is 4½ years older and he's the golden boy, the prince, and she's the ugly duckling. They are probably in their late forties now and on and on he goes about how angry he is with his sister because she has all these problems. And I said, "Yeah, have you thanked your sister for taking care of you in the family by being the family problem?" He was absolutely stunned. I said, "Just imagine if you didn't have a sister what would have happened to you." Now, that's something to think about.

Let's move on to your dad.

Jane: Okay.

Commentary

The therapist blocks any reaction about what he has just said to the couple. Not allowing them to take a position on the question or story forces the couple into a contemplative posture. The therapist believed that if he allowed the partners to respond to his reframe they would cite their old stories and the power of the reframe would be lost.

The therapist now moves into the middle of the session. Each session has its own beginning, middle, and ending. The beginning of each session, whether it is a beginning phase interview or middle phase interview, starts with some preoccupation with a problem. As the therapist shifts the focus away from relationship and the other to self, there is a movement to the middle stage of the interview. The therapist uses this stage to focus more on family-of-origin issues. The therapist wants to ensure that at least some time is devoted to family-of-origin issues in each session. At this point the therapist suggests that the focus shift to the wife's concern about her father. In actuality the fusion between this woman and her father is quite profound.

Now the therapist attempts to help her begin the slow process of differentiating emotionally from her father. She is very sensitive to her father's moods and feels responsible for his emotional functioning. The therapist has several objectives at this point. One is to begin questioning Jane's sense of responsibility about the father and help her become more curious about why she carries so much anxiety about her father's functioning. The second objective is to plant a seed in Jane's mind that it will be necessary to invite her father to a session so he can tell his own story. The third objective is to help Jane begin to understand how her anxiety about her father blocks her from having a safe father. This last point is quite important. Unless Jane can change her story about her father, she will not be able to allow him to be there for her and consequently will feel alone in the world. This feeling will get played out in her marriage so that whenever her husband does not seem to be there for her she will experience a profound sense of loss and abandonment.

Dr. F.: And you can think about this one later on.

Allan: That's a big bundle to just drop in her lap.

Dr. F.: I have found a lot of times answering a question blocks the thinking about the question; some questions are worth thinking about. But I would like to hear about your dad, Jane, and what your concerns are.

Jane: Except I just need to say that I felt already for years a lot of guilt about my sister. It wasn't just me comparing myself to my sister, it was my parents doing it to my sister. Some part of me has known that if she wasn't there it would sort of be very different.

Dr. F.: But your sister is in Vancouver, isn't she? Well, maybe we could do something about that.

Jane: Great. Okay, my father. This also will lead back into last session. He has had, I don't think it is any exaggeration to say a very serious crisis, a very serious depression. I guess actually when we first saw you, you were asking how do we feel about our parents, are we worried about our parents and that sort of thing and I remember saying, "Well, actually, physically my father is not doing too well right now," and he was bleeding, in fact, in his urine. I'm very worried. He had a prostate operation many years ago and all kinds of worries. That all resolved itself, the bleeding stopped and there was no apparent cause.

He quickly went into a bad depression and then sort of pulled himself out of it, but anyway the details aren't necessary but he came up to see us at Christmas and he stayed almost a month. He came up feeling a little bit shaky and then when he was with us he didn't stay right in our house. He stayed in a neighbor's house. They had gone away for Christmas. It was perfect. I had never seen my father like that. He was blissed out, he was calm, he was happy. He kept remarking, "I can't believe it. This is like a religious experience. I feel almost embarrassed. I feel loving toward everyone. It's like hokey or something." And it was really . . . I mean, have you ever seen my father that way? It was striking. . . .

Allan: I mean, we had an argument revolving around him. We were both worried that he was hurting or something, he was so distant from it. . . .

Jane: Yeah. It should have been a big warning sign to me but I just thought I don't know what's going on. Very, very different from my father and I have seen my father very depressed and I have seen him very manic. When he's manic it's not like that. It's aggressive, nasty. He is very belligerent when he's manic usually. When he's depressed he's just flat on his back. This was something else that I had never seen.

And he left on New Year's Day and within three days apparently just was utterly in pieces. And called crying over the phone. He's very scared, very frightened. He has been seeing a therapist for fifteen years now and his therapist is not an M.D., he's a psychologist, but decided, I guess, they jointly decided that my father needs medication. He's been on lithium also for about fifteen years. And that apparently had some effect on his mood swings but anyway he went to a psychiatrist who is sort of into pharmacological stuff and he got something called Xanax. I don't know if you know this stuff but apparently it's an anti-anxiety thing, some kind of miracle. But it took at least two weeks of him feeling totally shaky before he could even get this appointment and he called me a lot, and I called him a lot. He was just weeping over the phone and really in bad shape. He got the Xanax, and in two days the anxiety was gone. He was feeling better, and then it was like something very familiar to me. It was great, and I always find it so disturbing. To me it's like the wall goes up because my father's version of reality is so dependent on his inner workings. This isn't meaningful, this isn't real, this is just him.

Allan: Also you had concerns about side effects from the stuff, so you were sort of bracing yourself for something coming.

Jane: Well, that too, and I guess it's just very contrary to my whole, I mean I don't think taking a pill is the answer, although I also appreciate that I don't know what's going on biochemically with him. This thing is effective because it is doing something biochemically. Anyway, I was sort of feeling anxious about the whole thing. And the conversation we had here last time about Allan's response to my talking to my father, I don't know if you remember this one, we had called him on a question about the computer and when I was talking to my father I could hear that he was in bad shape again. This was after the Xanax high had started to go down again. I started asking him a few questions about the computer and then I could just hear, he was choking up, and meanwhile, Allan, this is when you were getting really uptight and saying, "Well, don't ask him, then," and whatever, and I handed Allan the phone, and I just said to Allan, "He's not well!" I mouthed that to him. Remember this, and you took the phone and you asked the questions and your version of it when we came here was that my father sounded like he had a cold and you weren't sure what was going on, and in the end the explanation was he had to go to the bathroom and that's all it was. Well, he did have to go to the bathroom, and there was all that stuff but the history is not relevant. And in fact he also really was not feeling well because after Allan had spoken to him and I got back on the phone right away he started talking about his anxieties and stuff. And you and I talked about that right afterwards.

Anyway, again he went really, really low and he's flailing around all over the place. He doesn't want to go back to this original pharmacological guy because he charges too much money and he is no longer seeing his therapist who he's been seeing for fifteen years. He went to his GP who got him a prescription which is an antidepressant. I just feel like he's all over the place. I do feel very, very worried for him.

Commentary

Jane tells a very elaborate story about her anxiety concerning her father. She depicts him as an emotional invalid who is volatile and suicidal. Leaving this story intact would prevent Jane from having a safe father. If the therapist bought into this story he would become part of the problem; however, if he challenged the story, he would encourage Jane to defend it. If the therapist moved too quickly, without being supportive about the impact of the story on Jane, then he would invalidate her need to have the story. This is the most important part of the interview. The therapist must walk a tightrope between communicating that he understands Jane's need to have this story and questioning the accuracy of the description of her father. This must be done in such a way that it does not stir up reactivity. The therapist understands the story about Jane's father as a metaphor for her sense of loss, abandonment, and general anxiety. The goal of the therapist is to set in motion the process of safely challenging the story and beginning to encourage Jane to develop a healthy dose of curiosity about the forces that have shaped her father.

The therapist begins by embracing the story, but in a slightly different way. He asks Jane to talk about her biggest worry concerning her father. He identifies the underlying theme in the story, which is her worry that her father will commit suicide, as his father did. By dealing with the most fearful part of the story the therapist frees Jane from preoccupation with that worry and allows her to shift into a more hopeful way of thinking about her father—that her father can say something to free her from her old story about his being an emotional invalid. It is important for the therapist to keep in mind that the grandfather's suicide has had a powerful hold on this family. Unless a different understanding of the grandfather's suicide emerges, it will be difficult for Jane not to identify her father with his father and carry on the legacy for yet another generation. An important part of Jane's story is that her father tried unsuccessfully to take care of his father and gave up. Jane is caught in a bind between wanting to let go of this responsibility but fearing that by doing so she will abandon her father and that that will result in depression and potential suicide.

Dr. F.: What are you worried is going to happen?

Jane: I'm worried he's going to die. That's the bottom-line worry.

Dr. F.: Do you think he will kill himself?

Jane: That's very interesting. Just about any other crisis that my father has had, that would have been my prime worry. It's not this time. He's not talking like that. He's not giving whatever suggestions about that that he has in the past, but I know one response that I had that was interesting to me is a tremendous anxiety response. I have to make sure that he doesn't get upset. I have to make sure that nothing I do escalates this. That somehow I have to be careful, and in the past that would have been so I don't trigger his suicide. You know, I have to keep Daddy happy. . . .

Commentary

The therapist goes deeper into Jane's fear of being responsible for keeping her father alive. As long as she feels it is her job to keep her father alive, she cannot allow him to be her father and take care of her in a fatherly way. The therapist must stay calm and involved with the theme of death and loss. If this issue made the therapist anxious he would not be able to make it safe for Jane to work on her boundary problems in relation to her father. Ordinarily when Jane tries to talk about this issue with other people they collude with her and give her suggestions about how to keep her father alive. The therapist offers a new way of thinking about the father and the relationship between father and daughter.

Dr. F.: Do you feel responsible for keeping your father alive?

Jane: Oh, as a kid I think that was a pretty heavy—

Dr. F.: Still?

Jane: Something shifted there, I'm not sure. I mean, this is so complicated because I had a dream that he died a few nights ago and it was the day that some of the fish died in the aquarium. I came home that night and I had a dream that my father had died. But even before that dream I was conscious, I'm worried, and we talked about this. He's old now. He's 66 and he's living by himself, which is also new.

Dr. F.: Is that getting old, 66?

Jane: He's an old 66. . . .

Allan: And his health has been deteriorating visibly.

Jane: Yeah, and again I've got so much stuff. No wonder I don't feel well. I don't know whether this is the first time . . . it's the first time consciously I've almost wished he would die. It's a horrible thing to say. I mean there is a part of me that has wished that. It's like I'm so tired of all this, I have to say this, it's something that I've felt. I don't want him to die. I love my father very, very much, but I'm so sick of this. I don't know how to say this. I feel awful saying that but I really am sick of it.

Dr. F.: What is the "it"?

Jane: His sickness. The emotional sickness and the feeling like he needs me, the feeling like I don't have a father that I can turn to. You know, feeling like this is an ongoing burden. It's just a burden, that's the most all-inclusive.

Dr. F.: You are sick of the burden. What is the process of getting unburdened without your father having to die?

Jane: No, I'm blanking out. My first thought was that he get well. But that's nothing that's in my control and I don't think that's going to happen.

Dr. F.: Do you really believe that it's not in your control? That you really cannot make your father well? Do you think your father thought he could keep his father alive?

Jane: I think he's punished himself all of his life for having behaved the way he behaved around the time of his father's suicide. I'm sure about that. It's nothing that we have really talked about explicitly.

Commentary

One way of becoming unburdened is to begin to make public what has been kept private. One of the interesting paradoxes in family relationships is that the unspoken is a powerful connector between family members. The job of the therapist is to encourage the unspoken to be spoken in the presence of important family members. Secrets bind family members to each other.

At this point in the session the therapist begins to ask Jane questions she cannot answer. The therapist must come up with questions that provoke curiosity. Asking these types of questions reduces the adult child's reactivity and puts the person into a more thoughtful, curious frame of mind. The therapist now introduces real doubt about the old story. When the therapist can accomplish this in a safe way, it helps the adult child become more motivated to bring the parents to a session and be open to their stories in a new way. In this session, the therapist introduces a series of questions that Jane has not been able to pose to her father and encourages her to think about how she would go about asking them. The therapist now begins the process of challenging Jane to think differently about her father and his history. In the beginning of the middle phase of therapy an adult child wants to be unburdened from the responsibilities of the parent, yet is ambivalent about letting go of the old story. By the middle of the middle phase there is a remarkable decrease in ambivalence about embracing the parent in a new way. As the adult child goes through the process of thinking about the emotional cost to self of carrying the old story, there is a greater willingness to want to embrace the important family members in a new way.

Dr. F.: Well, I think the process of getting unburdened is talking about this at some time with your dad. The thought I had was how burdened did your father feel about his father?

Jane: Terribly.

Dr. F.: How did your father's understanding about how burdened he felt about his father influence his trying to unburden you about him? I don't think you can answer that question, I don't think you have enough data to answer that question. But it is an important question.

Jane: Yeah. I think he hasn't, I hate my . . . This is part of the self-righteousness that you accuse me of. I'm always talking like I understand. I don't really feel like I understand it all but I feel like my father hasn't worked it through yet himself enough.

It's like all of us. What we haven't figured out we do to others, right? Well, our family was certainly just a mess, a mess. And he's been in therapy all of his adult life and I'm sure he's figured stuff out.

Dr. F.: Therapy doesn't necessarily help you figure things out. Sometimes therapy helps you stay stuck. The burden that you carry might be about your grandfather, not your father.

Jane: Certainly it was indirectly him and ultimately him.

Dr. F.: Well, you wonder how your dad freed himself of his burden so he could free you of your burden. If you had your dad here I sure would ask him those questions. Those are really very important questions. And how much both you and your sister carry that burden. Not that your father in any way premeditated this. Let me ask you about the women in the family. How the women balanced the men. I don't remember you telling me about your grandmother.

Jane: My father's mother?

Dr. F.: Yes. Tell me about her.

Jane: She was, this is the first thing that comes to my mind, she was manic-depressive. And she was hospitalized repeatedly all during her adult life for her depression. In fact, gosh, it is quarter to and you brought your letter in and—

Allan: No, it's okay, go ahead.

Jane: What I'm thinking is what I would like to do is bring something that my father wrote about his father and his mother. My father wrote something called "Portrait of My Father," which I would like to bring to the next therapy session. It evokes a tremendous amount of emotion and I obviously am not finished with that. So his mother was very sick and she was hospitalized after they left Austria. They just got out as the Nazis were coming in and apparently she was extremely depressed and my father has described to me that sort of border scene of getting her out of the country and how she literally was sort of propped up, on one side by her husband and on the other side by my father.

Dr. F.: By her son.

Jane: I guess both his parents were burdens for him in a heavy, heavy way. Anyway, when they got to the States they weren't there long before my grandfather committed suicide.

Dr. F.: How long?

Jane: I'm not sure. I think two years or something like that.

Allan: Then she was a total burden on him. . . .

Jane: Before my grandfather's suicide my grandmother was, I don't know at what point or for how long, but she was hospitalized in the state institution for the insane and my father describes this quite graphically in his short portrait. That it was a maze of . . . it's quite ugly. It was a big state mental institution and she received insulin treatment and electric shock and every possible thing. And there they were just out of the Vienna circle in Austria into this.

Dr. F.: The madhouse.

Jane: The madhouse. Yeah. Again, I don't know, this is information I can get, but I don't know how many years but she went back to Austria, where she converted to Catholicism.

Dr. F.: After your grandfather committed suicide, how many months, years?

Jane: I don't know.

Dr. F.: Your father knows this, though.

Jane: Yes, he does.

Dr. F.: So some time after her husband died, she went back to Austria and converted to Catholicism and stayed there. And your dad's relationship with his mom became what?

Jane: Oh, very fraught with problems. But I don't know if it became that, it continued to be that, they saw each other just very infrequently. See we went to Israel in 1954 and were there for three years. She came there, I know, and she got depressed there. I have no memory of this, I was newborn, but both my parents have talked about her trip to Israel. She arrived and she got depressed. They had to put her on the plane the same way they got her across the border and she went home to hospital in Vienna. She visited us once here and my father visited in Austria about half a dozen times. She died, I guess, in 1973.

Dr. F.: She was how old?

Jane: I guess in her eighties. She died in a Catholic nursing home. My only memory of her, which is from the time that she visited us when I was about 8 or something like that, and what I remember is of an old woman sitting embroidering a big cross that was for the altar. I remember being struck by how odd, it was odd to me, and I'm having layers of thoughts here because I'm thinking of Allan's mother and my accusation of her anti-Semitism. But I remember — these are not clear memories — but I have this sort of visual vignette of her sitting in our living room and embroidering this cloth and then sort of a memory that's superimposed on it of my mother making a snide remark about Ella is anti-Semitic and how my father is anti-Semitic. And of his having made some comment to my mother when they were dating. My mother is a Sephardic Jew who doesn't look Semitic at all; my father looks very Jewish. He apparently made a comment to her, "What's the matter with you, you could get anybody. Why are you going for a Jew?"

Dr. F.: What year did your grandfather commit suicide?

Jane: I think 1945, but I could be wrong. That information I have in a book at home.

Dr. F.: So Grandmother lived almost 31 years. . . .

Jane: Yeah.

Dr. F.: Didn't remarry?

Jane: No.

Dr. F.: And your father truly was an only child.

Jane: Yes.

Dr. F.: Did he ever ask his father if he truly was an only child?

Jane: I think I asked why they only had one child and he made some remark like he doesn't even know how they had one child.

Dr. F.: Does it seem odd for me to ask you that question is he truly an only child?

Jane: Yeah, I mean I guess it's something that I've never questioned. Have you heard something that maybe there was another, or you know . . .?

Commentary

At this point the therapist has expanded the definition of family. After discussing the grandfather and father, he begins to ask questions about the grandmother. Leaving the grandmother in the background and making the suicide of the grandfather the most important story would increase the family mythology. It is important for the therapist to begin to redefine what makes up family. Identifying proper heroes, guides, and mentors expands the family as a resource system. Although Jane describes her grandmother as an emotional invalid like her father, the therapist has stimulated curiosity about the forces that shaped her as

well. The reader will see in a future chapter that the grandmother was actually a herolike person. At this point the therapist does not know this but he is trying to give balance to both
sides of the family. If the therapist becomes intrigued just with
the family member the client presents, he becomes part of the
family problem.

The therapist questions all premises. For example, when he
asks if the father was truly an only child, he is suggesting that
there may be other sides to the family story. Possibly no one has
ever questioned the family composition. Just becoming curious
about that point can stimulate an adult child's curiosity about all
kinds of other family stories.

Dr. F.: What I have learned is that new people pop up now
and then. We grow up thinking that we know the family. Then
we realize that there has been another family somewhere that no
one has talked about. I had another couple I was just thinking
about where the grandson discovered that his grandfather had
another family, when they came to the funeral of his father. He
grew up never knowing anything about them until his father's
death. So you never know.

Jane: I think in that regard my father has a very small
family and most of them died in the Second World War.

Allan: It seems so striking the way you described this. I
mean, this is all new stuff for me, but it's almost as if for your
father's mother, it was a liberation to have him commit suicide.
She could go back to Austria, and the world was as if fresh
again. She could carry on happily, unburdened by all of that
stuff. It's just the image that it evokes in me. I may be way off
base.

Jane: Well, she didn't carry on happily. She was still sick.

Dr. F.: She carried on a little bit differently. So have you
asked your father what his theory is about his mother becoming
a Catholic when his father committed suicide?

Jane: No, I haven't asked my father that. No.

Dr. F.: What a good question, if he has a theory.

Jane: Probably.

Dr. F.: Probably he has theories.

Jane: He may. He also, isn't that odd, he probably has insights, too, real insights.

Dr. F.: Well, that's another way of using the word "theories."

Jane: I guess so. Somehow I felt like I had to come to his defense when you said that. It's as if he might have all kinds of explanations or something and that is also true of him. I also think he has insights. It hasn't helped him a whole lot.

Commentary

The therapist conveys the idea that it is important to think about one's family members without needing to figure them out. The goal for the adult child is to understand how the various family stories have influenced some of the decisions he or she has made.

Dr. F.: That's why I call them theories rather than insights. Insights imply that one knows. A theory allows for doubts. Theories do serve to guide us. If it's not a good theory it guides us badly. If it's a good theory at least there is some hope.

Allan: Or even bad theories you have to recognize as a theory.

Dr. F.: But he would have to have a very powerful theory about that one.

Jane: I can answer that one for you. I am sure he would say yes. That we have sort of talked about. He has said he never had a mother and I was named Joanna after his nanny because his mother wasn't there and he had a nanny.

Commentary

The therapist ends the session with a general comment about the need to get more information. He suggests that powerful themes such as abandonment and the stories we develop around them keep us stuck with certain preoccupations or points of view about our family. What is helpful is to obtain more data to understand how these themes got played out for each family member. He concludes by highlighting several themes in a way that will provoke greater curiosity about them.

If the therapist has been successful about increasing curiosity and raising doubts about old family stories, then the succeeding sessions will be ones in which the adult child brings in new stories, different questions, and more enthusiasm for wanting to understand the family better.

Dr. F.: Well, there are different levels of abandonment. Like that scene that you describe at the border with your dad having to be strong for Mum rather than Mum for Dad. And, as you were saying, your losing your dad in his depression; you don't have a dad. So you have a generational theme. There is another theme, about the deeper sense of abandonment or betrayal in leaving behind one's history. Becoming Catholic, what that is about. What your dad's theory is about that. And how that makes it hard, or made it hard for your dad to honor his dad around his dad's choice of saying good-bye. It's an interesting way that people say good-bye when they suicide. You can never really say good-bye because you have all these unfinished things. So it's like that person stays alive in a very peculiar way. These are all really interesting questions. I was just sitting here puzzling how to get at these questions, wondering how your dad would answer these questions.

Jane: I would love to have him come here. I mentioned it to him.

Dr. F.: Did he show any interest?

Jane: Yeah, very much so.

Dr. F.: Well, it would be wonderful to do that. Allan, you brought this letter. We won't have time to look at it, but I'm going to see you next week. If you could bring that one, too, and the "Portrait," and we will spend some of the hour on that.

Allan: Sure.

7

Middle Middle Phase: Going Home

Introduction

The middle middle phase of family therapy with couples focuses on helping each partner strategize how he or she will reposition with the family of origin. In the middle middle phase couples no longer present relationship problems as their major concern. When difficulties arise in the relationship, the partners reflect about how these problems are connected with historical themes. Each partner is essentially nonreactive and curious about his or her expression of anxiety. The adult children are more interested in reconnecting with their original families and applying their learning to their families of procreation.

Working on Self: Repositioning within Family of Origin

One of the tasks of the therapist in the middle middle phase is to prepare each partner for a series of family visits. It is important that adult children's agenda for these contacts is to learn more about the family rather than to validate their own stories and/or try to fix the family. Often adult children have secret agendas for their parents. Although they may have talked about being more curious about their parents, they may still hold on to a secret wish that their parents will finally validate their accomplishments. Or they may have hidden anxieties about their parents' functioning and hope that they can help them by involving themselves with their parents in a different way. Either of these two agendas will interfere with the repositioning of the adult child with the extended family.

The therapist has to ask numerous questions to discover whether the adult child has successfully worked through need for validation or anxiety about how his or her family is functioning. The adult child has to visit family with an open mind and a clear sense of self-limitations. It is important for the adult child to be curious about the parents' reactivity rather than being self-protective around it, or trying to change the parents' way of responding to the world. The therapist can ask the adult child a series of questions to see if he or she is ready to be more proactive with the parent when the parent becomes anxious, critical, withdrawn, and/or withholding.

The therapist should not try to convince adult children of the importance of doing family-of-origin work. By the middle middle phase adult children should have developed their own motivation and eagerness to do this work. The therapist should slow adult children down and help them become more thoughtful about how they will respond to the anxiety their new behavior will stir up. During the beginning of the middle phase the therapist encourages the adult child to visit with family of origin. However, in the middle middle phase the roles are reversed. The adult child is motivated to return home and ask various questions, but the therapist puts on the brakes. The therapist begins to ask provocative questions to prepare the adult child to be able to respond to a range of behaviors that can be displayed by the family.

It is important for therapists to remember that when adult children take a new position with their extended families, the response to that position will be critical, challenging, and generally anxious, principally because the family has not experienced this type of behavior from the child, and is confused by it. Family members may not be certain that the adult child is sincere in efforts to know more about them and are likely to try to reinstate the old emotional dance with which everyone is comfortable. If the adult child can sustain the new behavior over a period of time, there is a fair chance that he or she will begin to experience different types of family relationships.

Adult children need to be reminded that repositioning is essentially about learning more about self by allowing self to be exposed to the old family reactivity. It is similar to "putting yourself in the lion's den." To learn about how well self can deal with anxiety, it is necessary to put self in high anxiety-producing situations. When it feels anxious, the family will react in predictable ways. The adult child should allow these reactions to occur without intruding his or her old style of protectiveness. When the adult child is able to observe how the family deals with anxiety without responding to that anxiety, the child will have developed a greater sense of emotional functioning and will be able to embrace anxiety in others in more positive, connecting ways.

Rewriting the Family Story

Each time the adult child returns to the family and interviews various family members about their lives, he or she is engaged in the process of rewriting the family story. Each of us needs to do this at some point. The family story we have constructed interferes, to some degree, with our ability to deal with important people in our lives. The mythology we carry about ourselves and our families prevents us from learning how to respond to current events in creative, spontaneous ways. When we start rewriting our family story we begin the subtle process of giving up our old mythology about the world and how it treats us and become more curious and reflective about the forces we experience around us.

Each member of the family carries a different story. Our openness to our family members' stories is indicative of our openness to the stories of people, such as our spouse, children, friends, colleagues, and clients. When we were growing up, the stories our parents told us were based on the struggles they were having at that point in their lives and/or their anxieties about us. An adult child will hear a new version of the old story. The stories our aged parents tell us are quite different from the stories they told when they were young adults. And of course, what we were open to hearing when we were younger is quite different from what we need to hear when we get older.

Many of our parents are eager for the opportunity to tell their stories. Unfortunately, many adult children are not prepared to hear these stories, particularly if they contradict the old mythology. To be open to the stories of our parents, we must also be prepared to have a different type of relationship with them. This is the main reason adult children need a fair amount of time in therapy before they can shift out of the protection of the old story into the uncertainty of the new. If the therapist tries to change the adult children's stories too early, the attempts will be met with greater anxiety and defensiveness. However, in the middle middle phase of therapy the adult children feel more solid about themselves and are better prepared to deal with the sadness, vulnerability, struggles, and caring represented in the new stories.

Major Indicators of the Middle Middle Phase

It is important that the therapist recognize when adult children are in the middle middle phase of therapy. As has been indicated before, the therapist's rushing into this part of the therapy will undermine the adult child's readiness to embrace the family in a new way. A shift has to occur in the adult child's sense of self before he or she is ready to embrace the family's sadness. *People's stories about each other keep them emotionally safe.* As long as adult children hold on to certain stories about their parents, they need not look at their parents' struggles, sadness, and losses. Staying angry at, hurt by, and resentful of our parents allows us the safe distance we need to feel we are getting on with our own lives. When the adult child is able to embrace anxiety and sadness, he or she will be open to a fuller range of the parents' experiences.

The adult children have to become their own experts in this process. They have to be able to monitor their reactivity. The major tasks of the middle middle phase of therapy are to learn how to return home, to stay home and to leave home. The leaving is very important. How we leave will determine how we return. If adult children are their own experts, they will leave just prior to becoming reactive. This timing fosters returning with willingness and readiness. If adult children leave in anger and hurt, they shut down emotionally and are no longer open to hearing the family story without distortion and reactivity.

Self No Longer Needs the Other to Be Different

The adult child in the middle middle phase presents stories about how certain members of the family behaved in anxious, critical, negative ways, for the purposes of sharing what he or she has learned about that person and himself or herself. The therapist must listen carefully to how the adult child tells family stories. If the adult child is still blaming others and looking for evidence to support his or her point of view, then he or she is not in the middle middle phase. For this part of the therapy to be successful, the adult child must be able to learn how to embrace the family in a new way. Family members will respond in predictable ways when they become anxious. The adult child has to see this behavior as an opportunity to learn more about self. The adult child should not get discouraged when initial overtures are not received positively by a parent. If the adult child can persist to get to know the parents differently, eventually there will be a new opening.

The Adult Child Becomes a Family Researcher

The adult child does not rely solely on parents and/or siblings to learn about the family but also becomes curious about uncles and aunts, cousins, grandparents, friends of the family, and any written material on the family. It is important that the adult child go beyond the parents' definition of family. Siblings of parents often have fascinating stories to tell. It is not uncommon for parents to be cut off from a sibling or two. If the adult child does not reach out to these people and include them in his or her definition of family, he or she is deprived of some valuable data about the family.

This potential deprivation was illustrated by a story a client of mine told. She had been cut off from her uncle for over twenty years because of a fight her father had had with him. The family chose sides, and as a result this woman had no contact with her cousins, aunt or uncle for many years. It was a significant loss for her because the uncle was her favorite and she was close to those cousins. She grew up feeling that involvement with these relatives would represent disloyalty to her mother and father. During therapy she decided to visit this family and listen to their side of the story. She taped her uncle's story in which he talked about his sadness about the incident that led to the distance between the brothers. She asked a number of questions about her grandparents and how her uncle understood the forces that shaped the family. When she returned home she played the tape for her father. Her father was fascinated with the way his brother had talked about the family story and his sadness about being cutoff from him. The father then contacted his brother and reconnected with that side of the family. A year later, the uncle died. At the funeral the father talked about how important it was for him to be able to reconnect with his brother during his lifetime. This reconnection is a positive ripple effect but should not be the agenda for the adult child.

Planning a Family-of-Origin Visit

The therapist helps the adult child plan family-of-origin visits. This planning is done in the presence of both partners. It is not uncommon for one partner to be more motivated than the other. The therapist should not be too concerned about this. The therapist's task is to work with the one who is ready to take on these family-of-origin visits while at the same time remain sensitive to anxiety, reactivity, or confusion stirred up in the other by this process. The actual planning of the family visits is quite important. These visits may be initiated by the adult child or occur as a result of some special family occasion. In either case the adult child needs to have a strategy as to how to make this visit different. A series of visits that allows for the adult child to spend person-to-person time with various family members is preferable. Planned visits and visits around special occasions produce different types of learning. The planned family visit initiated by the adult child allows him or her to request special time with individual family members. It allows for the adult child to explain the purpose of the visit, to structure the visit, and to determine its length. The visit initiated by the family because of a special occasion, such as Christmas, anniversaries, weddings, funerals, and so forth, presents an opportunity to observe the family in interaction as a group. The special occasions are ordinarily accompanied by high expectations and a considerable amount of family anxiety. Observing how family members deal with each other at these occasions can teach one a lot about the family and the various roles, functions, and structures it has created for its members to be safe with each other. During those visits the adult child should learn about the family style by staying involved yet detached.

When an adult child is ready to initiate a series of family visits, the therapist helps develop a strategy that will produce new learning. The following guidelines offer some structure for the adult child who is planning these visits.

How Often?

Ideally, the adult child should make several visits over the course of a year. Assuming the family lives out of town, these visits should be three to four days long. Short, frequent visits allow an individual to put his or her best proactive self forward before anxiety takes over and the person withdraws and defends in old, familiar ways. A series of three- to four-day visits to spend time alone with certain family members is preferable. The adult child should explain to the parents how much time he or she has set aside for the visit and that he or she would like to spend time with each parent alone. Once the parents realize how serious the adult child is about reconnecting with them, their confusion and anxiety will lessen and their desire to have a more positive connection will increase.

Short, frequent visits may be a new pattern for many adult children and this in itself may stir up confusion and anxiety. For a short time the parents will feel awkward, and this will be expressed by their appearing ambivalent about the visit. However, it is important for the adult child to stay positive, understanding, and committed to his or her reasons for wanting to spend time with the parents. The adult child should not use the parents' ambivalence as an excuse to distance from them. It is important for the adult child to remember that when he or she begins to approach the parents in a new way, they will be confused and will express some of this with general distancing behavior. If the adult child can stay involved and positive about the connection, the ambivalence will disappear and a new type of connection will develop.

How to Structure the Visit

Does the adult child return to the family home? Does he or she stay in his or her old room? Does the entire visit take place in the family home? Can the adult child visit other family members during the same visit? Must the adult child spend the same amount of time with each parent? These are common questions. It is important that the adult child be in control of his or her part of the visit and explain clearly to the parents how and where the visit will take place. In certain families it may not be wise for the adult child to stay in the family home because it may be too difficult to feel in control of the visit when returning to the old, familiar family surroundings. Some adult children stay with a sibling and visit the parents; others stay with friends and visit the parents. Some adult children stay in hotels and visit, while others are able to stay in their family home without giving up their ability to structure the quality of the visit. The therapist should explore all these options with the adult child and help to choose the one that produces the greatest emotional freedom to experiment with ways of being positively reconnected.

The adult child must spend time alone with each parent, and should arrange this with them beforehand. When the parents realize that the adult child wants to be connected equally with both, any competition or jealousy will dissipate.

Whom to Visit

The adult child should visit both parents, if possible, and, at times, siblings. He or she should spend time with each parent alone. It is difficult to engage the parents in important discussions when others are in the room. To make these visits different and to provide new information, each parent must be taken from the family setting. Most parents have certain routines or rituals, such as walking or golfing. Joining the parent in such a routine or ritual may give the adult child an opportunity to see a different side of the parent. The adult child should then begin the gentle questioning about the parent's life experience.

Types of Questions

Coaching the adult child on how to question family members is an essential part of the planning for family-of-origin visits. How the questions are asked will determine whether new information is gathered. *The theories we have about our family will determine how open we are to the information they provide us.* If we feel we have "figured out" our parents, then we will fit their responses into our original theory. When adult children are truly in the middle middle phase of therapy they realize they have to let go of their original theories about their parents. If they do this, their questions will be neutral, nonjudgmental, and allow the parent to tell the story freely. The adult child must not preprogram the questions, but have general questions that encourage the parent to tell the story. The adult child should not ask questions that put the parents into a defensive stance. The adult child should acknowledge that the parents did the best job they could do with the experiences they had in the world. Many parents need to hear this from their adult children. Until that has been heard, they are likely to be defensive about their past and will justify or rationalize their choices. If the adult child can understand that the parents' behavior toward them was significantly connected with the parents' own family experiences, then they will be more curious and less judgmental.

When the adult child has worked through agendas of blame and hurt and has adopted a curious stance, the parents will respond by feeling safe enough to tell their story. A related dynamic is that many parents feel protective of their adult children, which leads them to change their story to take care of any real or imagined sadness they are worried the story may evoke in the adult child. When such parents see the adult child is becoming upset, they will stop telling the story and switch to safer subjects. Many adult children believe that their parents are not able to tell their story, when in fact the parents believe their adult children are not able to hear the story. The adult child must free the parents from this sort of preoccupation by letting them know they want to hear the story, even though they may appear sad or upset.

The adult child's questions should seek historical information, such as asking the parents to tell about their experiences with their own grandparents and what they learned from them and then about their parents and the experiences of each member of their own families of origin. These questions are safe. Gradually, the parents will talk about the sadness of losing their own parents or their difficulties with siblings or other family problems. This process allows parents to talk about their losses, sadness, and disappointments with safety. Parents vary greatly in terms of the amount of information they have about their family history. Some have a lot, some little or none. Parents cut off from their history tend to come from families in which their own parents and grandparents were similarly cut off. This dynamic is often connected with the immigration process. Sometimes leaving the family's homeland was so devastating that the family is unable to talk about it. Parents from families cut off from their own history because of sadness and loss are not able to communicate stories of hope, survival, and heroics to their children effectively. Such children grow up with very few family stories. On the other hand, parents whose parents left home feeling connected with their homeland and ancestors are able to communicate many positive stories. Their rich heritage, along with the ability to tell stories, is passed on to the next generation. When adult children realize that their parents' lack of stories have to do with their feelings of loss about being cut off from their roots, the children begin to appreciate, in a different way, their parents' stoicism, quietness, and lack of information.

Debriefing the Visit

After the adult child has had the family visit, it is necessary to debrief. The adult child returns to the family therapy session with stories about how the visit went: the things that worked, the areas of reactivity and disappointment, the positive connections and difficulties in making other connections. If the partner can be involved in this debriefing process by listening carefully without commenting, there is tremendous potential for learning in the relationship. When an adult child talks about the sadness of being unable to connect in a deeper way with a parent and how he or she dealt with that sadness, the partner learns something new that can translate into a more supportive and gentle connection between them. It is important for the therapist to encourage the adult children to generalize the learning to all key relationships.

The Therapist as a Coach

The therapist, as coach, helps the adult child understand the family and his or her reactivity around family issues. The therapist encourages the adult child to come up with more profound strategies to learn about the family, such as new ways to approach the family during the next visit. The therapist's role involves listening to the adult children's stories and posing questions that allow them to think of questions they want to ask family members during the next visit. There are no bad stories. Regardless of the type of story the adult child brings back, the therapist should encourage the adult child to use it as an opportunity to learn more about self rather than as an excuse to distance from family.

Telling the Story

After the adult child has attempted to reposition in the family of origin, he or she constructs a story about that experience. If that story simply remains in the adult child's head, it may become a new reality. The process of telling the story, and listening to ourselves as we tell it, helps us modify it. Unfortunately, many of the people we involve in our lives (spouse, friends, confidants, and so forth) join us in our old stories. When we tell them our new story, they often remind us of our old story, which can make us defensive and unable to learn. The therapist, however, stays neutral and allows the adult child to externalize the story and rethink it while it is being told. This is important, because there are few places where self can relate a story without others intruding their opinion about it. The therapist's stance also provides a powerful lesson to the partner on how to listen to stories without introducing his or her own agenda.

Checking Out the Reactivity

In listening to the adult child tell the story, the therapist looks for areas or pockets of reactivity. The adult child may not be aware of such areas. It is unusual to visit home and not encounter pockets of reactivity. The challenge is to return home and extend the length of time there before the old reactivity surfaces. Sometimes we don't realize that when we dismiss or avoid people or withdraw from certain types of discussions, we are in a reactive stance. When the therapist asks how the decision was made to take a certain position, he or she helps the adult child identify areas of reactivity.

Encouraging the Adult Child to Plan the Next Family-of-Origin Visit

After each family-of-origin visit it is necessary to plan for the next one as part of a series of visits. Each visit is a building block for future visits. It is important for the therapist to continue asking the adult child about what he or she would like to experiment with during the next visit. Each visit teaches the adult child something new about himself or herself. During the debriefing session, time should be set aside to plan the next visit.

Clinical Examples of Debriefing the Adult Child on Family-of-Origin Work

The remainder of this chapter contains two clinical examples of adult children in the middle middle phase of family therapy with couples. The first example follows up the session presented in Chapter 6. In this interview the couple has reached the middle middle phase of therapy. Initially, the focus is on the wife's story about what she is learning about her father. In the second half of the interview the husband talks about his struggles to reposition in his own family, particularly with his father and mother. This interview illustrates how one partner's work can stir up and motivate the other partner.

The second example concerns a couple who began therapy because of difficulties in their marriage. The presenting problem was the wife's affair. Over the course of the therapy the couple had developed a better understanding about what the affair represented in terms of their own emotional issues. Both began to realize that they had developed their own ways of distancing: the wife through getting involved with other people, the husband through losing himself in work.

After gaining a different understanding of what the affair represented, they decided they wanted to work on their self issues. The interview is a debriefing following a family-of-origin visit. The couple had visited the husband's family in Europe so that he could work on repositioning himself with his mother, father, and siblings. Prior to this visit the husband had maintained distant relationships with his family. The visit constituted a major repositioning for the husband. One of the consequences of his taking more responsibility for establishing connections with his family was that he was able to reconnect with his wife and approach his work with more balance. The wife no longer needed another relationship to feel safe once she realized that she didn't have to compete with her husband's work to feel special.

The following interview is with Jane and Allan, the couple presented in Chapter 6. It begins with the therapist asking what got stirred up in each of them after the last session. The responses to this question give the therapist a sense of the degree to which the couple has shifted into greater curiosity about their own families. The therapist discovers that the wife has significantly repositioned herself with her father. She tells a story about her anxiety about her father and her attempts to reposition around his losses and worries.

Dr. F.: Talking about stories, we have to start with where we ended. What happened when you walked out of here after the last session?

Jane: God, what actually happened was my father. It was my birthday last week and he came up this weekend, Friday, Saturday, and Sunday. So we did lots of things and I've got some information for you by way of his therapist's name and number. It's all written down.

Dr. F.: Okay, why don't you give it to me just before you leave.

Jane: It's an answering service and she said she'll call you right back. I guess you know when you asked what had happened since we last were here . . . I'm trying to sort of put this in some kind of meaningful. . . . I had some thoughts before my father's arrival but a lot of it is just like anticipating and so I was thinking about that. One of the things that struck me after reading my father's memoir to you was that shortly after my father left for graduate school his father left for California.

Within six months his father had killed himself and he made this comment that, you know, his feelings were like my father, it had been my father's absence, you know, my father had left his father and then he killed himself. I remember at the time thinking well, that is not quite right because in fact it's not that they had been together and my father had been gone over the years but he used to visit. But it doesn't really matter. It's the feeling that my father felt, the responsible son that comes through loud and clear in that essay. What I had never thought of is, you know, that so there is my father's guilt which I thought of a lot, but the flip side is the feeling of abandonment on my father's part when his father left him. I hadn't really thought about it although once it's out it's obvious but again, I'm sorry I always take so long to get to the point. . . .

Commentary

The therapist encourages Jane to go on with her story. There is no need to intrude with any questions. She is reporting on taking a new position with her father and her struggles to understand some of his losses differently. She could have shifted into some problem with her husband or the relationship, but she stays pretty well focused on trying to understand some of her father's struggles.

Dr. F.: You're doing very well.

Jane: Okay, I brought up the last time that my father had said his therapist mentioned that it occurred to her that maybe his father's inability to eat . . . that maybe he had Crohn's disease and that my father felt that when C., the therapist, said this to my father he said, you know, he burst out crying. He told me this weekend when he was visiting he didn't cry for fifteen years and he just couldn't stop crying and that he cried for three days afterwards, just intermittently crying about that and the tremendous relief he felt because it gave it meaning, and as I had understood it before my father and I talked about it in such depth that, you know, there is nothing he could have done. There is nothing my father could have done, because if it was a physiological thing he wasn't responsible for that. What occurred to me as a result of what you said is that it also means there was nothing his father could have done. I mean, his father was physically so sick. He wasn't responsible for that in a way, but for me, that brought me tremendous relief. I don't know exactly why, and I mentioned it to my father this weekend. I mean, one thing that feels really good is I feel good because although a lot of things my father and I talked about were very difficult to talk about, it wasn't as hard as I thought, so as a result we talked a lot. I guess I'm going through something and I said to him that I just wonder if that's something that you have ever thought about because in a way it is pretty obvious although I had never thought about it. To my surprise he said no. And he sort of thought about it and he said, "I've had angry feelings toward my father for other things. I have felt that anger, but I've never even thought about it in the context of his suicide. After all, I was 20 when he killed himself." I don't think kids stop needing their parents at 20. He just was very pensive about it and said he really had never thought about it. For me it felt, it still feels significant, significant for me anyway, in terms of my story.

The other thing that came up and that you had asked about was the letter that my grandfather had written to my father, the existence of which I was aware but it was one of those vague things. So I asked my father about that and I was very anxious. That is one of the things I was anxious about. Actually how it came up is that at one point shortly after he came I said there were some things I wanted to talk about but not right now. I don't know whether David was playing near and so then at some point an opportunity arose where David was actually out with friends and my father said, "You know, there were some things that you had said that you wanted to talk about." We had been chitchatting about other things and then suddenly he brought it up. So I said to him, "Okay, this is a kind of, it feels like a sudden shift but, okay, . . .," and he said, "Well, do whatever you need to do, it's okay with me. I'm ready to talk." So I said, "Okay, this is going to be hard for me." And then suddenly it wasn't so hard for me. I just did it, to my surprise. I sort of just said, "Look, I've wondered for years about . . ." I guess what I said is, "I know that your father left a short note with him in his office when he committed suicide but I've wondered for years about anything more than that that he might have written to you." And my father just said right away, "Yes, he did write me a letter." And I guess what I was going to say next was, "Would you consider showing me a copy?" or something like that but before I could he said, "I can tell you what was in that letter." I said, "Do you have that letter?" and he said, "Yeah, I do. I couldn't put my finger on it right away but it's in my papers and I can find it. I can tell you, let me try and remember," is the way my father said it.

All of this just surprised me because my father spoke so easily about it, casual is maybe the wrong word, but it's not as if, it's not really what I thought. But to use a symbolic . . . that maybe he kept it under his pillow or something, that it was so precious to him. But in fact it was somewhere in his papers. Anyway, what came out I think was significant. I don't know what to make of it but I know it's significant for me. The first thing was that although it was clearly a suicide letter he mailed it to my father. He mailed it the day that he killed himself. He never told my father that he was killing himself. What he said was, "I am writing you this letter because I have been so absent-minded lately that I am worried I'm going to have an accident." I think what my father said was, "I'm worried that I might get hit by a car and there are some things I want you to know." But he never addressed the fact that he was going to kill himself. That's important to me. I mean, it makes me feel very compassionate toward my father because I see it as such a loss, that they didn't have that kind of bond even for an act so final, that there was a pretext around it even for his own son.

My father talked about this, but not about any upset. I mean he was very genuine when he was talking but again this is my own fantasy, or I would have thought this would have been impossible for him to talk about. It wasn't the case. Probably three or four years ago it would have been but I don't know. So that was the first thing, that it was just a kind of, in case something happens to me there are some things you want to know. My father said he remembered that his father said that you need to expect that your mother will repeatedly get sick and that is something that will be a burden for you but that you need to know that this is really likely. It will happen. He also said that he hoped that my father would devote himself to his physics. My father was studying physics at the time, because he was so good at it and that he wouldn't get into, I can't remember the exact words that my father used, that he wouldn't become involved in politics. And here my father said, "Quote, 'because I know you,'" so what his father had written is not to get involved in politics because I know you, quote, unquote, and my father said, "Whatever that is supposed to mean. I don't know what my father meant by that." So that was never resolved for my father. But again of interest to me is that my father has been pathologically involved in politics all of his adult life.

Allan: Or call it intensely—

Jane: Intensely.

Allan: Pathologically is a little bit of a—

Jane: Well, that's why I'm saying that. I see something pathological about it but you're right, a much more neutral word is intense. You know he has been very provocative politically. On demonstrations he's gotten arrested, against the war in Vietnam, and the states' civil rights struggles and on and on, right up until a few years ago and I found that very interesting, too. The only other thing he said, and I have no feel for it, it was totally unexpected to me, whereas the other things I could right away connect with although I won't say I would have expected them to be in the letter, although they made sense to me. This I don't know. My father said again that his father had written, "I hope that you find a wife and have a good relationship. That is very important to me." As far as I know that's all that's in the letter. My father said, "For some reason my father was worried that I was gay." That took me totally by surprise and my father said, "I really have no idea why," he said, "but it came up between us because at one point I got a letter from a college buddy that was signed 'Love and kisses, Harry.'" He said, "It was a total joke, but my father saw it and really became concerned." My father said, "The more we discussed it, the more I tried to say that Dad, this is a total joke, the more awkward it became and it never got resolved." I don't know what that means but I know that my grandfather should not have written that in this letter, or what he wrote was, "I hope you get married and have a relationship," and that what sticks in my father's mind is that his father was worried that he might be gay, and again, you see with all of these things what struck me so much is of course they are things that never got resolved between my father and my grandfather because he wrote that letter and mailed it the day he killed himself.

So somehow I have a different feeling for my father's situation and what he was left with. In many ways it is, and I'm speaking off the top of my head now, but in many ways I feel a little disappointed for I guess if I had hoped for anything in a suicide letter it would have been something more, something that would have revealed more of the connection between them. I'm not sure why I'm saying this, but I guess that his father had to send a pretend letter, not a suicide letter, and that some of the issues that were discussed were based on misunderstandings between them.

Commentary

Jane's interpretation of her grandfather's letter is reactive. It is based on her old theory about her father and what happened to him in his family. She is sad that her grandfather was not able to give her father a "proper suicide note." She emphasizes that her father never really connected with his father and implies that her father in turn was not able to be a father to her. The therapist's task is to question this interpretation and help Jane become more curious about what went on between her father and grandfather. If the therapist allowed her interpretation to go unquestioned, he would inadvertently be colluding with the old theory. It is important for Jane to begin to question what actually happened between her father and grandfather. If Jane can see some connections between her father and grandfather, she may become more open to seeing how her father has tried to connect differently with her.

The therapist gently challenges Jane's interpretation by reframing the letter. Rather than defining the letter negatively, the therapist suggests that her grandfather was giving her father instructions for life. The last thing the grandfather did for the father was to give him a guide for how to be happy and safe in the world. This reframe is an important one. Jane can begin to question her old theory and actually see the letter to her father as one of caring and instruction. This reframe helps Jane start the slow process of rethinking her basic theory about the family history.

Dr. F.: I would just make a comment for you to think about, just to ponder. From your report of what your father remembers about the letter from his father, to the very end he was being his father. The gift that your father got from his father was directions for life. That was a positive legacy. He was trying to be a father. What parents do for their children is express their anxieties about their children's futures. When we begin doing this work on family, we have to understand what family members are saying in the context of their anxiety. Parents try to direct their children to do better than themselves. What we have to do is sort of get behind the anxiety to get our parents' stories. The anxiety comes out with shaping up suggestions like "study your physics. Get married. Don't go into politics." Your grandfather gave your father a special gift, which was directions for life. None of us ever appreciates those gifts from our parents. We have to find our own direction. But that is a gift, and actually seeing the letter and reading it would be more helpful. What do you think about what I am saying about it being an interesting gift? He didn't talk about death; he talked about life. He didn't talk about the past; he talked about the future.

Allan: Except the way you describe it, the way your father's words came out, it sounds like it wasn't very accepting because the way your father said, "Well, if he was worried that I was gay, then he was saying get married." You know, I mean if his father thought he was gay then you let it go and instead he is being told, "Get married." Instead he is being told, "You like politics. Don't get into politics. It will cause you no end of trouble." In that sense you know, nonaccepting. Now maybe I'm just saying it because I wish my dad would tell me, "Allan, these are the things you like. Just do them and succeed at them," or whatever. Maybe that's what I would like.

Commentary

This part of the interview illustrates how delicate it is for adult children to work on their family without some interference from their partners. Allan takes a position vis-à-vis Jane's story about her father. However, he has learned enough about his own themes to catch himself and conclude with a statement that acknowledges that the grandfather's letter may have stirred up feelings about what he did not get from his own father. It is important when one partner begins the process of repositioning for the other partner to stay on the sidelines. However, the closer one partner's themes and stories are to the other partner's the more likely they are to stir up the other. It is up to the therapist to gently nudge the partner out of reactivity and stay focused on the adult child who is doing the work. However, the therapist must recognize what parts of the story stir up the partner. When the therapist later shifts the focus to that partner the therapist can more quickly identify the themes the partner has projected onto the mate. If partners are left to their own devices, they can easily collude with each other's stories. If the therapist had not intervened at this point, he would have supported the collusion around the old theory about the letter and the father/grandfather relationship.

Dr. F.: Yes. I think that's a very interesting point. Getting back to what I said to you in the very beginning, the very first session, what our parents are not able to give us is connected with what they did not get from their own parents. So their struggles and their way of trying to make it safe for us is not criticism of us. It is anxiety about the self. Allan, remember the letter you read to me about your dad saying, "Don't send me those letters"? And you needed to understand that that was not about you doing something wrong. It would be nice to be embraced by our parents and to have them say, "That's wonderful. You sent this letter. It's wonderful that you are doing these things. I just want to let you know that I'm beside you no matter what you choose to do." Probably if that went on we wouldn't be having this conversation. It would be a different story. What I am saying is our job as adults is to embrace our parents without needing them to be different. We have to understand their sameness differently.

So Jane, your father's father gave him a gift. The only gift he knew how to give. His mind had already sorted out what the last gift he wanted to leave your father was. It was a gift of the future. You might read it differently. It was a guide for how to be safe in the world. It is our job now to embrace our parents differently. It is not their job, even though it would be nice, if they embraced us in terms of our differences. That is what you will do with your son. It is a different legacy that you are going to give your son.

Allan: I suppose I respond that way because I'm consciously trying to be that way with David.

Commentary

The therapist moves into teaching a bit about systems principles. He introduces the concepts of balance and boundaries. He suggests that if parents are not aware of their own themes, it is difficult for them to be proper guides to their children. It is important for adult children to remember that what they work through in one generation affects other generations. It is a matter of choice for the therapist how he or she wants to highlight the principles of systems behavior. The therapist can focus on the adult child's relationship with his or her aged parents, the adult child's relationship with his or her children, and/or the relationship between the husband and the wife. The task is to link the generations in some positive, cohesive way. The concepts of balance and boundary are significant. When there are boundary problems between the adult child and the aged parent, there are usually boundary problems between the adult child and his or her children.

Dr. F.: What you have to be careful about, and this is where the unfinished business repeats itself, are the opposite extremes. The opposites are the same, which is a very peculiar paradox. There are some guidelines and some structures that our children need. Structure that is given to a child out of anxiety is not safe structure. Structure that is given out of vision about how to be in the world is safe structure. Remember that point because that is going to be the delicate balance for you to achieve, not to err by going to the other extreme.

Jane: It feels like these are things one almost shouldn't have to think about but that in the course of coming to know oneself one can just act with respect and love and it works, but I guess that's the best of all possibilities.

Commentary

The therapist now attempts to highlight the importance of controlling anxiety. He suggests that when adult children can control anxiety they are more likely to be able to use their own wisdom to understand how to be different with their family. In the middle middle phase of therapy it is important that the adult children believe in themselves and be open to new learning from their parents. The job of the therapist is to highlight the wisdom within the family. The therapist helps the adult children realize that their parents have much to teach them, both from their accomplishments and their disappointments. The job of the therapist is to locate aspects of the family story that emphasize wisdom, survival, and connections.

Dr. F.: You are right and I believe that in us we have that wisdom. Anxiety blocks it. This process is about going back to your inner wisdom so you don't respond out of anxiety. It is there. It was there with your father. It is there with your mother. It gets lost somewhere with life events. There is a lot of wisdom in your father and you are getting it but you have to have your own anxiety under control to hear his wisdom. He can teach you a lot about survival. Now, his father taught him something about survival, too, some other things about survival. I am looking forward to meeting your father because I want to ask him about the legacy he wants for you and your sister to carry on. What is the letter he wants to leave behind that's different from the letter that his dad left behind? I guess that's the other way of asking that question.

Jane: It feels . . . I feel different. It really feels like a lot of stuff is leaving. I sort of want to say it quickly because I also want to talk about some stuff that happened when my father was there and this is also bringing up some stuff about my birthday.

I turned 37 and I was in the lab doing my thing. It was actually a day where I felt a lot of sorrow. It's not disconnected from this other stuff although it's not obviously connected but it was a sorrow like a recognition of some losses. At 37 I'm the oldest graduate student in the lab and what it was a mixture of was a recognition of many good qualities that I have, many abilities that I have that could have been blossoming when I was 24 or 25 and that didn't, and there was an acceptance but a real sorrow, a grieving almost. It was a sadness that didn't feel too bad. It was a sadness that was almost a healing sadness. I don't know how to explain it. I had a taste of it around New Year's, interestingly in my father's presence and I think this sadness had partly to do with my father; that's the connection, because I feel the same kind of sadness for him. I see him as an extraordinary person, extraordinarily gifted in many ways, and so I don't always like my choice of words because they are blunt but so crippled. You know, I could see so much what could have been. Well, it won't be now. He's 67. There is a sorrow with that but also an acceptance, I don't quite know how to convey it better but the taste I had of it at New Year's was we went to the Celebration downtown and one of the things we saw was a youth symphony although it wasn't a symphony. It was soloists playing from ages 7 to 13. Very young kids playing violin or piano or whatever. Well, I played piano when I was a kid and I see now I played really well. I loved it. And when I sat there listening to them I was so moved and I had visions of myself. I mean it was totally unexpected but I saw myself and I said, "God, what a gem you were, what a gem you were." And yet that never got nurtured and in fact as soon as my teacher really started saying, "You're very good!" which she did, I dropped it. That was exactly what I did, I quit. And of course my parents never, they were so caught up in their own stuff that I just quit. They didn't try to figure out why or what was wrong. They didn't have time for that. It was my choice. I was 13 at the time but I can see so clearly now, it fits into a whole series of quittings, right when I was being told I was so good. And I experienced that then with such sorrow, but a kind of acceptance and this was just more of that. And I feel changed, somehow.

Commentary

The therapist picks up on the phrase that Jane introduces of "healing sadness" and emphasizes that this is a positive way to think about how the family has to heal. The therapist then reframes Jane's description of herself as "quitting" as her way of honoring the family. The therapist takes these two powerful terms, "sadness" and "quitting," and uses both to show how the family has struggled with connecting. The therapist tries to highlight the internal wisdom that exists within the family but that got lost in the anxiety the family members experienced at times of loss and disappointment.

Dr. F.: I like your phrasing "healing sadness." I like that a lot. I think that is what we need to go through. The anger keeps us unhealed. Anger really keeps us unfinished, stuck. Sadness has the potential to heal us and I think we have to change our story from anger about other to sadness. As you were saying that I was thinking about legacies and honoring and mostly about the story you made up about your grandfather. I thought it was a wonderful metaphor, the story about how he died. How we make up stories about safety and what we need to do to honor our family. Like success. Can we honor our family by being more successful than our parents? Or do we dishonor them or take something away from them? Do they give us permission to go beyond them? We can convolute all that stuff. What is our quitting really about? A form of honoring? When we are freed of that honoring, then we can move on.

Jane: I hear you. I think I really hear you on that one. I mean, yeah, I really hear you on that one.

Commentary

The therapist checks out whether his comments have stirred up more reactivity. If he is moving too quickly in reframing the story, the adult child will react defensively. In this situation it is clear that his timing is appropriate. Jane seems to be quite open to the reframe.

The therapist also wants to check out the reactivity of Allan. To this point most of the session has focused on Jane's discoveries about her father. The therapist wonders what is being stirred up inside Allan. It is important to give balance to both partners' struggles and stories. However, in the middle middle phase of therapy, one partner is less likely to feel offended or shut out when the other partner uses most of the session for his or her own issues. The partner fully realizes that his or her turn will come and is learning about self issues as well. The therapist now shifts to Allan's story.

Dr. F.: Well, that's good. Just stay with that one. Is it okay to shift the load to Allan? One of the things I thought was wonderful, really wonderful that you did last time when Jane was reading the memoirs, was to say you were really struggling with how to let her know that you were there but not to interfere with her process. I think that was absolutely right on. It's the struggle we all have once we get into this new thinking. You're there if you want to be, on the sidelines. Now you've had a chance to think about what Jane was dealing with, how it ties in with your family. When that happens it is hard not to react. What was happening with you?

Allan: I still have very much of a hard time staying on the sidelines. I mean, even as you're speaking now I find Jane's descriptions very convoluted and very wordy by comparison to myself and I keep holding back, telling myself, "Jane, get to the point." God, I have a hard time with that. I want to ask myself why am I having such a hard time with that.

Dr. F.: That's a good question.

Allan: That's just strictly the mechanics of it.

Commentary

Allan's comments illustrate the difficulty partners have in separating their own reactions from their partner's struggles. Allan clearly recognizes that he has to separate his own issues from those of his wife. The therapist supports his recognition and begins to highlight the wisdom in Allan. It is important that the therapist honor Allan's struggle as he honored Jane's. The therapist supports Allan's struggle and at the same time encourages him to talk about his own themes of loss and loneliness.

Dr. F.: There is a shift in what is going on. There are two types of questions. One asks "Why is the other doing it this way?" The second is, "Why does it concern me that the other is doing it this way?" Once you are into this type of question there is no holding you back. Some people take years before they can ask themselves this question because the first question keeps them safe. That is a really good one to watch. When you are anxious you ask the first one. When you are solid inside yourself you ask the second one.

Allan: I feel solid enough, not *very* solid, though.

Dr. F.: I think you're doing very well.

Allan: I guess actually there is something there. I have experienced, when I lived on my own, being supportive of other people, being quiet and listening to what other people have to say, acknowledging what they have to say. It was so important to me because it was perhaps the first time it happened to me, that others could do that for me, that I could see it. And because I now realize how unsafe I feel and how careful other people have to be with me in order for me to open up, I see that now and I kind of have a feel for how I can be that way for Jane by sort of staying on the sidelines. I also see how that wasn't the case for me when I was young. All of last week and maybe even the time before that has been a process of looking back and how it wasn't the case for me when I was young. Everywhere I turn that question just pops up at me as a reflection of what I see here and now. As an example, I brought David to his music lessons and one of the parents there was saying, "Isn't it wonderful that boys are now taking music lessons. Before you used to give girls them." And I thought, goddamn it. I loved music. My father loved to sing. I was too damn shy, afraid of how it might sound to even venture and try singing. I was afraid of how people might look at me and I now see I was afraid to ask my dad, what he would tell me. And I wish he had been there picking up on the fact that I listened to all these records at home, that I listened intently to the music on the radio and otherwise. But I would never sing. I didn't sing in the presence of other people, even in my own presence, other than in my mind until David was born. And then I heard Jane sing and I could bring myself to sing and believe me it was very tentative at first but it was great. I could do it. And only now that I feel okay about it do I ask myself the question of why, and that is the kind of process I've gone through, asking myself why couldn't I ask my dad this, whether it is to play baseball or soccer or just everything around me strikes me that way. And I can feel it so sharply now because I felt after I separated from my father what it means to support somebody, what it means to be there for somebody, how it feels because I had never experienced it so differently. I'm not sure so much I'm addressing the question you had asked.

Commentary

The therapist is trying to reframe Allan's story about his father and to help him become more curious about his father's struggles and losses. He reminds Allan about a story that Allan told several sessions back about his father's anxiety about his relationship with his own father. The therapist increases Allan's curiosity about his grandfather as a way of shifting his theory about his father.

Dr. F.: I just want to remind you of a story you told me about your father. After you came back from that visit back East and you told me the story of your father with his father and the camera. Remember that story? Your father was in his father's workshop or work area and being a curious person took this camera down and then broke it. He was terrified to tell his father because he thought he would be punished for his tampering. Instead his father embraced him for his curiosity. I got thinking about that, about how your father felt embraced by his father and how his father recognized his specialness. Did he feel safe within himself because his father admired that? You know you ask yourself how do we become our own heroes. I think it is from having someone recognize our specialness and validate that specialness. Then we are able to introduce that specialness into the world. It just reminded me of that.

Allan: I mean the way I am with David or I try to be with David . . . he takes toothpaste and spreads it all over the place, on the mirrors and everywhere and I will tell him, it's great, you had a lot of fun, it felt good, but we also have to clean it up. And I will dwell on the cleaning-up part, which makes sure it's heard. I mean that's the process I wish—

Dr. F.: What do you think would have happened if *you* had taken the toothpaste and got it all over the place? What lesson would you have been taught?

Allan: You know there are times where I feel there was an unspoken anger. My father wouldn't speak so much, I don't think, to praise or to berate but you knew how he felt, and in any event—

Dr. F.: You felt you knew how he felt.

Allan: Yeah. I was going to say my mother would probably

catch it first and my mother would give me heck for it. Yeah, that brings the second train of thoughts I've had, which is about my mother. Very, very different from my father. I'm beginning to see how needy she was or self-centered. And it's been disastrous in terms of the consequences for me. I really see that. What struck me a few days ago so strongly was when my parents separated and my father moved East, I followed with him because my mother and father for a year at least had just been going at each other. A lot of anger and antagonism toward each other. Well, after I moved with my father the onus was on me to reestablish a relationship with my mother, do whatever I needed to do. And it struck me just recently, Goddamn it, I was angry at my mother. I had all that stuff and I was supposed to set it aside and reach out for my mother and nobody ever validated that pile that was staying there. And as I thought that, I felt, I still feel that anger and never had anybody taken it seriously, anybody validated it or anything like that and why the hell should I keep pretending it's not there?

Jane: Boy, something just struck me. It was your father you said who encouraged you to make amends with your mother and what just struck me—

Allan: He kept saying it would be very important for me if I maintain a relationship with my mother and the onus was on me clearly to forgive my mother, so to speak.

Jane: It just, I guess because of the context it struck me that's not unlike his sending you back your angry or critical letter. You know, don't send me letters like this, don't be angry at your mother. I don't know. "Be good," that's how I hear it. I don't know if there is a connection but I mean your father, I guess fundamentally what strikes me is that your father didn't want to really talk about the real feelings. He just wanted it to be okay so the same way with the letters, let's just have it okay, with your mother. Let's just make it okay. I don't know if that was really what went on, but that's what strikes me.

Allan: No, you're right to a large extent about that. I mean, I have never had that kind of support where somebody will ask me how do you feel about things. I think to a large extent it has also been a source of tension for us because you haven't been particularly good and you're just beginning to learn how to sit back and hear me out and draw it out of me and ask me, "What do you feel? How do you feel? What do you think?" All these things rather than come forward with your suppositions, perceptions, or whatever it is. I haven't had that.

Commentary

The session is concluding. The therapist attempts to encourage each partner to become a teacher about self to other. He introduces the concept of the downside of change and encourages the partners to think about what they would lose by giving up their theories of family. It is important for partners to realize how they reinforce each other's theories. Although most people think they want things to be different, they behave in a way that keeps things the same. Introducing the concept of the downside of change helps people to understand their own part in staying stuck better. It is a way to help partners shift from blaming to owning up to their part in avoiding change. The therapist now encourages both partners to think about the anxiety they have about giving up old behaviors that they report as upsetting and yet that in some ways keep them safe.

Dr. F.: Is there a downside to that for you? If Jane is better able to do that, is there a loss for you?

Allan: It hasn't happened enough for me to know.

Dr. F.: Well, my hunch is there is a loss. There is always a downside to getting what we fantasize we need. That's the hidden agenda in any issue, that most of us aren't aware of. When I ask people, "Well, just imagine getting that, exactly the thing you say you want, what would be the loss for you in getting it?" And the first response always is "No loss. What do you mean? It would be wonderful. It would be great.". . . .

Allan: No, I think you're right. You know I've been meaning to raise why the hell didn't I have it way back then all along when I needed it? That's the kind of feeling that it brings but it's still too far back inside to really be tangible.

Dr. F.: So, on that note the direction I think we should take now to balance this is to talk about mothers, is to get mothers back into the picture. We have spent a lot of time with fathers, and fathers are only half the puzzle. We have to do justice to mothers.

Allan: The timing is good because it's more and more intriguing anyway.

Commentary

Just before the interview ends, the therapist introduces the issues of mothers. Because so much of the interview has focused on fathers and grandfathers, he introduces mothers and grandmothers to give balance. For an adult child to develop a solid sense of self, he or she needs to have stories about both parents. If the therapist had remained involved in just the fathers' and grandfathers' stories he would have violated that principle. He concludes by opening up an area that leaves the couple slightly confused but also challenged to go beyond their stories of fathers to their stories of mothers.

Dr. F.: I'd like to get more stories about each of your mothers and what happened to them in their remarriages. If your mothers are in any way coming into town or through town, please let me know. Maybe we will get them in here and let them tell their stories. It would be wonderful. There is something special about hearing a parent's story, letting them tell their story to you through me because the questions I ask, hopefully, are not hampered by the stories you have already told me. If I'm doing my job, they shouldn't be. It's much harder for you to kind of clear your mind and ask your parents about their stories.

Allan: You kind of see how it works but not like doing it.

Dr. F.: Both should happen. Both processes should happen. It's just that it's nice to get those stories on tape. Your son needs to have those stories of his grandparents anyway, so it's for your boy's record as well. So we will stop with that.

Debriefing Session after Family-of-Origin Visit

The following interview provides an example of a debriefing session after a family-of-origin visit. The clients were the couple described previously who visited the husband's family in Europe. The role of the therapist in this session was to help the husband highlight the learning that arose from the visit and identify additional themes he could work on in the future. The session begins with the husband telling his story about how the visit started.

Brian: I guess what happened was that Sally left in the middle of July and she went to Montreal for a couple of weeks. I joined her in August, and the following day we flew to Europe and had three weeks there. It was really interesting to be back in Amsterdam. I found it interesting to be there with Sally. Because you always have a pattern of relating to each other that's very familiar but all of a sudden I felt myself in a place that was very familiar to me and it was hard to imagine it being totally unfamiliar for Sally. I was really interested in seeing how she responded, with real curiosity. I guess I was taking a lot of stuff for granted, saying let's go see this and do this. I was really impressed and taken by that. One of the things that occurred that was interesting was there was the old family house still standing, and on my part there was a real reluctance to go and knock on the door and it had to do with I don't know these people, I don't want to hassle these people. . . . Sally was adamant that we go in. So we drove off and lots of tears and whatnot, and then we went in. It didn't turn out to be that bad.

Sally: I had come all of this way, I was not going to leave without going in there.

Brian: I was very resistant. We knocked on the door. There was just a maid there. I had to talk quickly. She was black and a bit suspicious. It was a bit of an exotic story, coming from Canada to look at the house. But she let us in. And the place had totally changed. The only thing that had stayed constant was the roof. But Sally sort of poked around and got a sense of the place and garden and so on. It was quite interesting.

We were basically in town for about one week and then went to Paris. It was very different. I think I mentioned to Sally on the way back on the airplane that I was really happy that we had gone. We were together constantly for three weeks, and we had been on a holiday before which was really disastrous so I was really happy for this opportunity and that we were able to do it. For me it was very important. There were a number of times where we tried to initiate conversation inasmuch as we set a goal for ourselves . . . and in retrospect it amounted to various friends and acquaintances. We thought we would go there, make a decision, and our whole life would change. The momentous occasion didn't come and the conversations were struggles, very difficult.

Sally: Nonetheless, they were conversations.

Brian: Oh, yes. They were conversations. That was good. What I found, all I could project was some sort of deep-down emotion, but I couldn't really connect it to any pragmatic, functional direction. You are sort of operating in a vacuum and you have some abstract things that you can relate to each other . . . I went to Montreal, and all of a sudden my thinking was focused on how to operate in Montreal, and all of a sudden I am in Vancouver, and I had totally blocked out Vancouver, and how do I operate there? Anyway, that's a generalization. But I think one thing that we did come to a conclusion about was that, and I think this is a positive one, I think we are able to work much more closely together and it is our intent to come to terms with our financial situation and to try to put all of Sally's earnings into a savings. I think for us that's important, and it's an attempt to structure our financial life, which is something we haven't really done. So that was one thing.

But I can't give you all the details of the trip itself. I don't think that's part of the reason we're here. But the next two weeks in Montreal for me were very heavy. There were a number of weddings. I was a best man at a close friend's wedding, and then quite to my surprise I was asked to be both the master of ceremonies and also toast the bride at my sister's wedding. That came as a great surprise.

Sally: It surprised some other family members as well. Brian is looked at as the baby.

Brian: One of my middle brothers said, "Well, how come you're doing it?" and I don't know. And also what I did, I asked my older brother, James, out for lunch and that was very fruitful. He was quite taken by surprise that I took the initiative to ask him out for lunch. And I was very frank that I was asking questions, and that I was in fact taking the initiative. Because I gathered from our conversation that he had basically written me off some time ago, so he started questioning why I was doing it. And I said it was basically an interest in trying to find out about family because I had already asked my parents what the nature of experience of our family had been, and the nature of their experiences and it was partly curiosity of what his experiences were. Also, I remember a couple of years ago at a family event, at my father's 70th birthday, and I had some really nice conversations with my brother James, and so I felt that at least intellectually there was an interest. He was really appreciative of it. I also got him into a position of . . . I pressed him on when he came up with this notion of dismissing me. He used the word that I had been the black sheep, which I thought was interesting, and I asked, "How did you perceive me as the black sheep?" To him, it's interesting, he's an academic. He said, "Well, you went to university. You were flunking your courses left, right, and center. You didn't give a damn," and he threw in my nervous breakdown in the same vein. Well, it was all part of the same pattern. And then on top of that, also, my parents had been totally supportive to me throughout and I had never been appreciative of that fact. I wouldn't acknowledge birthdays, etc. And to my mind, I think all my brothers and sisters are really good at remembering my parents' birthdays, but the nature of that relationship was what I had always questioned. It's easy to send a card on the right date, but I didn't get into that conversation. But what I did say was that certainly whatever I was doing I felt it was imperative to do, and it was certainly never with any malevolence toward my parents that I was operating under. Then I asked him about his own family. He was talking about his wife and the concerns he had about her. He admitted that she was much brighter than he was, but he was always the plugger. I think I also mentioned to you the last time I was back I had a meeting with his wife, so I had been able to talk to her and have some sense of what was going on, so it was interesting to hear what was going on. And he talked about his concerns about his older son Daniel and the lack of rapport that had been there. And that made me think about what I always felt was a lack of rapport with my father at an earlier time. And I think I had mentioned that my father felt the same about his father. This time I didn't write things down.

The overall thing was that he was really happy that I had taken the initiative. I had told him as well that he should feel welcome to send his daughters out here anytime they wanted to come.

Sally: Actually his remark to me about that was he would

like to come himself. And my feeling is that he's been somewhat straitjacketed, he is very much that steady influence. And other people in the family and his parents relate to him that way. Well, he had been thinking about it over the last couple of years. He saw, in fact, especially intellectually, parallels with Brian but he never really worked at them before, because he always considered Brian a young renegade.

Brian: I think that came out in the conversation as well, here we were talking on a one-to-one and age wasn't an issue, but that I had been basically put into this category, so I think it was a relief to be able to break out of that. And it was interesting, too, because I was at the same time trying to think about my sister. I had also been best man at this other wedding of a man I had known for seventeen years and it was quite easy to look at and talk about Sam. Then to think about my sister it was very difficult all of a sudden, even though it was my sister. I stayed two nights before the wedding at my parents', and I had a very nice evening. What I did was I found a whole bunch of family albums, and that was very fortuitous because in going through them and looking at them it triggered a bunch of things about my sister or that came back to me about her, and from that I was able to put together a toast to the bride. And I think I was very anxious about it. Again, I had no problem doing one for Sam, and there was a much smaller gathering at my sister's, but I felt a real anxiety. I felt my voice was going to crack. And I had a great time giving that. When it actually occurred, it went really well. I thought everyone was very positive.

Sally: Everyone was dumbstruck. The other people in the family . . . Brian joked afterward that he had repositioned himself as macho man of the family.

Brian: I guess it was really a sense of . . . more comfortable in the family. Again, I had always felt a certain funny way about things that I had never been able to articulate. But certainly this time around made me feel a lot better.

Commentary

The therapist encourages Brian to go into more detail about how he started to reposition with each family member. The therapist knows from previous sessions that one of the family members Brian was most cut off from was his older brother, Steve. The therapist asks about this brother to gain a sense of how willing Brian is to approach relationships that have the potential to create a great deal of discomfort and anxiety. The therapist listens very closely to Brian's description of his contact with Steve. Steve is his greatest challenge in his attempt to be proactive.

Dr. F.: What about your brother just above you?

Brian: My brother Steve? Well, he was the one I called. What had happened was James gave me bits of information and I also phoned Steve to see if anything came to his mind about my sister. What was interesting is in doing that neither my sister or my brother James could remember any special moment. And of course he made a remark, "What are you doing this for?" I had to say that I must admit that I was surprised myself that I was asked. We didn't talk on the phone that long; but then the following day we had a couple of fairly friendly chats, but I don't recall anything special being addressed. I think I was asking about his work. He had been traveling a lot more. I was just trying to continue a rapport. A much friendlier rapport was started when he was here in town. I met him here for dinner. Again, I don't remember anything of importance, but there was the time constraint. But I felt that this time going back I wanted to talk to Steve because he had been away the last time.

And then a day or so after we left Montreal, my mother and father were up at Sally's parents' place a couple of days and my father was quite anxious to have a talk with me. He always has a way of trying to have a talk with me and all of a sudden, oops, another talk, so we went walking on the property. My parents are remarkable. They remember snippets of conversation and they piece together a whole scenario. . . . I never actually told him, but he was aware that I was in my mind trying to imagine a scenario of moving back to Montreal because I had mentioned talking to colleagues and feeling out situations and so on. He was of the opinion that it would be unwise at this point in time to move from what he perceives to be our financial situation, the burdens we have now, and my own professional work, to reregister, to make contact. And also recognizing that I was slowing establishing myself here in town, and also being generally of the opinion that there is more opportunity in the West than in the East. So he tried to put that point forward. I tried to explain what I was trying to do was explore all avenues. Part of the issue came down to risk-taking and he felt I would be taking a risk. I said, "I grant you that, but on the other hand, I am of an age and energy level where it would be possible to take risks. Also, in a sense I would never take the initiative on my own." I did go on to say that I felt decisions had always been made for me, rather than my making them myself. What I did say to him about finances was that on the finance end of things, certainly our family had never been that strong, in fact we never talked about it. It was homework that each one of us put together for ourselves.

I got a sense that he had a sense of guilt that motivated his wanting . . . I don't know, maybe this is me being pessimistic, there is a sense of "You should be doing something for me." In fact, he had written a whole letter because he felt that he might not have an opportunity to chat with me. I appreciate it . . . the way he worded his letter, as *his* experience of being an engineer, and wanting to share some of *his* experiences and feelings.

Dr. F.: Is that consistent with him?

Brian: I think that's the first time he has actually put it in that sort of almost "sharing" of a professional opinion approach.

Commentary

The therapist asks about the possibility of Brian developing a more person-to-person adult relationship with the father.

Brian's answer will indicate whether there has been a fundamental shift in his relationship with his father.

Dr. F.: Professional to professional instead of father to son.

Brian: Well, there was a bit of both. Certainly his letter indicates he was trying to put it on a more professional level.

Dr. F.: More adult to adult.

Brian: I guess. I got a sense of there being father-to-son and professional-to-professional rather than adult-to-adult. I think the other thing was that he did feel, and this was from his experience, that it was important for me to have a working situation that was positive because of the impact it would have on my relationship with Sally. So I'm assuming that he had been in a situation where for himself, vis-à-vis my mother sometime—

Dr. F.: I was wondering what your thoughts were about that because I recall you mentioning that he felt that he had to give up something for family, professional goals for the family.

Brian: And yet on the other hand, what was coming out this time, it was important to have a working situation as a positive contribution to the family.

Commentary

The therapist introduces questions about the mother in an attempt to give balance to the story. It is important for Brian to have worked as hard on trying to reconnect with his mother in a new way as he had with his father.

Dr. F.: Did you have a chance to build on any of this with your mother, what you had started?

Brian: No. Because basically she had sent us on this trip. One of the things we spent most of our time on was filling her in on this trip, slide shows, etc. There was a lot of talk regarding the trip. And then what also happened, there was a lot of talking about Mary's wedding, a rehashing of the wedding. Those were top priorities for them. But they will be coming out in the new year.

Dr. F.: So the big breakthrough was with your brother.

Brian: Oh, definitely. But as I say, I felt that the ten days was for me very active and turbulent. In retrospect I really appreciate being asked by my sister to propose the toast.

Dr. F.: Do you have any fantasy as to why you were asked?

Brian: Well, my speech to her was constructed on the notion of Mary the mother, the little girl. I played with that notion. I appreciated in the past her role as the mother toward me and how supportive she had been, so for me she was throwing her support behind me again.

Dr. F.: That's what you felt?

Brian: Yes.

Commentary

The therapist now shifts to the wife to see if she has been able to remain on the sidelines and avoid colluding with various parts of the story. It is clear that the wife is quite excited about observing the changes in her husband. She is beginning to see him in a different light. Her old theory about her husband was that he was cut off from his family and overly involved in his work. Now she sees a more balanced husband. This shift in her thinking is important. For partners to begin the process of embracing each other differently, they have to change their basic story about themselves and each other. One powerful way to set this process in motion is for one partner to observe how capably the other partner deals with his or her family differently. However, when partners need to hold on to their old theories about each other they do not perceive the changes as new information. Rather, they convolute them to reinforce their old story.

Dr. F.: Sally, do you have any fantasies about why Brian was asked?

Sally: I think there's a special connection there. She has often said that to me, and in fact, she said that she immediately knew she wanted Brian to do it but she thought about the family and whether her other brothers would be insulted. And then she decided, "It's my wedding and I want him to do it." Which is interesting because she has always . . . I mean, I see the family as always trying to second-guess the other person and I actually think it was good for her to say what she wanted and do what she wanted. I think she was really delighted. I sensed a real sense of pride from her and her parents, because they have never seen you in that role. In all the family situations, your family is very structured, your father invariably gives the speech and is supported by your mother physically because his knees shake and he gets emotional when he talks about the family. He's a fabulous man, very articulate, but as soon as he gets in the realm of the family . . . Brian's mother is physically right there and that is the way they operate together. And then James, the together serious one, he gave the spiel at the fiftieth anniversary. His was all very ordered, and he had notes. This is not only that it was Brian which is a breakaway, but the style and ease that he did it with. It's different. The other men have a lot of difficulty with that kind of thing and they get very ordered. The father always says something that is very thoughtful or special. He had structured the telegram to the groom's parents, which was very moving . . . they always manage to do something like that.

The children say that the parents always manage to one-up them in some way. Whatever they try to give them, the parents have always thought of something more wonderful. So they maintain themselves as parents, even though they're approaching their eighties. They are sort of indomitable. But I think that speech and the way you handled it really turned them around.

Dr. F.: What did it do for you watching Brian do this?

Sally: I was proud of him. He did it beautifully.

Dr. F.: Have you seen him before in roles like this?

Sally: Earlier in the week.

Dr. F.: How about in the relationship?

Sally: I would say that where I've seen Brian more at ease with himself and in a situation where there are people watching or more public like that has tended to be more around work. I've seen him do presentations. He's developed an ease with that and a way of working people to listen. But not in terms of the family, so that was a change. I think my parents have never seen him in that light, either.

Brian: I scored points there.

Sally: You did actually. My father . . . there were a lot of Dutch people there and a lot of connections from Amsterdam, and a lot of real characters there. My father's comment was that he thought it was so emotional that he thought it was an Italian wedding. It was that kind of event.

Brian: In terms of public speaking, I've always looked to Sally as well as she comments on physical posture and so on, partly related to our yoga practice and how things go positively. I was curious what her response was in that sense. There's a closeness about it for us, at least for me.

Sally: That's right.

Dr. F.: That's exciting. Let's hear what you've been working on.

Sally: As I said, I feel that there's a lot to assimilate and I haven't done that yet. In terms of the trip I was really interested in finding as much history as I could. It was hard to find because people there don't really care that much about it. I did manage to find one museum after a lot of searching, but it was very good. I felt a real interest in imagining what it was like when his family was there. I found it interesting to visit the home, but I was more interested in imagining what it was like for him, which is why I insisted on going to the house. Now that I've been there I can look at the photographs that they have and understand what it was like to have lived there. And the same thing, going around and looking at the shops, the area right around there, and I realized for them that they considered that the best time of their lives. I can especially see it in terms of Brian's father. He went down there as a young engineer and basically had to work very hard. He built the airport, the hospital . . . in terms of the scope of work that he did I can see why it would have been the best time of his life. Especially leaving his family and getting out of his father's office. It was a real strain on his mother but ultimately she came to believe that it was the best time of their life, too. Mainly because of his work and also because of the friends they had there. And coming back to that wedding was a lot of those same people from those days, big, tall characters. Really indomitable people. I really enjoyed getting a sense of all of those connections.

Brian: Looking at those buildings, they're good buildings. I took some photographs and so on.

Sally: I look at a lot of buildings through being involved with Brian and I know what's really good and I did get a very nice sense of him, looking at those . . . They're small and careful and thoughtful buildings, just like he is. I appreciated seeing them. We took a lot of photographs. It was very nostalgic.

Commentary

The therapist now shifts the focus from the husband's family to the wife's family. It is helpful to understand how Sally has started the process of changing her theory about her family. The therapist comments that in previous sessions the focus was more on Sally's family; now there is a new sense of balance. The change in focus allows Sally to reassess her thinking about her family. This shifting focus gives each partner the opportunity to become his or her own expert about his or her family. This in turn gives the marriage more balance.

Dr. F.: Seems like more of a balance now between these two families. I was trying to think back to when we first started. I think I had a sense of more involvement with your family, Sally.

Brian: I think that was true. I think in our relationship that was my perception, not in a negative way, but family seemed to be an element that was stressed on Sally's side of things. But I feel, partly, obviously because of your encouraging me to explore it and some of these later events, I think, have been more positive for me and drawn my family into it more. I feel less of a pressure from Sally's side of the family.

Dr. F.: Now that there is more of a balance between the two of you, do you feel as though there is a loss for you? What are your thoughts about that?

Sally: No, not at all. I like Brian's family. I love some of the people. I have always felt that in some way Brian negated his family. I always felt that it negated his starting his own family. I always felt that there was a connection, that he distanced, and there was a need not just for him but for other people in the family to share more with each other. I think for them it's been really good. There's been a nice spin-off for me. But I think for him it's been very valuable. I don't feel a loss for me at all.

If anything, I know my family is very strong and they still are. I've looked at my own family a bit more realistically. I went to Toronto with my mother and it was interesting. She's the eldest in the family and her position in the family has . . . She shared a lot of things about her own family with me; about her mother, her sister, and her father; and about her relationship with her grandparents. I went to see my grandmother's grave, which I had only seen at the burial. I had been 14 at the time and I had a very skewed image, the memory of it. I knew it wasn't really intact, and I wanted to go back there. At first, my mother didn't want to go. She said, "You go, I'll give you directions." But then she decided to come with me, and I just needed to see that. That started off a lot of stuff. Then I got her to take me. You have to understand that this family is rooted in family, so much so that actually I feel, and my mother feels, that it has limited their growth.

Two sisters married two brothers. My grandfather continues to live in the house that he was born in and will die there. His family was three blocks away. The other side, the grandmother's house was four blocks the other way. The two brothers married the two sisters. My mother was the first grandchild to be born into that situation. So she had this incredibly rich childhood. She related very little to her own father—he was just Father, the family was the women, and except for the grandparents, the grandfathers, who were very feisty old people, but who were real softies to the first granddaughter. So she had this old structure. We went for a walk, and we went to the back parts. We didn't use the street. It was hilarious because we were sort of sneaking around, what she had done when she was a child. She was really excited relating a lot of anecdotes about the family. But then she started talking about her own situation and how much love and devotion there was. Her mother, eventually as those people died, sort of became the matriarch of the family. She is the one that everyone in the family says that I'm like. I knew her until I was 14.

But it's interesting that my mother really feels . . . like all the way we were driving . . . she basically went down because we had to look after my grandfather for a few days because he wouldn't go to the hospital. She was really hesitant about going back there. This was related to her relations to her two sisters and she is very much envied by her two sisters and what that has done is sort of cut her off in a way and she feels very bad about it. Because at the same time she feels there isn't much to do about it. And she shared a lot of when she was growing up in her teens. She was always seen as the competent one. The middle sister was very flirtatious and went through her life having a number of affairs that didn't mean anything. They were just something she needed to do. She married someone who had all the family credentials but turned out to be a bad businessman. Basically she's kept at the father for funds and has taken a lot of money from the family estate. It's quite uncomfortable.

The youngest sister, probably the beauty of the family in some ways when she was young, finally married someone with impeccable credentials in terms of family, all of which was very important. Again, he became an alcoholic and a terrible businessman as well and drank away both families' money and they are still together. But they are still both children and she remains a 48-year-old child.

It's interesting, there is so much in that. When her own mother had her, the grandmother moved back into the house when she was 13. Basically my grandmother's whole attention was on her mother, so she basically lost her mother for those years. I think my own mother, being the elder sister, has something to offer the younger sister in terms of what—that is something I talked to her about, which I think she's going to pursue. It's all very tied up with the middle sister.

There was just a lot but I really appreciated all of that information. I haven't assimilated it totally. But it helps me to look at my mother's situation and her family. She married someone from W——, which is nowhere, but he was a professor. So that was the only reason she was allowed to marry him and it continues to be a marriage of love. Her sisters see her family as successful, all of us, the children as successful, but what I realize is that through their jealousy they have cut her off. They can't deal with her success, which I think is very sad. It makes me very determined not to have that happen with my own brothers and sisters, however our lives go. I think that's really a shame, the fact that they are not able to be proud of her so they basically stay away.

Dr. F.: I am just curious about your aunt, your mother's youngest sister. Is she married? The two brothers that married sisters —

Sally: No, that was in the previous family, my grandmother that married the brother. And in fact the third sister was engaged to the third brother, but he was killed in the war. They had just an enormous family in Montreal. And the way that gets down to me, my mother and I never talk about, "Are you moving or not?" But she said to me, and I know it is very hard that I am living away. This is another thing I realize that is probably hardest for me — to be away from my family. I went out to dinner with just my mother and father one night, and my father's comment to me that I was very fortunate to have such good relationships with everyone and I sort of felt a lot of pressure on my role.

There are just little things there and I found it interesting that they saw me that way. Our family sort of runs in terms of matriarchs; there was my grandmother, now my mother who is that way, and I think in the family dynamics I am the person who would take that one on. Yet having moved away I have had big changes. So I think my coming to terms with my own family has to do with that and how to still maintain contact, which is very valuable and I know it is to them. I find it very difficult to leave them, and yet my mother's comment to me . . . she said, "I don't know what you're deciding, it's up to you and Brian to decide but whatever you decide don't put too much stock in family." What an incredible comment to come from her, because I know how important I am to her! I know that she misses me, but she still feels, and I think this comes from viewing her own family . . . she sees her sisters and there is a cousin and a whole other family, they're all gnarled up together. She really feels that a lot of the women were never really allowed to grow up and expand. She feels that although she hated Montreal with a passion, and that when she had to leave Toronto she was heartsick for several years, she really feels now that this is how she was able to grow up and live her own life. In a sense I really appreciate her saying that to me. It gives me a freedom not to have to worry about her feelings although I am still concerned about her.

Dr. F.: It sort of releases you?

Sally: Yes, but there are some other issues I would like to figure out about my family.

Dr. F.: How about for you, Brian?

Brian: Yeah, I've been observing and watching things develop. It seems to be making a difference in our marriage.

Dr. F.: Well, each of you has become much more curious about your families and each other. It would be interesting to hear what more you can learn about your families and how this new learning affects each one of you.

Commentary

The session concludes with the therapist's suggestion that the couple continue the process of learning more about their families and bringing that learning back into the marriage. During this phase of the therapy the therapist consistently encourages the partners to take credit for the overall changes in their family connections. He emphasizes the theme that family-of-origin work never really ends and will continue to affect how the partners relate to each other.

8 _____

Ending of the Middle Phase: Family-of-Origin Sessions

Goals and Objectives of the End of the Middle Phase of Therapy

Middle-phase work is quite complex. Many therapists do not stay involved with families long enough to become involved in middle-phase work. When the middle-phase process is handled appropriately, it has significant implications for how the couple terminates therapy. The therapist's task is to increase the family's sense of ownership around change. To enhance this ownership, the therapist must continue to work on family connections. The overall goal of the therapy is to encourage the adult child to make deeper connections with his or her family. In the beginning of the middle phase this goal is accomplished through reframing the presenting problem. In the middle of the middle phase the adult child is encouraged to return home to work on repositioning. The end of the middle phase is characterized by the involvement of the adult children's parents in the therapy process. This intervention has proven to be a powerful one. It allows for the adult child to be open to the parents' stories, and thereby increase the depth of story-telling between the generations.

There are seven major objectives in the end of the middle phase. Each honors the overall goal of seeing the family as a positive resource in its members' lives.

Consolidating Gains

Prior to the end of the middle phase the adult child has made a series of visits home to attempt to reposition with family members. He or she usually reports mixed success in these attempts. Inviting the adult child's parents into the session provides an opportunity to consolidate the gains. The child is likely to become even more open to the parents' stories and to process them as new learning. Family-of-origin sessions with the parents encourages a broader range of storytelling. The parents become the experts on family history and provide a gift to the adult child by telling their story. Structuring the session to allow the parents to tell their story so they will not be judged, evaluated, or blamed provides for a deeper sense of connection between the parents and the adult child.

Recording the Family Stories

It is important that parents' stories do not get lost. When adult children return home to hear these stories, they seldom record them. It is helpful to videotape the stories, which are then available for review over the years. Taping also provides a resource for subsequent generations. Organizing a formal series of videotaped storytelling sessions creates a record of the family history. Many families have lost their history. In our society there is a tendency to become more removed from history. The general value of our society is to stay present-oriented or to plan for the future. We do not place much value on the past or learn from the past. By involving parents we not only honor the past but also use their experiences as guides for the future.

One adult child told me that both her parents had died some time after I had conducted family-of-origin sessions with them. She was thankful she had the videotapes of her parents telling their story. Whenever she missed her parents or felt sad about them, she played the tapes and almost felt like she had them back. This story is not unusual. We need to be able to honor our parents throughout our lives; how we do that will teach our children how to honor us in their lives.

Deepening Family Connections

The goal of the therapist is to encourage the parents to tell their story in such a way that family connections between the generations are highlighted. When there has been tragedy, loss, or abandonment, the therapist can frame these experiences as opportunities for learning, coping, and survival. The therapist does not look for failure or loss in the parents' stories; rather, he or she helps them tell about hope, competence, and mastery. As the parents reflect on the past and talk about what they have learned to help them deal with life, the adult child begins to rethink the parents' struggles. There is a tendency for adult children to be critical and judgmental about their parents' choices. However, when they listen to their parents' stories with open minds, they learn about their parents' coping and general mastery over difficult life events.

Often parents have not told their children about how powerful events in their lives have shaped them. When the therapist asks the parents about what they have learned from developmental losses and crises he or she gives the parents an opportunity to share with the child how these events have influenced them and shaped the way they respond to their children, spouse, and the world in general. The understanding the adult children gain helps them become less judgmental and more open to learning from their parents' experiences. It also allows for deeper connections between generations. When adult children understand that certain choices of the parents were based more on anxiety, loss, or sadness rather than indifference, lack of love, or general withdrawal, they can begin to connect around behaviors that separated them in the past.

Initiating a Process of Storytelling between Generations

Family-of-origin sessions with parents of adult children actually begin a process. The task of the therapist is to set in motion a process of storytelling. When the therapist provides a positive experience for the parents it is not unusual for them to comment that they have become more curious about their own history and plan to obtain more information from other family members. It is also common for these parents to start sending their adult children pictures, diaries, and other documentation about their family history that they had previously felt no one else was interested in.

Embracing Sadness

The parents tell their stories to the therapist in the presence of their adult child. Often parents have attempted previously to tell their children sad or hurtful stories. When the adult child has responded with any strong emotion, they have tended to change the story. Many parents try to protect their children from sadness. Adult children often say that their parents are not willing to talk about difficult subjects; however, at times the adult children by their emotional reaction to the sadness or hurt, block the parents' opening up these areas.

One of the major objectives of the family-of-origin sessions with parents is to give the parents the opportunity to discuss difficult areas without worrying about their children's reactions. Many parents in their seventies are ready to talk about losses that they were not able to reflect upon as young people. Adult children tend to forget that when they were in their twenties their parents were going through their own changes and were not then willing to talk to them. Parents in their forties and fifties often go through a process of distancing from the pain and sadness in their extended family. Those same parents in their sixties and seventies have ordinarily worked through these losses and become ready to reflect on some of their history. Unfortunately, many adult children only remember their parents' reticence about talking about certain issues and don't provide them with an opportunity to tell their stories later in life.

The therapist will ask questions about loss, death, and illness. A number of parents have expressed relief about finally being able to tell how their parents died or how they have prepared for dying without having to worry about upsetting their children. The children tend to find these comments remarkable.

Often when a parent becomes tearful about a certain story the adult child will weep. When a parent delves into an area of family sadness the adult child becomes anxious and doesn't know how to react. These common responses highlight the importance of doing some of the family-of-origin work in the safety of a structured session. When the therapist is able to remain calm, nonreactive, and in control of his or her anxiety, the therapist provides a powerful model for family members to emulate in telling each other their stories.

Videotaping Stories for Future Learning

The emotional atmosphere of family-of-origin sessions is so charged that adult children often find it difficult to listen to the entire story. From time to time their minds may drift, or they may be intrigued by a certain aspect of the story and fail to hear what else the parent is saying. A later review of the videotape provides a powerful learning opportunity. The adult child has a chance to feel the parents' story in the session; then, by watching the story on video, he or she is able to think about it.

The therapist should encourage the adult child to become more thoughtful about, rather than emotionally reactive to, the family story. If the adult child has only the emotional memory of the session, much learning is lost. The videotape provides the opportunity for reflection. Some adult children have reported that they watched the tapes half a dozen times, each time learning something more about their parents and themselves. Any procedure that enhances the ability of the adult child to become more thoughtful and reflective about the powerful emotional forces in the family of origin also helps the adult child become more detached and thoughtful about his or her spouse, children, and other important relationships.

Looking for Lost Heroes and Guides in the Family Story

One of the important tasks of the family therapist is to search for lost heroes and guides in the family story. Often parents coming into a family-of-origin session think that the focus will be on the failures and losses of the family. They are primed to talk about what has not worked. The family therapist must encourage the parents to tell stories about the positive forces in their lives. The therapist asks each parent about the role of his or her parents and grandparents. What lessons and legacies have they taken from their parents and grandparents that have helped them in their lives? Who were the most important role models and mentors in their lives? If parents reveal they didn't have any heroes or role models the adult child begins to realize what a struggle it must have been for the parents to be role models for him or her. When parents reflect on important, powerful people who helped shape their lives, the adult children begin to appreciate the reasons their parents made certain choices.

It is important for the therapist to look for the other side of any story. If a parent talks about a loss or disaster, it is helpful for the therapist to ask who assisted the parent through that period. Who were the most supportive people in their lives? Who did they feel safest with? Many people get so stuck in the intrigue of the loss or disaster that they forget that powerful principles of survival have come from those experiences. When parents reflect on a difficult experience they had when they were young adults or teenagers, it usually follows that somebody helped them through it. The family therapist should ask who that person was. If there was nobody, then the adult child gains a deeper appreciation of the struggles and sense of loneliness the parents may have experienced. The essential job of the therapist is always to look for strength, hope, survival, and connections. It is important for the family to leave the session with a clear sense of the heroes, mentors, and guides who helped them in their life struggles.

When Should Family-of-Origin Sessions Be Held?

The therapist raises the possibility of involving parents of adult children when he first meets with the couple. The usual response is caution or outright refusal. As the therapy continues, the adult child becomes more open to the suggestion. After a number of attempts to discover new stories about one's family, the adult child usually becomes motivated to involve the parents. One reason the adult child becomes more open is that he or she is no longer defending against the parents' stories. The adult child has learned that being open to these stories produces more gain than loss. During the beginning and middle of the middle phase, the adult child remains ambivalent about new stories. However, once the adult child emotionally shifts from worrying about closeness and intimacy to feeling ready to embrace the family's sadness, struggles, and difficulties, the family-of-origin sessions become appropriate.

During the end of the middle phase the therapist does not

encourage the adult child to bring in the parents. Rather, it is the adult child who expresses a readiness to involve the parents. If the therapist had to convince the adult child to invite the parents, then it would be premature to have a family-of-origin session.

When adult children say they are ready to have the parents involved, it is important for the therapist to ask the adult children why. The therapist must play devil's advocate at this point and give the adult child the opportunity to convince him or her of the appropriateness of this type of session. The therapist wants to be certain that the adult child is no longer judgmental or maintaining a defensive stance regarding the parents. Often adult children say there are many areas they would love to hear their parents talk about but they're not sure how to elicit all the information. This type of comment is a sure indication that the adult child is ready for a family-of-origin session.

A family-of-origin session should not be conducted during a family crisis. If the family is in a period of high anxiety or reactivity, the family-of-origin session will be seen more as an attempt to deal with the family crisis than as an opportunity for storytelling. It is difficult to reflect on stories when highly anxious. It may be necessary to work with the family around that crisis and later structure a family-of-origin session. Family-of-origin sessions are much more constructive during calm, nonreactive periods. *The family-of-origin session is not designed to do therapy on the family but rather to allow for a deeper sense of family connections around storytelling.*

Prior to scheduling a family-of-origin session the therapist should be satisfied that the adult child has worked through most of his or her powerful self issues. The adult child should not be in a generally reactive phase. If the adult child is still holding on to his or her story about the family, or has pockets of high anxiety about the family, then the family-of-origin session is not appropriate. The therapist must continually check on the readiness of the adult child. The therapist may do this by introducing different scenarios of conflict and concern and asking how he or she has learned to understand these dilemmas differently. It is also helpful to ask the adult children to reflect on new theories they have developed about themselves and their families. If the theories are based on curiosity and openness about the forces that have shaped the family's experiences, then it is likely the adult child is ready for a family-of-origin experience. In contrast, if the adult child's theories still involve figuring out or blaming the parents for certain life decisions, then it is premature to initiate a family-of-origin session.

Structure for the Family-of-Origin Sessions

It is important to follow several guidelines when conducting family-of-origin sessions.

Role of Therapist as Guide

The therapist is more a guide than a therapist to the family during the family-of-origin sessions. His or her job is to encourage the parents to talk about their history without feeling that they are being offered therapy. The therapist-guide asks questions and keeps the storytelling focused. He or she looks for openings in the parents' stories and encourages them to go into more detail about important connections, life events, losses, and pockets of anxiety that influenced the lives of family members.

The parents may attempt to cast the therapist-guide into a more therapeutic role. This should be avoided at all costs. The therapist-guide must be clear about his or her agenda. The major goal is to allow each parent the opportunity to voice his or her history. The therapist-guide makes sure at all times that the parents remain safe, are treated with respect, and are never put in an embarrassing situation.

At the beginning of the first session the therapist-guide clearly explains to the parents the structure and purpose of the sessions. He or she will ask the parents how they understand the purpose of the sessions, thereby gaining a quick reading of how anxious, defensive, or open the parents are to the experience. After explaining the agenda and structure of the sessions, the therapist-guide will ask the parents if they have reservations about participating. The therapist-guide should at all times respect any reservations that may be expressed. The therapist-guide should convey to the parents that they are the experts and storytellers. There is no attempt to interpret the parents' stories, but rather to allow them to be heard without interference.

Who Attends the Family-of-Origin Sessions?

The adult child attends the sessions with the parents but does not invite his or her spouse or children. The main reason the adult child's spouse is not invited is that the spouse's presence interferes with the ability of the parents to tell their story. When spouses are invited parents tend to become preoccupied with how their son-in-law or daughter-in-law hears the story.

It is important that the adult child be there with both parents if both are available. However, if there has been a separation or divorce, it may be necessary for the adult child to attend the family-of-origin sessions with each parent alone. If the adult child has only one surviving parent, it is important to structure the sessions so the parent tells his or her story rather than use the time to focus on the deceased parent.

Role of the Adult Child in the Family-of-Origin Sessions

The therapist-guide must prepare the adult child carefully for the family-of-origin sessions. The adult child must remain quiet during the first two sessions with the parents. If the adult child intrudes on the parents' story there is a risk that the parents will not tell the story the way they need to. The adult child has to be comfortable enough to listen to the parents' story without needing to modify or explain it. It is a powerful experience for adult children to remain silent while listening to their parents. Many adult children have commented that in the absence of specific instructions to remain silent, they would not have been able to resist intruding their feelings. They find, however, that by remaining silent they learn a great deal about their parents and their struggles. The parents are often confused about why the adult child hasn't interrupted them as is the usual family pattern.

During the initial part of the family-of-origin session the parents may even tell their story to provoke a reaction from their adult child. This behavior is their attempt to reduce their anxiety and set in motion the interactions that are most familiar to them. When the parents realize that the adult child is not going to intrude on their story, they begin to relax and go into greater depth about their struggles throughout life.

Number of Family-of-Origin Sessions

It is productive to schedule three structured $1\frac{1}{2}$-hour family-of-origin sessions, over a three-day period. Each session focuses on a different part of the family history. The first hour and a half deals with the parents' experiences in their nuclear families and with their grandparents. It is important to talk about experiences with both parents and grandparents. The therapist should always remember that with the exception of Native Indian families, all families have immigrated to North America. The stories about how families arrived in this country are powerful. The losses involved in leaving one's homeland are not to be underestimated.

The second session focuses on how the parents met, their courtship, and how they brought their families together. This segment also focuses on the parents' vision for becoming a family in their own right, that is, how they got the job of family living done. The therapist also asks about the legacies passed from one generation to the next. The parents are encouraged to talk about lessons they learned from their own families that they used to establish their new families.

The last session is devoted to the adult child, whom the therapist encourages to ask questions that would expand on parts of the story the adult child would like to know more about. When the adult child is truly in the proactive phase, he or she will ask questions that allow for further elaboration on important themes in the family. However, if the therapist-guide has misjudged the timing of the family-of-origin session and the adult child shifts into reactivity and/or blame, then the therapist-guide needs to take over the session and continue questioning the parents about their story.

The last session presents a powerful learning opportunity for adult children. When they review the sessions, they learn a great deal about their reactivity around their parents' stories. If they have asked good, curious, proactive questions, they will experience a sense of freedom about being able to connect at a deeper level with their parents. Even if adult children are defensive and reactive, reviewing the videotapes will help them learn more about where they are stuck and develop better theories about their reactivity.

Role of the Parents in the Family-of-Origin Sessions

The parents are the storytellers. It is necessary to honor both parents and each is offered 45 minutes per session to tell his or her story. The therapist-guide should discourage one parent from telling a story about another parent. If only one parent is present the entire session should be focused on his or her story. At times parents may shift into problem areas they are experiencing with each other. This focus should be avoided. The therapist-guide must remain in control of the process at all times. He or she should not allow the parent to be tangential, triangle the therapist-guide into a family story, or put the therapist-guide into a therapeutic role. When parents become anxious about some aspect of their story, they may revert to criticism or anger, or shift to a concern about another member of the family. It is extremely important that the therapist alleviate this anxiety by slowing the process, and helping the parent become comfortable with his or her story by refocusing on some safer area of the family history. After the anxiety has subsided the therapist-guide can refocus the discussion on these more sensitive areas.

The therapist, as the guide, gently maneuvers the parents into telling their story so they feel safe and honored, while at the same time eliciting many of the developmental struggles that represent their life—struggles about death, loss of abilities, disappointments at work, regrets about dealings with family members, and so forth. The therapist-guide gently asks questions about these areas without pressuring the parents to deal with them in ways that feel unsafe.

End of the Family-of-Origin Sessions

At the end of the third session it is important for the therapist-guide to summarize the experience. It is appropriate to ask each parent what it was like to tell his or her story. If the adult child was clearly proactive toward the parents, it is also appropriate to ask him or her about what the experience was like. It is helpful and appreciated when the therapist-guide concludes the sessions by thanking the parents for telling their stories and reiterating that they have left an important legacy for their children and grandchildren. The therapist-guide may mention that much of what the parents have discussed shows us what we can learn from the past to help us through present and future dilemmas. The therapist-guide will wish to end the family-of-origin experience on a positive note. One way to do this is to ask each parent what legacy they would like to leave behind for their children, grandchildren, and great-grandchildren who watch the videotape. In posing this question, the therapist guide honors the parents as the senior elders of the family clan and implies that their wisdom will be carried on throughout the generations.

What Are Some of the Problem Areas of Family-of-Origin Sessions?

There are a number of concerns to be considered before scheduling family-of-origin sessions. It is a relatively new concept to come to therapy not to discuss problems but to tell stories. The word "therapy" still suggests that something is wrong with somebody and/or the family. It is unusual for a parent to approach a family-of-origin session with the idea that this is about doing things right. It is very important that the parents not experience the family-of-origin session as a sign of unsuccessful parenting. Many parents doubt their abilities in this area and are quite defensive about their roles. They need to be honored and complimented for their efforts as well as asked about how they learned to do what they did. The first task in a family-of-origin session is to communicate to the parents that their coming in is an indication of their doing things right. Once they are assured the process is not about blame or criticism of their parenting, they begin to relax and involve themselves more fully.

The issue of when to involve siblings in family-of-origin sessions must be addressed. As mentioned in the previous section, the session involves the adult child and parents. The therapist has a relationship with the adult child and has worked over a period of time with this person to prepare him or her to hear the parents' stories without judgment. The siblings have not had this experience. Primarily because of this lack of experience, it is unpredictable how the siblings would behave in a family-of-origin session. Many siblings are reactive to their parents' stories, and feel they must intrude their own story. My approach is to exclude the siblings from direct participation in the family-of-origin sessions unless I have worked with them for some time. However, the siblings are entitled to their parents' stories—they do not belong to only one child in the family. If the family therapist is asking the parents the right types of questions and has blocked any parental attempt to triangle in other family members, then it is probably safe for the siblings to listen to their parents' stories. When siblings watch the tape of their parents they are often able to benefit from it even though they have not been involved in the process. Listening to them on tape only prevents them from intruding reactively. Siblings thus seem to listen to the stories more intently than if they were in the room interacting with their parents.

If siblings express a need to tell their own story after receiving the tape of their parents' stories, it is important to make that opportunity available. Many adult children join their siblings in watching the tape of their parents. This can be a connecting experience between siblings. For a more detailed explanation of how to work on sibling relationships see Freeman (1991).

The therapist must not allow the parents to use the family-of-origin sessions to focus on their own struggles in the world or difficulties in certain relationships. Some parents attempt to use the time to talk about problems in their marriage. It is crucial that the therapist maintain his or her role as guide for the storytelling. When the parents shift the focus to themselves the therapist must shift it back to storytelling. When parents talk about difficulties in a marriage, the therapist can shift the focus by asking the parents what they observed about their own parents' relationship and how their parents dealt with difficulties in the family. Each time parents reflect on a present personal problem, the therapist should ask about how they experienced that sort of problem with a family member in the past.

Parents become sad, some extremely so, when they reflect on certain past losses or painful situations. Parents have said, "If these stories will be helpful to my children, I am willing to tell them, but I would rather not have to think about them if I had my own way!" The therapist must be gentle about these painful areas and allow parents to tell their story in the safest way they know. One has to be respectful of the parents' need to find safe ways to talk about sadness. The therapist should assume that the parents have survived all these years with their history and will find their own way to feel safe telling their story. Many family therapists mistakenly try to push parents into areas they are not prepared to look at. The adult child must remember that areas parents cannot talk about or need to sidestep have important stories attached to them as well. The therapist should not open up all these areas in the family-of-origin sessions but provide a safe process that can be built on in the future between the adult child and the parents.

A therapist should never buy into the adult child's story about the parents. Parents' behaviors seldom resemble those attributed to them by their adult children. If the therapist basically accepts the adult child's image of the parents, the therapist's questions will be biased. It is essential that the therapist have no preconceived theory about the parents; otherwise the parents will, at some level, feel judged. The therapist must clear his or her mind of all stories told by the adult child about the parents. The parents must be able to tell their story any way they wish. The therapist may be aware of some powerful family themes and wonder how these themes get played out. However, the therapist does not need to structure the sessions to bring out these themes; if they are powerful, they will be revealed in the parents' stories. Themes of abandonment, loss, separation, and so forth, will all be evident when the parents tell how they dealt with their own families.

Family-of-Origin Sessions: Case Illustration and Commentary

The following three interviews which all involve the same family, illustrate family-of-origin work. The family presented was initially discussed in Chapters 6 and 7. This adult child, who initially presented with a relationship problem, progressed into the end of the middle phase of the family therapy process. At that point she became motivated to invite her father to a session to begin the process of storytelling. Her parents had been divorced for several years. Her plan was to begin with her father's story and then invite her mother at a later date. The sessions were structured as described earlier in this chapter. The first session offers the father an opportunity to tell his story about his parents and grandparents. The next session focuses on the father's story about the family he tried to create for himself. The last session focuses on the impact of the experience on the adult child. The last session took place after the adult child had an opportunity to review the videotapes of the earlier sessions. The principles of family-of-origin work are highlighted throughout the commentary to each session.

The first session begins with the therapist asking the father how his daughter explained the sessions to him. After the father responds, the therapist describes the structure of the three sessions to the father.

Dr. F.: I assume your daughter has filled you in.

Dad: Pretty much, yes.

Dr. F.: We could start with your understanding of what this is going to be about.

Dad: Well, what she has told me is that basically you want me to talk about my story. I don't know the specific things you want because obviously I could talk a long time about my story. So you are going to want to direct it somehow and I don't know quite how that is going to work but whatever it is, it is fine.

Dr. F.: Was there anything about the invitation that you had reservations about?

Dad: Not at all. No. As a matter of fact, I have been talking with my therapist and she suggested that both Jane and Karol come to town and that we do something there and it wasn't very definite, but she just mentioned that that might be something that we would want to do. And you talked to her, didn't you, yes? So I have no reservations about that at all.

Dr. F.: What I would like to do if it's okay with you is to have three sessions and divide them up and for Jane mainly to listen today and tomorrow and then, Jane, have you ask your father questions on Saturday about anything you want your father to elaborate on. For today and tomorrow, divide it up from the beginning of your memory, your earliest memories of family history to the beginning of your family when you had Karol and Jane and then on Saturday expand on your story.

Dad: You mean tomorrow it is family?

Dr. F.: Today we will start with the beginning of the family and tomorrow take it from there to now if you like and then on Saturday Jane will ask questions she wants clarified. So let's go back to your earliest memories. How far back does your memory go on family?

Dad: What do you mean "on family"?

Commentary

The therapist encourages the father to go back at least two generations. He asks the father to tell his story about his grandparents. It is important for the therapist to make sure the interview begins with stories about the past, not the present. Some parents believe that notwithstanding the explanation given, the therapist is really searching for problems in current relationships. It is necessary for the therapist to establish from the beginning that the exercise is about storytelling, not problem resolution.

Dr. F.: Your grandparents. Your great-grandparents. How far back does it go?

Dad: Oh, okay. All right. My maternal grandfather was dead when I was born. My maternal grandmother lived till I was about 3 or 4 but it's hard for me to distinguish between what I remember and what I was told and of course I have seen pictures of her. I have seen pictures of my grandfather, too. My father's parents. Well, my father's father lived till I was about 6 or 7, and his mother lived till I was about 10 or 11. So I have some definite memories of them.

Dr. F.: She was the longest-surviving grandparent, your dad's mother?

Dad: Yes, but see, both my parents were in their thirties when I was born. Well, my mother was just barely 30 when I was born. My mother was by far the youngest in her family, so her parents were a lot older and my father also was the youngest but by not as much. It is my impression that, well, like I said, my maternal grandfather was dead when I was born. My mother's mother must have been in maybe her late sixties when she died, and that is about the impression I have of my paternal grandparents, too, that they lived until about my present age. Something like that.

Dr. F.: So your stories, the stories that your mum told about her parents—give me an example of a story to illustrate their lives.

Dad: First of all I was born in the same apartment in which my mother was born and in which her father established his practice. He was a doctor. And I mean that is sort of typical of the way housing was in Vienna at that time.

Dr. F.: It was handed down.

Dad: It was handed down. It was actually an apartment that consisted of, in my lifetime, two apartments because the part that had been his practice was sublet and it was two separate apartments next door to each other. And so it was that kind of thing and it was very definitely sort of, what seemed like a very solid kind of existence.

Dr. F.: So the story that your mum would tell about her parents, what would she convey to you or want you to remember about them?

Dad: Well, first of all her father was a district physician. I guess you would call it district medical officer maybe. I am not sure what the corresponding thing here would be. In the district of Vienna where we lived under the Empire. This is before World War I. It was, I guess, a fairly elevated and bureaucratic position. I think he was in charge of seeing that the various medical cases were in good shape and examining things and so on. I'm not really sure what his function was but he was also a practicing doctor, but what my mother was particularly stressing about her family was that he was the first Jew to ever have that kind of position in Vienna.

Dr. F.: That was very important.

Dad: And they were, my mother's family was very highly assimilated and very non-Jewish, as a matter of fact. My mother converted to Catholicism later, after she went back. I mean the fact that she went back afterwards, you know, after the Nazis, also shows some of that. She was, I mean they were blond but I was more or less a dark blond and except for my nose not Jewish-looking at all. And that was true of my mother and from the pictures I saw also of her parents.

Dr. F.: Do you still have those pictures? Are they available?

Dad: I have pictures of my mother. I don't remember having any pictures of my grandparents. Actually, a lot of my pictures got drowned when my houseboat sank. I have some of them, but they are all curled up and, you know, not very good. But I do have some available.

Dr. F.: Did your mum's family change their name?

Dad: No. Her maiden name was B——, which could be either Jewish or non-Jewish. Her family used the non-Jewish version of the name.

Dr. F.: Was it considered a safe name for a Jewish family to have? So you have the story that your grandfather was the first Jewish doctor to hold that position. Even though they played down being Jewish they played up that story?

Dad: Well, my mother. I don't know what the "they" is in this case.

Dr. F.: I mean your mother's parents. Did they tell that story?

Dad: They must have. I don't know where she got it and it was a very solid bourgeois kind of existence in Vienna, at least under the Empire. She also told me there was a great-uncle of hers who was a well-known writer and involved in the revolution of 1848. So they went, at least part of her family was in Vienna that long ago, whereas my father's family came from Germany. My father was also born in Vienna, but his father came from Germany, and even though they were all German-speaking, because all those Jews from the western part of the Austrian Empire spoke German, whereas the ones in the eastern part spoke Yiddish. That was an enormous distinction in terms of social status and all kinds of things. My mother's family was definitely a more established, assimilated one. I think that was something that was of some importance to her.

Dr. F.: To your mother?

Dad: Yes.

Dr. F.: Did your mum ever explain to you her understanding about why her family played down being Jewish? Why the emphasis was on assimilating?

Dad: This was almost universal when my mother. . . .

Commentary

The therapist directs the story about fitting in, safety, and belonging. These appear to be major themes in the family. The father tells a story about the family being the outsider in a community that was basically anti-Semitic. The father relates an interesting story about how part of the family tried to fit in and assimilate, while another part maintained its Jewishness. This paradox between wanting to fit in and taking pride in being different gets played out throughout the father's story.

Dr. F.: Well, tell me the story then as you understand it about your mother's family playing down being Jewish.

Dad: My guess would have been that it was a matter of career, a matter of fitting in. We lived in a non-Jewish district and the area was one of the middle-class suburbs which was incorporated into Vienna at the time but was, you know, used to be, it is one of the ones on the edges of the Vienna woods, which means, you know, going up into the hills. There was an enormous amount of internalized anti-Semitism among the Viennese, the old-time Viennese Jews. I think rather generally. I don't know whether my mother's family was particularly remarkable along those lines, but certainly the fact of having been in Vienna a long time, you know, ancestors and well, actually her maternal grandmother apparently came from Varostin, which was in Dalmatia, so that is a non-German part now a part of Yugoslavia. Also not a place where there were many Jews. The mass of more recently immigrated Jews into that area were from Poland around World War I and they were the Yiddish-speaking ones. I mean, in addition, of course, in my parents' generation a lot of that took the form of being socialist, which among other things, was a complicated way of not being Jewish.

This takes actually some explanation. In my grandparents' generation they essentially tried to become good, solid Austrian professionals with incidentally, certainly on my father's side, they to some extent kept Jewish customs. I don't think on my mother's side they did at all. At least I have no impression of that at all. My parents were atheists and socialists.

Dr. F.: Both equally, with equal passion?

Dad: Well, my father was actually quite prominent in the Socialist Party, which was at that time in Vienna. I mean, this is now after World War I, the dominant party and remained that way in terms of population until the Nazis came, but the government became Catholic fascists quite a while before that. Sort of supported by Mussolini and the end came when Mussolini and Hitler got together. But the Jewish intellectuals particularly, I mean Vienna had a large Jewish intellectual population, were the backbone of the leadership of the Austrian Socialist Party. This was true not only in Austria but also in Germany and goes back to Marx and that whole thing. And all of this among other things was part of the sort of emancipation of the Jews who came out of the ghetto and the Enlightenment. So this goes way back into deep eighteenth century in actual fact. While there was the, well, let's say the identification with the underdog and with the oppressed became identification with the working class and so on. It was a way of, I'm talking in a rather cynical way about this now, but this was an extremely important thing in my childhood, this identification with socialism.

Dr. F.: This came from your father and your mother, or more from one?

Dad: Well, my father was really prominent as a socialist intellectual.

Dr. F.: But your mother, did she speak with passion about it as well?

Dad: I would say so.

Dr. F.: Did she get it from her husband, your father, or did she get it from her own family? Where did it come from in your mother, that passion? What is your theory on that?

Dad: Well, in neither case did it come from the family. This was part of the revolt of that generation against the . . . I mean, there was the story which I am sure Jane knows where my parents refused to have me circumcised when I was born. This caused an enormous uproar in my father's family as totally going away from tradition and so on but my parents did it. This was part of the socialism and part of the Enlightenment and the rebellion against tradition. It was . . . well, I don't know. I mean my mother told me that my father's oldest sister came to her in the obstetrics, while she was in the hospital to plead with her not to do this thing, which was going to kill my father's father, she said. My mother told me this story much later.

Dr. F.: What age were you when she first told you this story?

Dad: I think she told me that story in New York, probably after my father's suicide.

Commentary

The circumcision story is an important one. It illustrates the extent to which this man's parents went to have their son fit in and play down their Jewishness. This fitting in was at the expense of alienating half the family. The therapist does not take a position on this story but stays curious about it by asking the father to explain the timing of its revelation to him. The questions also subtly emphasize the importance of this major developmental incident.

Dr. F.: The first time you heard that story you were a grown man?

Dad: The story about the controversy. I mean, obviously I

knew I wasn't circumcised. I also knew that that was an expression of the Enlightenment and the socialism and probably at that time, I would think that the primary . . . I mean there was this peculiar Viennese culture which also involved psychoanalysis and all of that. I would guess in this particular case it was more a rebellion in terms of the castration and all of that than it was the socialism, but I'm not sure.

Dr. F.: Yes. So you didn't grow up with this story. It wasn't like you were told all your growing-up years this story about not being circumcised. You were told in your twenties, I gather.

Dad: But that had been a real big deal.

Dr. F.: That was a real big family issue.

Dad: On the other hand, it was also true when I started in school when I was 6 that they formally left the Jewish religious community because that way I didn't have to take religious instruction in school. You see, the setup was that there was religious instruction and the kids went to whichever one that their parents' community was in, I mean, the community their parents were in. They had never officially left the Israeli Cultural Community or the Jewish religious community until that time. That was done so that I wouldn't have to take religious instruction and I was a freethinker officially in school and didn't take religious instruction. Almost all the kids were Catholics and there were maybe three or four Protestants in my class and a couple of Jews and a couple of freethinkers. That made us very marked. That was a very ideological thing to be a freethinker.

Dr. F.: It separated you from the rest in some way.

Dad: Yes. But I grew up with sort of the understanding that all this was a sort of a very advanced and progressive and even elite kind of a thing. It was a very strange business in my childhood years, certainly up until the beginning of the '30s that there was this really sort of elite feeling about these socialist intellectuals, most of whom were Jews but who didn't think of being Jewish as being at all important. This was in the midst of enormous anti-Semitism, which was there all the time but which we sort of pretended not to see. It didn't exist. You know, Vienna was this great socialist city and all the workers, and you know, we would go out on May Day into these enormous May Day marches with hundreds of thousands of people.

Commentary

The therapist highlights the paradoxes in this family and asks the father how he sorted them out. By encouraging the father to talk about the ways he developed to feel safe around these confusing messages, the therapist is also providing the daughter with some important lessons about how to sort out her own confusion. The daughter has her own powerful stories about her father's battles with the world. Listening to how her father struggled as a young man to honor his family while at the same time trying to be true to himself provides the daughter with new information about the father and his way of surviving, and new ideas about herself and how she wants to resolve her own paradoxes in life.

Dr. F.: Sounds like a lot of paradoxes.

Dad: Oh, hell, yeah.

Dr. F.: Did you ever sort these things out to your satisfaction, or did it confuse you as a child?

Dad: As a child? I don't know how to answer that. I mean, the contradictions obviously were there, but at the same time they seemed to be a sort of given. I know from my own therapy and looking into things later and so on, that I had a lot of feelings about hypocrisy, which were among other things related to the socialism of my parents and their circle. It was the socialism of an elite, or people who felt themselves as an elite. Similar phenomena exist elsewhere, but this was very marked there. And I knew that some of the kids in my school were Nazis, you know, already then. Some of my friends were Nazis, you know these were little kids. I know there was an enormous discrepancy and contradiction between this sort of feeling as an elite and feeling hunted, both of which were there. So that on some level I think I was aware of these contradictions but all of that seemed absolutely natural to me somehow. That was the way it was, and there couldn't be anything else.

Dr. F.: You know, the story of the circumcision kind of fascinates me because as a child you weren't told what was behind that symbolic act. It's a very powerful decision that your mum and dad decided to make. He went against his own family, which as you tell the story, was very upsetting to the point that it might kill Grandfather. You knew you weren't circumcised, of course, so what did you tell yourself as a child. Well, two questions, one is what did you tell yourself as a child not being circumcised was about, and secondly, how did it change your relationship as a grandchild in that family, your father's family?

Dad: First of all, hardly anybody I knew was circumcised. You see, the kind of medical circumcision that exists in the United States didn't exist there at all at that time. I don't think it ever really came up very much. Certainly not until I went to the *Gymnasium*, which is like starting with the fifth grade. When I went to school where there are lots of Jews but even then it didn't seem to be a big deal. You know, religious Jews were something I didn't see much of, so I don't think that was a big deal, certainly, I don't remember it as being a big deal. But a lot about the business of being Jewish at least partially was sort of shut out and repressed. You know, we were these socialists.

Dr. F.: Your father's family stayed Jewish, as I follow your story.

Dad: The grandparents did. Yes, and even also to some extent his sisters and their husbands. Now, you see they were lawyers, my father's father was a lawyer and lived in a much more Jewish atmosphere and they were not socialists. Also, both his sisters married lawyers, one of them in fact became a partner in my grandfather's firm and even my cousin G., who was about ten years older than me, he was the son of that lawyer who was a partner in my grandfather's firm. He studied law and became, I don't know what you call this, where you are sort of an apprentice lawyer in a firm . . .

Dr. F.: Where you article.

Dad: Something like that, yeah, in that same firm but then the Nazis came and he never practiced law in Vienna. He managed to get to the United States also. The lawyers probably had the hardest time of anybody because the law was totally different. They couldn't practice and they would have to start all over again basically.

Dr. F.: But your grandfather was a Jewish lawyer?

Dad: Well, I don't know exactly what you mean by that . . .

Dr. F.: Well, different from your mother's dad who, as you tell the story, was played down as being a Jewish doctor.

Dad: But he was also an official, you know in the bureaucracy. Where basically before World War I, in the Empire to be a Jew in the bureaucracy was almost unheard of. But in the three professions it was very different.

Commentary

The therapist stays with the theme of being different. He asks about how this man's father dealt with his own father about being different in the world. He is drawing out the multigenerational theme of being encouraged to be different yet pressured to fit in. The daughter struggles with this issue in her life. She makes choices to accentuate her differences, yet simultaneously feels alienated from her community and tries desperately to gain acceptance. The ambivalence between wanting to go one's own way and fearing being ostracized for it has a powerful history in this family.

Rather than take a position on this theme, the therapist asks the father to reflect on what he learned from watching his father deal with his grandfather and how that influenced the way he learned how to deal with his own father.

Dr. F.: What I'm curious about is your father's relationship with his father. If I follow your story very carefully, and it is a very fascinating story, correct me, of course, if I'm getting the wrong flavor, but your father chose to take a different course in the world from his father.

Dad: Absolutely. I mean his father was a real patriarch. And my father was the only son but he was the youngest of three children.

Dr. F.: The firstborn son.

Dad: Firstborn son, yes. The girls both were like married off to other Jewish lawyers and it was like that. My father studied philosophy and got his Ph.D. in philosophy and this was, of course, this was all at the time of World War I. My father was born in '91 and the Empire was collapsing at that time as well as the patriarchy and everything else. The socialists, the Austrian socialists, were already quite strong before World War I but came into power in Austria itself, which was the sort of fragment that was the German-speaking part of the Empire. In many ways the breakup of the Austrian Empire in World War I was very similar to the breakup of the Russian Empire at the same time. All these nationalities and also very similar to what is going on in the Soviet Union now. I mean, there are enormous similarities in my perception of that situation.

Commentary

The father becomes tangential at this point. One can speculate that when the therapist asked about the conflict between this man's father and his grandfather it stirred up some of the conflict between himself and his father. Becoming tangential and preoccupied with some side issue in the family history is usually a sign that the parent is anxious. If the therapist allowed the father to become comfortable by remaining tangential, then the power of the family-of-origin session would be diminished. However, if the therapist moved too quickly to focus on unsafe areas, then he would violate the important principle that the session should be safe for the parent. The therapist chooses to bring the father back to the discussion of his father's relationship with his grandfather. He asks about the age of the father's father when the father's grandfather died, encouraging the father to shift the focus back to family matters.

Dr. F.: Your father would have been how old when his father died?

Dad: He was born in '91. My grandfather died probably I would say in '29 or '30, because I said before it was about when I was 6, I think, that is my impression. And so my father was about 40.

Dr. F.: Do you remember as you were growing up your father telling you how he made peace with his own father? How he worked out these differences?

Dad: No.

Dr. F.: He didn't talk about that much.

Dad: No. What I remember him telling me was that he felt very intimidated and hostile and rebellious against his father. I mean he mentioned how his father had beaten him, more in sort of explanation of his own neurosis than anything else.

Dr. F.: What age were you when your father began to tell you these stories about his father?

Dad: This also I think was after we left Vienna. It was in the period where essentially my father was already . . . I mean, you know, he had a terrible time in Chicago. I think it was at that period.

Dr. F.: Not while you were in Vienna, he didn't talk much about that.

Dad: We didn't talk about that at all.

Commentary

The therapist is assessing the father's readiness to talk about family matters. He asks the father what his theory is about why his father was ready at a certain point in his life to talk about his history. By asking the father to reflect on his own father's readiness to deal with loss and important changes, he is also encouraging the father to talk about his own readiness to do the same.

Dr. F.: Do you have a theory about that? Why your father began to talk more about it after you left Vienna? Any speculation about why he did so at that point?

Dad: I think he was talking about his own difficulties more than anything else. Also telling me how much better a childhood I had had than he had had. You know, I was having difficulties also, but he felt that I was basically on much more solid ground than he was.

Dr. F.: You were how old when you left Vienna?

Dad: I was 15 when I left. I was 14 when the Nazis came in.

Dr. F.: So you have very vivid memories of that period.

Dad: Oh hell, yes.

Dr. F.: Did your mum and dad stay connected with their families, or did the socialist movement become like a substitute family?

Dad: Well, there certainly was a connection with actually

both. My mother had a sister, my Aunt D., who was maybe eight years older than herself. She had had a brother but he was dead. He was a doctor also, and he died from some illness. He was a surgeon. Something that happened in the course of an operation. So I never knew him. That was also before I was born. I knew the aunt and we had sort of an arrangement where every Saturday I would eat lunch at her house with her and her husband. They didn't have any children. Then Saturday afternoon I would go to somebody I also called an aunt who wasn't really an aunt but somehow a friend, actually I think mostly a friend of Aunt D., same age group, older than my mother. I would sort of spend Saturdays with these two women. I'm not sure how close the relationship between my mother and her sister was. I think there was quite a bit of antagonism there.

Commentary

The therapist encourages the father to expand his definition of family. By asking about cousins and other extended-family members he tries to gain an understanding of the extent of family resources and connections. When parents talk about their connections with extended family members, one gets a sense of either a family with resources or family that has lost its way. Some parents reveal they never knew their cousins, uncles, and aunts and grew up in a fairly isolated nuclear family. Others describe an early extensive family network that became lost to them later in life. Others describe ongoing connections. No matter what the description, the adult child listening to it learns important lessons about the depth of family cohesiveness and when, in some cases, the splintering or distance arose. It is always helpful to ask parents their theories about what brought about the changes in the family.

Dr. F.: Your cousins didn't play a large part in your growing-up years?

Dad: Okay, I had three cousins on my father's side. One is this cousin George that I mentioned. He was a lot older than me but we had a rather close relationship in many ways and which extended into the United States. Well, they lived in the South and so we didn't see too much of them but then he died . . .

Dr. F.: And the other two cousins, what happened to them?

Dad: Now the other two cousins were the sons of the other sister. We had some relationship with them, but it wasn't terribly close, and . . .

Dr. F.: They were much older than you, too?

Dad: Somewhat older. One of them is still alive, Paul, living in Britain. The other, Otto, was, there was something . . . I mean he . . . people in the family regarded him as feebleminded. Both of them managed to get to England, whereas their parents did not, and their parents were killed in Auschwitz. But both of these cousins managed to get to England and were then sent to Canada during the war and interned in Canada and stayed on there. And Otto lived in Toronto until he died, married into a much more Orthodox Jewish family there. Paul became, well, I'm not sure about everything that happened with him but eventually he became an interpreter for the United Nations and that is how he went to England. He worked for UNESCO in London. And there has been some contact but not a hell of a lot.

Dr. F.: Well, you really kept track with what has happened to these cousins.

Dad: Oh, yes, yeah.

Commentary

The therapist shifts the focus of the story to an important developmental event, the family leaving their homeland and moving to North America. The way the family handled this important shift gives an indication of the strength of the connections between the family members and how they were able to make things safe for each other. The way the father tells the story about this time in the family life is significant. Does he talk about his parents as his heroes, or does he see himself as having been the hero to them? Did his parents make the move safe for him, or was it his job to make the move safe for them? Were connections maintained with family in the old country? If the family was not able to provide safety for him, then how did he provide it for himself as a young man? This family lost its way around the move to a new country. The father tells a powerful story about how the parents decided to move to offer him a future. Does he now have an obligation to be successful to prove to his parents that they were right to make the move? Much of the story the father tells about the move to the new country concerns the losses for the parents and the gain for himself. One gets the sense that the father felt obligated to take care of his parents. In some ways, after the move to the new country, this man lost his parents. One of the major themes of the daughter was her sense that she lost her father to his "illness." The father now talks about losing his father and mother to their sadness and depression.

Dr. F.: The story I think would be so interesting to hear you tell would be your memories of how your mum and dad prepared you for this huge move, to leave Vienna for the United States. What do you remember about how they prepared you for that?

Dad: Prepared me for that? You mean when we knew about it, or how my upbringing prepared me for it?

Dr. F.: Any of them, all of them.

Dad: How they prepared me for it . . . Well, my mother was deeply depressed when she, I'm told that she was depressed after my birth, but this, of course, I don't know. . . .

Dr. F.: Told by?

Dad: I think by my father first of all. Some of this is mixed up in terms of I don't know when I knew what, you know. She got very depressed in '34 when she lost her position. This is when Austria went fascist, Catholic fascist, and she was, she taught in a *Gymnasium*, which I don't know if you know what that was but this was for girls and she taught English and German. Both she and my father were employees of the state and at that time, I guess in '33, '34, I don't know the exact timing, they put in a law, this was in the middle of the Depression but it also had ideological and political implications that no two members of a family could both be state employees. Ostensibly because of the Depression and the shortage of jobs but actually as a way of getting the women out of these professional jobs more than anything else, I think, because there was this big tendency to get the women back into the kitchen. The socialist movement also had a lot of feminism in it, though not quite the sort of current type of feminism but the feminism of equality in employment and so on. Although I guess that is part of the current one also. My mother had a Ph.D. as well as my father. . . .

Dr. F.: Her Ph.D. was in?

Dad: In German and English, linguistics.

Dr. F.: And his was in philosophy?

Dad: My father's was in philosophy and science, philosophy and physics. And I was basically raised by maids. I mean, in those days a two-profession family had a maid in Vienna. But this whole thing collapsed for my mother in '34 and she had a very serious depression then, was hospitalized for several months, and then tried to do some private lessons and she had this whole group of former students of hers. I don't know how to describe this exactly but also it was connected with the socialist youth movement and so on and a lot of those students of hers came and took private lessons with her in German and English.

Commentary

This part of the interview is quite important. The therapist gently begins to question the father about his mother and father. If the therapist accepted of face value the father's story about the mother being sick and depressed, and the father giving up on life when he immigrated, then there would not be much hope to build on. The challenge is for the therapist to look at the other side of the story and help give voice to that. The therapist does not want to leave the story on a note of despair, failure, and victimization. He begins to ask questions about the competency, hope, and abilities of the parents. By encouraging the father to talk about these other aspects of his parents, the competent sides, he gives balance to the family story. The adult child needs to discover that both her father and her grandparents were survivors. As it turns out, this man's parents were more than just survivors, they were quite competent and capable people. The father's most emotional stories were about the way his parents dealt with the move to North America. It is understandable that the father overemphasized that part of his parents' lives because the move represented a significant loss to him. As the therapist helps the father develop a more balanced picture of his parents, the father begins to see himself a bit differently in relation to them. This process also helps the daughter recognize the positive legacies in the family.

Dr. F.: They were very loyal to her.

Dad: Yes, which sort of kept her going, you know, for a while. Emotionally.

Jane: Can I just ask a question? Were these Jewish girls or mixed or non-Jewish?

Dad: I think most of them were Jewish but mixed. The *Gymnasium* where she taught was where again sort of free-thinking Jews sent their daughters. But there were also non-Jews there and in fact the director of that *Gymnasium* turned out to be a big Nazi, whom my mother was extremely tied to emotionally. The whole thing was a sort of a family affair in a way. And the business when the Nazis came into power and all that, I mean it was an enormous wrench, I think also for this woman who was the director. Who, of course, never, I mean there was always this business about, you know, the Jews are terrible but I have these Jewish friends who are not like that at all.

Dr. F.: You would be how old now at this time?

Dad: When are we talking about?

Dr. F.: When she got the depression.

Dad: All right, this was in '33, '34, so I would be 10, 11.

Dr. F.: So this is about three years before the move, two or three?

Dad: Well, this was '34, the move was in '38. But essentially things were falling apart already then and also even though he didn't lose his job, my father had been teaching in something called the People's University, which was a joint thing of the city of Vienna and the Trade Union Movement. It was essentially adult education, evening stuff but much more sort of general intellectual than the kind of practical thing that is usually done here with that sort of thing. So he was the head of the Philosophy Department and he taught philosophy and physics and did research at the same time, wrote books and things like that. Now, he had been refused a professorship in the university on apparently ideological grounds. See, the university was not Vienna, the university was the state of Austria, which was very Catholic and anti-Semitic and so on. There was this enormous conflict between the city of Vienna and the rest of the country, see, the city of Vienna, which was a city of 2 million inhabitants and had been the capital of the Austro-Hungarian Empire, was now the capital of a country of 6 million. I mean, we used to talk about it as a big blown-up head of a very small body. And enormous ideological differences. Like I said, the city was overwhelmingly socialist. The socialists had a two-thirds majority in the City Council, which was also a province. I mean, Vienna was one of them, Austria had nine provinces at that time, and Vienna was a province and so had a lot of autonomy but was in enormous conflict with the federal government, which at that time was already Catholic, though immediately after would also have been socialist, okay?

Commentary

The father is becoming tangential again, getting lost in detail about the historical developments in his homeland. The therapist refocuses the father on the family story. The parent should not totally control the content of the session. However, the refocusing must always be done in a nonconfrontational, noncritical way.

Dr. F.: Do you remember listening to your mum and dad talk about things unfolding, I guess unraveling?

Dad: Yes. That was very clear, and it was also clear for my father, who couldn't teach at the People's University because all the socialists were cleared out of there, and that was made Catholic so he had to go and teach at a *Gymnasium.* They didn't fire him but they made him go teach at a *Gymnasium.* Things were really falling apart. I remember after the Nazis came in when my mother was again totally depressed and my father was almost immediately fired from his *Gymnasium* job also, and pensioned off. I mean, he did have his pension. I remember discussing with him, you know, "What are we going to do?" and the impression I got is that they were going to stay except for me. Because I had absolutely no future with the Nazis. That's why they decided to leave. It was an extremely difficult thing for them to leave, not only because of the general situation but because of my mother's depression. I mean, my father had a horrible time. He was pretty depressed himself, but he kept going. I mean basically, the thing was I was going to make it because I was such a, you know, I was always first in all my classes. You know, I was going to make it as a brilliant student. As a matter of fact, I did make it that way, whereas my father did not, not to mention my mother, who spent most of the time she was in the States in a state hospital. And my father lived on grants for refugee scholars type of things.

Dr. F.: Do you clearly remember your dad saying the move to, where was it they moved to?

Dad: Well, initially to England to wait for the American visa and then we moved to Chicago.

Commentary

The therapist brings the father back to an underlying theme by asking him to talk more about the reasons for the move to North America. He emphasizes the father's point that the move to North America was for his future. He encourages the father to talk about what the move represented to him as a young man. The therapist wonders if the father felt burdened by the move and how he made peace with his parents around the meaning of the move.

Dr. F.: So the move out of Europe, out of Vienna, was for your future.

Dad: That's what tipped the balance. He was thinking what would happen if we stayed and people were having all kinds of illusions about how this Nazi thing was going to go and sort of like, well, I have my pension and so on and we could probably survive. It would be very unpleasant and so on but we could probably survive but there would be no future for you at all. Talking to me.

Dr. F.: Do you remember trying to convince him otherwise, that this was safe? You didn't want to go.

Dad: Me? No. I wanted to go.

Dr. F.: You wanted to go. Why did you want to go? Why? You were 12, 13 years old. . . .

Dad: No, 14.

Dr. F.: 14. What was your thinking about that for yourself at that time?

Dad: Well, for one thing, I mean it was already totally obvious that we were outcasts. That I couldn't keep on going to school. Immediately after the Nazis came they threw all the Jews out of the *Gymnasium* where I was. There still were a couple of *Gymnasiums* where I could go and I had to scramble and get into one of those. This was for the remainder of the school year. The Nazis came in in February, March, and so for the remainder of the school year I had to find another school and we managed to do that but it was horrible in that school. I mean, the teachers were all Nazis who hated having to teach us, and treated us like dirt. Whereas before I had been sort of, at least in our own minds, we had been some sort of an elite, you know, the intellectual cream of Vienna. Now we were these "dirty Jews." The anti-Semitism had always been there but it wasn't in power in the same way. And I felt in '38 when the Nazis came into Austria they had already been in power for five years in Germany, so people knew a lot about what was coming, what happened to the Jews. Except that it got much worse after they came into Austria, and, of course, progressively worse later.

So I don't think anybody was thinking about the Holocaust at that time but that being Jews under the Nazis was certainly no life for a teenager to grow up into. It was clear. Clear to me. Of course, this was also my adolescence and a very important part of the Nazi thrust at that time was the sexual thing about, you know, the Jews polluting the German race and all of that. I was terrified of my own sexuality, for one thing. The husband of my Aunt D., my mother's sister, who had a mistress at that time who was not Jewish and my aunt had already died, and I think he lived with her but certainly he had a very long-standing affair with a woman who worked in his business. He killed himself immediately when the Nazis came in because he knew what was going to happen to him.

Jane: He was Jewish?

Dad: Yes.

Dr. F.: This was before you left?

Dad: Yes. I remember going to his funeral. It is the only funeral I went to as a German.

Commentary

This last story is a powerful one about family loss. The father had mentioned his own father's suicide in passing earlier in the interview; he now tells the story about the suicide of his uncle in such a way that it implies a heroic deed. The therapist asks more about this story and its meaning to the father as a prelude to talking about the meaning of his own father's suicide. It has taken two-thirds of the interview to move into the area of significant family loss. The theme of the father's father's suicide runs through the family and has haunted the father's daughter all her life. One of the objectives is to help the father talk about the meaning of his father's suicide so his daughter can understand it differently. To this point the daughter has viewed her grandfather as a failure who gave up. Although she does not see her father as a failure she does feel that in some ways he has given up. She struggles with the desire to give up within herself. Later in the interview the father discusses his own father's suicide in heroic terms. However, at this point, the father continues to talk about how life events affected various family members.

Dr. F.: Do you remember what you told yourself his suicide was about?

Dad: We knew. I mean, I knew.

Dr. F.: What did you say? What did you know?

Dad: That he killed himself because he knew the Nazis were going to get him for having a non-Jewish mistress. I mean, that was the first, everybody knew about that. And I remember her being at his funeral, you know, and weeping. And actually thinking at the time that this was an extremely courageous thing for her to do, to be there. I knew that. I was 13 years old.

Dr. F.: How soon after that did the family leave?

Dad: Well, they sent me off ahead.

Dr. F.: You went first?

Dad: I went first alone to England, because there was a horrendous amount of red tape to get out and there was also a horrendous amount of red tape to get in. But the red tape was easier for a teenager than it was for my parents because it had to do with making sure there was no property and making sure that they got everything and that no taxes were owed and all that kind of stuff. And I spent days in long lines at various police agencies to get the okay to leave and I got it before my parents did obviously. That was the way it worked. So my father said, "Okay, let's get you out of here," and put me on a plane to England, where I was picked up by some friends of the family who were already there and went to a Quaker boarding school that school year. Actually, my parents came several months later and then went to Chicago very briefly after that so I both got to England before they did and left after they did because I stayed to the end of the school year.

Dr. F.: So they set up residence in Chicago and then you followed.

Dad: That's right. And I never lived with them again because when I got to the United States, which was in the summer of '39, I had a scholarship, a refugee scholarship to a college in Virginia. How I got that was it was essentially a lottery, I think. There was this thing called the International Student Service, which was placing Jewish refugee kids in various colleges through money raised by the student body. I mean it was this kind of a student action. And the student bodies picked their refugees, and I was picked by this college at Virginia, which was an enormous cognitive dissonance. I mean, there I was in a totally segregated Virginia, which was in fact sort of still living in the antebellum period essentially at that time. With this impoverished pre-Civil War aristocracy. I was the mascot, the Jewish mascot, in this college.

Dr. F.: You were 15 now?

Dad: Yes. Wait, by that time I was 16. I had spent a year in England, and whereas I had been the nigger in Germany, here there was this whole population which were the kikes. It was, I mean, the cognitive dissonance was . . . But the sexual problems were not as extreme as with the Nazis but of the same type because even though I was the Jewish mascot at this antebellum college, of course the girls were all taboo for me. So my whole sexual development was very strongly warped in that whole period. In fact, I felt sort of liberated in many ways when I went to graduate school at the University of Pittsburgh in '43, which brings me almost up to the time when I met M.

Commentary

It would be easy for the therapist to shift into a therapeutic role with the father at this point. The father has opened up certain problem areas in his own life. However, the therapist stays true to the structure and encourages the father to tell stories rather than shift into problem areas. The therapist sidesteps the father's opening about his struggles with his sexuality and stays focused on how his parents said good-bye to their own families. How one generation says good-bye to the next generation is always an important theme.

Dr. F.: Yes, but before we jump to that, one thing I just became aware of is that you didn't see how your mum and dad said good-bye to their families because you weren't there.

Dad: That's correct. But I know my father was haunted in his Chicago years by the fact that he couldn't get his sister and her husband out. Because the other sister got out also.

Dr. F.: That was one of the major losses for your dad, not being able to get that sister out?

Dad: Well, apparently. I mean he was extremely guilt-ridden by that. Not being able to manage and they got sent to Auschwitz and he sort of watched that.

Dr. F.: So one sister got out and one sister died. And your father didn't forgive himself for that?

Dad: Yeah, I mean he talked about it a lot. I mean the conception that people over there had is once you got to America essentially you were all-powerful, whereas he felt totally powerless.

Dr. F.: When he got here to America.

Dad: Yes.

Commentary

The therapist begins the process of questioning the father about the heroic qualities in both his parents. He does not want to end this part of the interview leaving the impression that the parents were unsuccessful. The therapist differentiates between the parents' pre- and post-American days. When the father talks about the competence of the parents in their pre-American days, it helps balance what happens to them in their later post-American days.

Dr. F.: Now, there is a period that I'm confused about. In effect, you never lived with your parents again after you left?

Dad: Yes.

Dr. F.: So the changes that you saw happening to your mum and dad you saw from afar and then in visits.

Dad: That's correct.

Dr. F.: You saw these massive, as I understand, changes occur. So in your own mind I would imagine there was your mum and dad pre-America and post-America.

Dad: Well, actually the changes began before we left. I mean, I guess I could say that things really seriously started going downhill. . . .

Dr. F.: For both of them?

Dad: Already in '34, I would say. It was a sort of a doom is coming.

Dr. F.: But here you are this young, midteenage son. Can you talk a little bit about what was happening to you, seeing what was happening to your parents in America? What did you try to do? How did you try to make it safe for yourself?

Dad: Okay I spent the summers in Chicago while I was a student in Virginia. The way it went was that my father was living in, sort of subletting in these sort of brownstone houses in Chicago and he would get another room usually in the same house for me in the summer. So I saw a lot of him in those summers. My mother most of the time was in the hospital. The hospital that she was in most of the time there was a state hospital. It was a real nightmare. They had these huge brick fortresses. They looked like prisons. A whole bunch of them. There was a special train on the weekends that went out there with, you know, I don't know whether it was really thousands, but my impression was thousands of people going out there to visit their relatives, like visiting friends in prison at least, and probably worse in many ways. Those places were real nightmares.

And that's how I interacted with my mother during that period. There were some exceptions and particularly the time when my father killed himself. She was out of the hospital, and I then spent six months with her. Me being the one who told her. But this was in '44. After I was already at Pittsburgh, but that is the only time I remember being with my mother in Chicago when she wasn't in the hospital.

Dr. F.: After your father killed himself.

Dad: Yes. I don't know, there were a couple of other . . . when I first arrived in Chicago in the summer of '39 they were staying at a place on the lake which was a big estate that somehow the Quakers had gotten and were using as a summer place for these refugees. They were both there when I arrived but my mother was, you know, my mother was weeping, I mean she was—

Dr. F.: Wasn't the same mother that you remembered?

Dad: Well, it's not true that she wasn't. I mean, I remember her like that from Vienna, too, from the last years in Vienna.

Dr. F.: But you never saw the other side of your mum again, the competent, professional teacher?

Dad: Yes, I did.

Dr. F.: You saw that, too, in America?

Dad: No, not in America.

Dr. F.: That didn't come back.

Dad: No.

Dr. F.: That got lost. That was left behind somewhere. Did you have peeks of it, little windows of that old person?

Dad: Well, see, my mother was a big storyteller when she was not depressed and I think a lot of her professional activity basically was that also. You know, she taught literature. Okay, I think the high point of her life in Vienna was a time when Thomas Mann visited Vienna. Two of her students were the daughters of a famous publisher which was sort of *The New York Times* of Vienna. Thomas Mann either stayed with those people when he was in Vienna or at least there was a big social thing and my mother was invited to dinner with him and this was something. She adored Thomas Mann. And basically a lot of her professional life was in going through literature of that kind and telling about it and so on. And I saw some of that when she was happy in Chicago, you know, telling me stories from Thomas Mann, that kind of stuff.

Commentary

The therapist concludes the interview by emphasizing positive memories of the mother. Restructuring the story about the mother provides a herolike person to two generations, the son and the granddaughter. When the father returns the next day it is interesting to note that he has already been affected by the telling of positive stories about his mother. He mentions he has not really had much opportunity to think about his mother in a positive light, and acknowledges she had areas of competence that got lost somewhere. When the therapist hears this type of comment he knows that he has struck the right balance in the storytelling.

Dr. F.: So you have those memories of your mum. Those stories.

Dad: Those stories I have.

Dr. F.: Did you record any of her stories, or did anyone record any of her stories?

Dad: No.

Dr. F.: Did she write stories?

Dad: No. My impression of my mother is basically that she fluctuated between two personalities. When she was happy she was essentially childlike, caught up in literary romance and so on and the other personality was depressed. Somehow I never thought of my mother as competent. As you said before, her competence as a professional. Somehow her profession was tied up with this fantasy life and you know, the storytelling and so on. Now, this is, of course, looking back on things.

Dr. F.: Sure, I hear you. Her competent side got lost somewhere.

Dad: Yes.

Dr. F.: It was there but just got lost. We are going to stop now. We're just at the point where I wanted to ask you more about your dad, but we could start with that point tomorrow. How has it been to talk for an hour and a half with me?

Dad: Well, you see, I'm very bored with myself. An hour and a half, it hasn't seemed that long.

Dr. F.: You okay, no surprises yet, in terms of what I've asked?

Dad: Yeah.

Dr. F.: And Jane, was it okay for you?

Jane: It seemed very good.

Dr. F.: Well, I look forward to tomorrow.

Second Family-of-Origin Interview

The focus of the second session is on how the father tried to create his own family. However, before getting into these stories it is helpful to ask the father what thoughts he may have had during the night that he may wish to add to the stories he recounted the previous day. Often parents remember more family stories after the first session and may wish to add to or revise a story told the previous day.

It is a good indication that the first session was positive when a parent talks about allowing old memories to come back. Usually, the stories parents recount on the second day have a bit more balance than those of the first day.

Dr. F.: Maybe we could start with the question I ended with yesterday. Do you want to add to some of the events that you've started talking about? Any new thoughts or ideas come to mind overnight?

Dad: Not so much events but when you asked me yesterday at the end whether anything new had happened yet, I said no at the time. I mean suddenly all the things that I talked about, I have thought and talked about before. But there was, not very strong, but a sort of a feeling of synthesis when I was lying in bed last night. I'm not sure that I can formulate it very well yet but there was a feeling of some stuff falling into place and it had to do with something that you were emphasizing rather strongly and that is really the extreme degree of assimilationism in my mother's family, which I have never thought of in that way quite before. Almost the thought that, well, just how this relates to what happened with my father I'm not sure, though there must be a relation there, too, but that my mother's really very strong inability to sort of look the world in the face. You know, this business of either she was in a fairy-tale world or she was totally depressed must have had something to do with the, well, I said cognitive dissonance about something else yesterday, but I guess I'll use that term again.

Dr. F.: With your mother?

Dad: With my mother, yeah.

Commentary

The therapist takes advantage of the opening regarding the mother and encourages the father to tell a more balanced story about her. The therapist believes that there is another side to the story about her. If he colluded with the father in regard to his story about his mother, the family-of-origin session could create additional problems for the family. The job of the therapist is to float between the stories. The therapist must remain curious, not challenging, about why stories are being related in a certain way and wonder if, in fact, there are other aspects to the story that haven't been told. It is difficult for people to give up their old stories that keep them safe in some way. When someone challenges our stories, we look for more evidence to support them.

Dr. F.: It's interesting how you start because your mother in your story really intrigues me, what happened to her and how her competence and her creativity got lost somewhere in the story. To make that come more alive is, I think, important. To put her more in balance as a competent, creative person who was betrayed at all kinds of different levels. It sounded to me, if I were to venture a hypothesis about your mother, I was struck with your telling the story about the school she was teaching at and she was really involved with the principal or the head of the school. . . .

Dad: Director, yeah.

Dr. F.: Director of the school who turned out to be a Nazi. She had that. This was like family, the way you described it.

Dad: Yes.

Dr. F.: I was so struck with that part of the story. What it would be like for her to have lost that.

Dad: Well, she actually met that woman again after she returned to Austria. She told me that she met her on a streetcar and the way she described it was that, she seemed extremely, well, first of all very worn out. You know, this was some years later, and she had lost all of her confidence, and, in fact, from the way my mother related the story to us, was cringing when she saw my mother and I don't remember, sort of sat down next to her and. . . . Anyway something like that.

Dr. F.: I guess the sense of betrayal runs through.

Dad: Oh, yeah, absolutely.

Commentary

The therapist should maintain balance between both parents. This man's father's suicide was a significant part of the family history. To this point, the therapist has not focused on it. The therapist must use the time he has with the parent wisely. He now shifts the focus to this major life event. Part of the therapist's agenda is to help the father tell the story about his father in a balanced way. The daughter's story about her grandfather's suicide is that he gave up and was a failure. The father has a slightly different story and a significantly different understanding of the meaning of his father's suicide.

Dr. F.: So if we could just pick up with your father. On Saturday we'll spend a lot more time on your mother because I wouldn't want to leave that but I wanted to hear more about your father, too. We didn't really talk about him. . . .

Dad: We didn't talk about him very much.

Dr. F.: Maybe you want to pick up where you think would be important to get a sense of your father.

Dad: Okay, my father's identity. I think I said at some point yesterday that the socialism and all that was a complicated way of not being Jewish. In a way my mother was much more simplistic about not being Jewish. You know, with all this business with her family, whereas my father's way of dealing with this whole situation, and I identify very much more with my father than with my mother, was first of all the socialist thing, but I mean, this whole socialist culture was actually very Jewish. I once wrote something which apparently Jane hasn't seen in that same magazine, Z–, where the thing about my father appeared. There was a whole issue on Jewish identity and in talking about sort of the way I was thinking about it, I think this on some level represents the way my father was thinking about it, though I'm not sure that he would have formulated it that way. But it was very definitely a Jewish identity. I mean, my father's identification with a philosopher was primarily and in the first instance with Spinoza. In all kinds of ways, and I don't know how important, at least explicitly, the fact that Spinoza was a Jew was there, but I'm sure the identification with the iconoclastic Jew was extremely strong. That is sort of the way that I have resolved this to the extent that I have resolved it myself. I mean there could be a whole pantheon in this socialist Jewish tradition, one could rattle off, starting way back with Spinoza but then people like Freud and Marx and if you like, Trotsky. . . .

Dr. F.: These were like mentors for your father, I imagine?

Dad: Well, traditionally and there was the Vienna circle, which he was involved in. Of course, that was not primarily as much Jewish. There were a number of Jews in the secondary positions involved there, but the big philosophers were not Jewish. I don't know if you are familiar with that tradition at all. . . .

Dr. F.: Just enough to ask questions.

Dad: I mean, there was a professor of philosophy at the university who in 1936 was assassinated by one of his former students who claimed, I mean, who was clearly disturbed, but who gave as his motivation that this professor had destroyed his religious belief. Now, this guy was a Catholic, the student, but it would work for Jews, too. I mean, these people were extremely rationalistic, antitraditional, and the socialism was in there. I mean, the main thing was they were positivists but combined with Marxism, there were all kinds of contradictions there, too.

Dr. F.: These people were the community your father was involved in.

Dad: That was one aspect of it, the Vienna circle. The other aspect was the Socialist Party.

Dr. F.: That was the second community.

Dad: Yes.

Dr. F.: These two very powerful communities in Vienna.

Dad: Which overlapped but were not identical.

Commentary

This part of the interview is significant. The father gets a bit lost in detail again. The therapist understands this as a manifestation of the father's anxiety and brings the father back to a discussion about his own father. The therapist asks how his father tried to take care of him. One of the big questions in this family is how parents parent. The adult daughter never felt parented by her father. One of the consequences is that she has felt she had to be her father's caretaker. This stance has blocked the father from being a father to his daughter. One of the problems the daughter presented initially was that she felt abandoned by her father. She now saw this problem reoccurring in her adult relationships with men. The father's story about how his father tried to teach him and take care of him can potentially shift the daughter's thinking about him and facilitate her seeing him as a resource in her life.

Dr. F.: Now, when your father came to America, this is the part of the story that I would really like to understand both from the point of view of a 14-year-old and a 20-year-old. And then now looking back as a grown man. What did your father try to do? How did he try, as he told you, and as you felt it, to replace those very powerful communities in the new country?

Dad: Well, he didn't. I mean, he really rejected what was available. He became essentially a total loner and an outsider.

Dr. F.: It was different from how he behaved in Vienna.

Dad: Well, it was getting more that way in Vienna, too, of course. As you know that whole thing collapsed. I mean it collapsed in Vienna. Not just with the Nazis but with the onslaught of the Catholic reaction and the essential impotence of the socialists who couldn't cope with it at all.

Dr. F.: You remember yesterday, I asked you how your mother and your father prepared you for the move to the new country and you pondered that word. I remember you thinking about the word prepare. Then I got thinking about how he prepared you for the changes when he got here.

Dad: There were some real contradictions there, too. When I spent the summers in Chicago largely with him there was a question of how I was going to support myself. Now, his general tendency was that I should become Americanized. I made several very abortive attempts to do things like house-to-house salesmanship. I remember trying for two days to work for a firm. I can't remember the name but they were selling socks mainly. It was one of those things where you got a sample and the people would make orders. I couldn't do this at all and my father obviously couldn't do anything remotely like it but he thought I ought to do it and actually I had a lot of resentment against him thinking that I ought to do it, whereas he obviously wasn't able to do any of this practical stuff. And he had in fact a great deal of contempt for it. The most successful of the Viennese refugees in Chicago was Dr. P., who became a very big deal in sociology in the United States. At that time he was having something called the Bureau of Sociology, which later became the Bureau of Applied Social Research at Chicago University and he became the head of the Applied Sciences Department there and all kinds of stuff like that. But what he originated was the market research and public opinion polls. Not only to market stuff but also to political stuff. He had started something like that in Vienna, where they did a study of the effect of the Depression on an Austrian small-town, working-class community. You know, the demoralization with the unemployment and so on, using the kind of questionnaire and mass-interview kind of techniques which I think they originated at that time. And which he then brought here and he had tie-ups with a broadcasting system and they did something on early voter studies. I think this must have been in 1940, the 1940 election.

Eventually I sort of pressured my father, who knew P. very well. In fact, P. was in that generation about half way between my father and myself and was in a group. My father also had this large circle of students who were largely university students but who went to take courses with him at this People's University, where things were less rigid, less stultified, and P. was one of those people. P. was employing all kinds of refugees in Chicago, doing some of his interview stuff, doing statistical analysis, and I actually worked three summers for P. I managed to get my father to give P. a call, though I could have actually gone cold to talk to P. and that would have worked quite easily but I, you know, I wanted to get the introduction. I didn't really at that point, I guess, realize that I could have gone cold. My father called him and P. said, "Yes, of course, send him over." I went over and I worked there for three years in the summer mostly doing statistical analysis of stuff and met a bunch of other people who were working there and, you know, getting their beginnings, but my father would never come close to asking P. to do anything for him.

Dr. F.: Did that upset you, that he wouldn't do that?

Dad: Well, in a way. My father wasn't going to change, dammit! And he played out this role of the total outsider who was destroyed. But maintaining all his . . . well, it wasn't only his principles it was also his hang-ups.

Dr. F.: Now, looking back, you say this to yourself, but did you understand it a bit at the time, too?

Dad: Yes.

Commentary

The therapist now asks the father his theory about his own father. The theories we have about our parents affect the way we use them as resources. If we carry a theory that a parent is inadequate or a victim in the world, it is hard for us to learn positive lessons from that parent. It is important for adult children to see their parents as having valuable experiences they can draw upon to teach them about the world. The therapist's teasing out of the father his theory about his own father, has the potential to help the daughter rethink her theories about her father.

Dr. F.: As a young man, what did you say to yourself was going on with your father?

Dad: Well, to some extent I think I even formulated it, though I probably would not have said it explicitly. . . that he was sort of maintaining a sort of aristocratic . . . In fact, there were certain similarities with the destitute southern aristocrats in Virginia. You know, their maintaining the antebellum thing but who really came across like, what is the name of the woman in *Streetcar Named Desire*, the Tennessee Williams thing, you know who I'm talking about?

Jane: No, I don't.

Dad: Who wound up insane because she was this southern lady in twentieth-century New Orleans. This total sort of refusal to live in the real world. I could also see what it was. First of all, he clearly had a lot of resentment against people like P., who he felt, and lots of people felt, was selling out. Some of the worst aspects, from where we were sitting, of American capitalism. For instance, what came out of this same circle as P. was D., who is the father of motivational research and subliminal advertising and all those things. And were using essentially psychoanalytical methods to get people to buy stuff. And that was considered, you know, we thought of that sort of thing as a total sellout and my father refused to sell out and it killed him as a result.

Commentary

The therapist now introduces the notion that this man's father had heroic features. He encourages the father to talk about his father as a person who was true to himself and lived according to his values rather than perceive his father as a failure and a victim. To this point in her life this man's daughter has seen her grandfather as a victim. She has fought desperately not to be a victim in her own life and becomes enraged when she believes her father is presenting himself as a victim. In actuality, the family has been anything but victimized. They have been able, in their own way, to honor their values and beliefs. Unfortunately, prior to this point, the daughter had never heard her father talk about how his father taught him about loyalty and belief in yourself.

Dr. F.: That is what I was going to ask you about. Your father, from the way you tell the story, was betrayed, but he, as you tell the story, wasn't going to betray himself.

Dad: Well, he was the last of the Mohicans.

Dr. F.: You knew that at the time?

Dad: Yes and no. I mean, somewhere I knew it.

Dr. F.: Somewhere you knew it.

Dad: And somewhere I wasn't going to be that anachronistic and ridiculous myself except that I felt an enormous amount of guilt at the same time for the fact that I was betraying it, at least to some extent. And later on, of course, I became a supporter of all that. I mean, after my father killed himself that sort of, in many ways, compelled me to sort of take up where he left off in a way.

Dr. F.: In a way, and in a way not.

Dad: Well, but I see this enormous ambivalence and conflict about making it in this setting. On some level I was in enormous conflict about succeeding but having to do myself in.

Dr. F.: The ultimate paradox for you to sort out. You told the story yesterday about your father saying to move to the U.S., where you had a future. He came here, and as you tell the story this morning, it was important he didn't betray himself. Yet he wanted you to become American-like.

Dad: That's right.

Dr. F.: That wasn't betraying him. Your father knew that if you did those things that wasn't a betrayal of him. That was a way of honoring him by having a future.

Dad: But he was very ambivalent about the advice he gave to me, too. Because it was a question of can you make it with integrity. And the answer clearly was no, you couldn't.

Dr. F.: He came to that answer, or you came to that answer?

Dad: Well, there were very mixed messages. I don't know whether he was doomed not to be able to do it with integrity. I sort of tried in a way to have it both ways, which meant having it neither way.

Commentary

The therapist now asks the father to talk about what his father's suicide meant to him. This area has not really been discussed between father and daughter. The daughter feared that if she raised this issue with her father she would in some way, provoke him into a depression and/or suicide. The therapist, by remaining calm about the areas of suicide and death, permits the father to describe the meaning of his father's death to him. The therapist encourages the father to talk about how he said good-bye to his father and the meaning he attached to his father's way of saying good-bye to him.

The therapist assumes that if the adult daughter is able to hear how her father made peace with the way his father conducted his business in the world, she will be freed in part from feeling responsible for her father. She will then be able to view her father as a more positive force in her life.

Dr. F.: That takes us into your career and your family. Before we move into that, tell me about the suicide and what it meant to you. How did you understand it and how did you make peace with it? Can you speak to that?

Dad: How I made peace with it?

Dr. F.: How you understood it and then the process you went through, over the years, to make peace with it.

Dad: There were all these things. The last Mohican, Don Quixote, and a lot of tragic Jewish heroes of that type. Trotsky comes to mind, Marx, Spinoza himself. I had both great admiration and great contempt for that because it was another case of cognitive dissonance. Over the years I, more and more, have suppressed the contempt and emphasized the admiration. When I felt good about myself was when, at least temporarily, I made the grand gesture of defying.

Dr. F.: The contempt for it was what?

Dad: Well, first of all, the self-deception involved, you know, like Don Quixote, the posturing, which was something I did very much. In a way I'm doing it now, right now.

Dr. F.: How's that?

Dad: The sort of looking at the whole thing and understanding it and in a way being above it all by understanding it and by talking about it.

Dr. F.: Well, what would be a better way of honoring it?

Dad: I don't know that there is a better way. I don't know that there is a resolution of this contradiction.

Dr. F.: Because I wonder about that. What is a better way of honoring the important lessons from all of those people that you just mentioned? How do we find a way to honor them without becoming like them?

Dad: See, I'm not even so sure that becoming like them is worse than other available alternatives. I guess where I finally wind up is that it is all part of the human what, tragedy, comedy, tragicomedy, whatever. And that all of those elements are there, and, you know, including what I see and including what I am and what we all are. And I don't know, this whole problem of what the hell do Jews do with all their heritage and history and so on. I think all the extremes are equally absurd.

Commentary

The father has become tangential again, and the therapist brings him back to his issues with his own father. He asks the father about the last communication he had with his own father. This communication was in the form of a suicide letter that the daughter had discussed in a previous session. The daughter had seen this letter as evidence that her grandfather was unable to say good-bye to her father properly. From the father's discussion of the letter we see that in fact the letter was very fatherly.

Dr. F.: Jane mentioned to me that your father wrote you a letter. His last letter was to you. When she came back after seeing you she told me what she remembered you telling her was in the letter.

Dad: And I can't find the letter. I don't know where it is. I've been looking for it.

Dr. F.: I want to ask you about the meaning you attached to the letter when you got it. What did you tell yourself the letter was about?

Dad: Well, there were various things even then. But, of course, the period immediately after my father's suicide was one in which I couldn't think clearly at all. I sort of did read, glimpsed various things, and so on, but I went to Chicago to tell my mother. I had that job to do that. This was in March '40, so I was in the second semester of my first year of graduate study at the University of Pittsburgh. I simply quit and went to Chicago and spent until the following fall with my mother. So however I saw it at that time I certainly didn't form any clear picture of any of it. But there was a lot of irony in it, looking at it. In terms of feeling about it I remember that. I mean, all this advice he was giving me, which was all stuff which he himself couldn't do. He was also trying to make me feel that I was not doomed to the same kind of fate. That was when he was talking about how my childhood was. Everybody loved me and I was very much appreciated, and so on. Which on some level was true but it was also largely being part of that dream world which didn't really see the contradictions which were going on in our life in Vienna and the life of that whole Jewish community in Vienna. Which has been satirized very well by some Israeli writers since then. I don't know if you know A., but there was this one novel about these clearly Viennese Jews, though it wasn't identified that way, living in this spa, which was clearly Baden, which was a spa near Vienna. You know, after the Nazis came in and sitting there and sort of calling each other "Herr Professor" and all that kind of stuff. And in the end when they found that the transport that they were being sent in consisted of cattle cars, they were saying, well, this obviously means that they don't mean to take us very far. Which was basically the government was benevolent. That whole kind of business. I'm sort of getting off the point.

Dr. F.: You were saying that your father wanted to really make sure you weren't doomed to the same outcome as he.

Dad: Yes and partly, at least, he was telling me about contrasts between what he considered to be his very unhappy childhood and my very happy childhood and at the same time I always had to count on the fact that my mother was going to get depressed and that I had to deal with that. You know, that I should form a good and loving relationship with a woman for my personal life and so on. He, for some reason which isn't clear to me, very strongly suspected that I was gay, which absolutely wasn't true. But I remember there was this guy who was one of the people in Virginia at the college at whose house I was living part of the time with his parents, his family. These were mainly local people at the college and so they were living at home. They put me up and I had a room there and all that. He sent me a postcard while I was in Chicago staying with my father which he signed "Love and kisses, Harry." Which was sort of the jargon of the day. My father took this very seriously and was very worried about it.

Dr. F.: Well, he had anxieties about you.

Dad: Yes.

Dr. F.: He tried to make sure that you had a future different from what he felt he had, at least up to that point.

Dad: Yes.

Dr. F.: You got married and had two children.

Dad: That was after he was dead.

Dr. F.: That's right. In that letter there were instructions that he wanted to leave with you about how you could be happy and successful in the world.

Dad: Right.

Dr. F.: They were instructions, and they were anxiety.

Dad: Yes, very much so. He also tried to make it that it was not a letter which he had written before committing suicide; I mean, he apparently thought he could conceal that fact from me. Though how the hell he thought that I don't know.

Dr. F.: But you think he tried to do that?

Dad: Well, the letter said something about it was written because he was almost run over the other day and he was afraid.

Dr. F.: He wouldn't have time to finish it.

Dad: Yeah, and that, but he left it open on his desk when he killed himself to be found to be sent to me.

Dr. F.: He didn't actually put it in the mailbox himself; it was someone else.

Dad: They found it. There were all these obvious contradictions.

Commentary

The therapist elects to spend the remaining time in this session on how the father tried to build his own family. He asks about the legacies the father carried from his own family into his family of procreation. The therapist uses the term "legacy" purposely to emphasize the link between the generations. The therapist encourages the father to talk about how he tried to father his daughters. It is helpful for his daughter to hear these stories, to dispel her own mythology about her father's behavior in the family.

Dr. F.: Very interesting. Maybe in the next session we'll come back to that. You might have some more questions about that. But one thing that really has intrigued me is how we carry on certain lessons, certain legacies from one generation to the next. I would like to hear you talk a bit about your own children. What about this history did you feel was important? What about your father, their grandfather, did you think was important? What did you want to make sure got carried on as they were growing up?

Dad: You are now asking me to think back how it felt then?

Dr. F.: Right.

Dad: The integrity was extremely important. You know, speak the truth no matter what. I remember recently reading something which said, "The function of the intellectual is to speak the truth." That could have been written by my father in exactly those words. One of the things my father said at one time was, and this was a quote from some Greek philosopher way back, "I would rather write the nation's songs than rule them," or "I'd rather be right than president," or something like that. That kind of thing. In other words, integrity was more important than material success, which sort of in a way was justifying himself. Intellectual clarity was extremely important. That is part of integrity but also sort of integrity in terms of not allowing yourself to kid yourself about things, which was a really ironical thing, because while on the one hand he had that and in many ways could follow it through, in other ways there was an enormous amount of self-deception involved in this whole setup obviously. Which I think I also already felt as a child. I always had this very strong impulse about the emperor having no clothes, including my parents. My father had that role also in terms of the powers that be. But my parents were in the same position. All of that was certainly something I tried to communicate whether by word, but more by example to my children.

Dr. F.: Do you remember telling them stories about their grandfather as they were growing up?

Dad: Apparently not very much. See, there is this whole business with the portrait that Jane has told me about where I even repressed the fact that I had that at that time. I thought my mother had it, or rather I couldn't remember what had happened to it. I know I had it, but somehow I thought I had gotten it from my mother from Vienna, whereas I had it all the time. Jane told me I sort of alternated between displaying it and hiding it, depending on, I guess, how I felt. All of that I have completely repressed.

Dr. F.: How many years after your father's death was your marriage?

Dad: I met D. when I returned to Pittsburgh in the fall of '44, so that was like six months after my father's suicide. We started our relationship very soon after that. We were both highly disturbed at that time. I guess we found each other. We didn't get married until '47, and that was basically because I moved from Pittsburgh to NYU because the professor moved from Pittsburgh to NYU and took a whole bunch of us with him. There was no way in which D. could be with me in New York without us getting married. I mean, in terms of her family, without us getting married. Whereas in Pittsburgh we were both students there and basically her parents didn't know what the setup was. But she couldn't be a student at NYU, as an undergraduate at that time. So when she wanted to move, when I went to NYU, she went back to the family home but then we wanted to live together and the only way we could do that was to get married.

Dr. F.: Do you remember how much of this history you shared with D. and how much of her history she shared with you before you decided to get married?

Dad: We talked a lot about these things, but a lot of the way I'm talking about it now I wasn't conscious of myself. As far as her history, well, I knew a little. They were non-Ashkenazi Jews. This was all very interesting. I met some of her family and she talked about her other uncle, the one who had muscular dystrophy, I'm sorry, multiple sclerosis, who had apparently made an extremely strong impression on her. I knew all about that, and of course, I met her parents. And I saw what I felt already at that time, an extreme dissonance between the story about her father and the way her father seemed to me. . . .

Commentary

The father has attempted to triangle the therapist in around stories about his former wife. This dynamic is common when parents are divorced. The therapist must avoid this therapeutic trap and stay focused on how the father tried to make the family safe for his children.

Dr. F.: So both of you came together with each of you experiencing a lot of losses.

Dad: Yes, and a lot of conflict.

Dr. F.: A lot of conflict. How did you protect your children from those losses? What did you decide to do to protect your two girls from those losses?

Dad: I don't think that we would have ever formulated it that way.

Dr. F.: This is more of a retrospective question, looking back. What do you think you did, not consciously, but what was the pattern?

Dad: My pattern basically was to pretend that it all was a big success story. I was trying to show that it was all a big success story. See, this was part of that very complicated business there because one of the things I was trying to do was to sort of rehabilitate my father by showing that actually it could be done the way he was trying to do it here and do it that way. To do both, to make a big success out of being the great outsider. It's been done, at least on some level, by others, but I couldn't do it.

Dr. F.: You made a tremendous effort.

Dad: Yes. To have my integrity and eat it too. I think that was sort of what—

Dr. F.: That was the driving force.

Dad: Yes. And then I guess by building that I would at the same time make a positive identification for my kids with that history.

Dr. F.: Well, the other side of my question is what were you worried would happen to your girls if they knew more about this history. Not the success story, but the other side of the story.

Dad: I guess that the way I would answer that is that if I could turn this whole thing into a positive thing while knowing all about it, then that in itself would make it possible for them to also do good. Does that make any sense?

Dr. F.: It makes a lot of sense to me.

Dad: I mean, I don't know that I ever thought of it, but I think basically that was sort of my script. Maybe it was the benefits of adversity or all kinds of stuff, I don't know. The overcoming of fate.

Dr. F.: Do you remember the first time you told either one of your daughters how your father died?

Dad: I never did tell them. I mean, how they first found out, from what Jane has told me is that I apparently left a letter in a typewriter which is sort of, I mean, thinking about it now, is sort of my father leaving the letter when he killed himself. Both trying to conceal it and to show it because this was when I left, when we were in Pittsburgh and basically I felt I had to leave and I moved out. And somehow that letter was, I still don't know how I did that except it must have been half intentional, half unintentional. That is the only way I can honestly account for it, because the idea that it was just a total accident I don't buy. But I don't remember it even now.

Commentary

The therapist concludes the interview with a powerful reframe. He suggests that the father kept the memory of his father alive through his behavior. Rather than talking about his father he honored him in the fundamental decisions he made about the way he assumed the roles of a father, a professional, and a man. This reframe offers the daughter an opportunity to rethink her father's behavior toward her, in the family, in his career, and in the world at large.

This type of reframe is important. One of the purposes of the family-of-origin session is to challenge the family mythology to allow for new learning between family members.

Dr. F.: So if I follow you, you kept the memory of your father alive in the family in a very unusual way. Not by talking directly about him but by organizing your life in a certain way.

Dad: I don't know how much I talked about him. Did I talk about him? You don't think so. I mean, there was this business with the portrait, right?

Jane: Yes.

Dad: Did we talk about that ever?

Dr. F.: Let's leave that question for tomorrow. Jane, you will have a chance to ask your father some questions about this and other things then.

Impact of Family-of-Origin Sessions on Adult Child

Following is an interview with the adult child (Jane) and her husband that took place after her family-of-origin sessions. It illustrates the impact of the sessions and the subsequent review of them on videotape. The interview is divided into three major parts. During the first part the therapist questions the adult child about what she learned from watching the sessions on video. The questions are consistent with those that would be asked of any adult child after a family-of-origin experience.

The second part of the interview examines the impact of the sessions on the couple's relationship. If the timing of the family-of-origin sessions was appropriate, one would expect to see a repositioning of the partners with each other. The therapist will want to determine if the nonparticipating partner experienced the family-of-origin sessions as a positive experience in the family's life. In the third part of the interview the therapist will assess whether the partner benefited from observing the family-of-origin sessions. An indirect benefit is that the nonparticipating partner often begins to think more about his or her family-of-origin issues after observing the other partner's experience.

The therapist helps the couple evaluate the overall experience. If the timing of the family-of-origin sessions was right, the couple will be near the end of therapy. If each adult child has significantly repositioned in his or her family of origin, then he or she will use ongoing sessions more as consultations for further repositioning moves in the family. At this stage, the intensity of the therapy decreases significantly, and couple is no longer seen on a regular basis. The sessions are governed more by the adult child's need to debrief from experiences with family than by reactivity toward the partner or being stuck in emotional struggles.

Case Discussion and Commentary

The therapist opens the session by asking the adult child, Jane, about her reaction to the tape of the session with her father. He is especially interested in the difference between how she experienced her father's story in the session versus her experience of watching it alone, on tape.

Dr. F.: Tell me what you experienced after watching the tape.

Jane: It has mainly to do with myself and my interaction with my father more than the contents. But my feeling about that is that I know I want to see them again and again, after I graduate and I have time, at which point I'm sure all kinds of stuff will come up with the contents. More and more. There were basically two things that struck me from the last session, where I was talking with him, and the first was that for years Allan has said to me, and my father has said to me, how irritating it is for them to interact with me at certain times because I go around and around and around asking a question. I can't just say "I wanted to ask you this," I end up sort of interrupting myself at least three times and so, I saw myself doing that. I couldn't believe it because I've been sort of aware of it but I've never seen it. It was very striking to me and I guess it is particularly so with my father and it was for the very reasons that we were talking about. It was clear that although I felt like I just wanted to be frank with him, I constantly had to make sure that he understood and couch it in a way. I just saw it and it just blew me away. So that was the first thing. And having seen it I honestly feel like I don't have to do that anymore. I mean, I'm sure that I still do, but it's like something is gone. It feels wonderful. I actually spoke to him the next day. I called him to say I had seen them and that conversation was different, you know, because it was gone. It felt wonderful. It really felt wonderful. So that has sort of been almost like a high for me. It's a very liberating thing.

The other thing that I think I got an insight into had to do with the content of one of those questions. It was the one that I kept going around and around and saying, "I couldn't quite feel what it was that was wrong between us," you know, it came up at several points, and yet at one point you said directly, "Look, Jane, is there anything you feel like you still want to ask your father that hasn't been dealt with yet?" And I said, "Not contentwise but there is something. I don't know what it is, it's more the feelings," and then I said something to the effect that my father told all these stories about things and that was all very well and good but there is something about the feeling and . . . When I saw it it became clear to me what it was that I wanted or what it was that I felt was missing and it was that I didn't feel at any point in the session and also in my life as his child, not so much adult child but child, that he approached these issues, questions that I would ask him from a perspective of his impact on me as a child. From the perspective of my needs basically but that any explanations or any behaviors really were centered around his own fears, around his own unresolved stuff but without regard to this is my child, my needful child to whom I need to be responsible. It wasn't there. That is what it was, you know, and I was able to tell that to my father, too, in our conversation over the phone and he was very quiet and said he would have to think about that but that he knew that one of the things that he was consciously terrified of as a parent was that he was responsible, that he was having an impact in that kind of way. So he just left it that he would have to think about it. But it felt, it all felt very good. First of all, I felt like my need for that was diminished by recognizing that that was my need so I don't feel like I was, I guess in your words, telling him that you need to change and do this because I know he can't change and do that. Those needs were not met as a child. I know that now. That lessens the need in me. That's my feeling about it now and he didn't feel at all from what I could gather, defensive about it. He just wanted to think about it. So that felt very good. I can't tell you, very, very good.

The only other thing that I want to make sure I mention is that I was also more acutely aware watching the video than I was at the time, although even at the time it occurred to me, that when Karol sees it there are two points when she comes up in a way that I know she is going to be hurt. One was when you asked my father something about how he feels about the openness of our relationship, my father's and mine. He said, "I would say it is open and has been for years. Now, if you ask me about Karol, that's another story," and you said, "Well, I won't ask you about Karol." And then the other point was when I said that I had been struck on a few sessions earlier on describing Ella, my grandmother, to you, that the first thing I had said was she is not a well person and that I had realized that I wouldn't say that about any other person except maybe Karol. When I saw them I realized that she will see it and hear those things and that it will be very hurtful to her.

Commentary

Jane presents an interesting dilemma when she talks about her sister's reaction to seeing the tape. As was mentioned earlier in the chapter, it is not certain how adult children will hear their parents' story. However, it is a story that should be made available, at some time, to all members of the family. The therapist should never encourage the parent to speak negatively about family members. One way to learn how to make this procedure more positive for families is to continually assess how each family experiences the family-of-origin exercise. The therapist asks Jane to inform him about her sister's reaction to the tape. This type of feedback helps one understand how delicate this operation actually is.

Dr. F.: So you're concerned a bit about your sister's reactions to those two points.

Jane: I don't want it to put distance between us.

Dr. F.: We'll talk about that. I have some reservations about sending tapes to siblings who have not been involved in the process.

Jane: She's got it already.

Dr. F.: Well, then we'll learn something from it and then it'll help me with figuring out my reservations. I would appreciate you tracking that because I have some concerns about that. That is one part of the process that I'm not too certain about. People who are not involved in the process seem to hear the tapes differently, and that is what I wanted to ask you more about. I think people tell stories that are important to hear. Whether we hear them with new ears, or we hear them with old ears is really the important thing.

Allan: Certainly she will be aware that there was no censorship going on. So whatever people feel that is how it is and that has an impact.

Commentary

The therapist checks on the degree of detachment Jane had while listening to her father's story. Asking about what was different between hearing her father's story during the session and watching it on tape helps the therapist to assess Jane's ability to be observational about her parent's story.

Dr. F.: Yes. On that note, about how one hears things, you were in the room and you remember how you heard it in the room and then you watched it and you heard it once removed. Can you make a few comments on what was different, hearing it in the room and hearing it once removed?

Jane: Gosh, well, again, and I feel sort of embarrassed saying this, but it is definitely the session with my father where I was seeing, hearing myself that was definitely the most striking for me. I feel like the first session, which is the only other one I saw of the video, there wasn't a striking difference. I feel like I was actually very attentive at the time. I guess there might have been places where something my father said triggered a thought that then didn't allow me to be as fully attentive as I otherwise would and so seeing it the second time I could catch some things that I didn't the first time, but there wasn't a sort of tangible difference in perception. I don't think, at least for that first one.

The second one, which I have not seen yet, which had more to do with him being my parent, I'm very eager to see it because, you know, I'm not sure what will be new there for me. Seeing myself, seeing yourself on video is very powerful stuff; it's unbelievable. I mean, to me, because I never have . . . it's just a revelation. My sense of myself is very different from what I saw. And as I say the dynamics of our interaction—I had no sense of that. During the time of that third session I remember telling you later that I felt somewhat shut down. So although I was there and asking questions, there was something foggy almost because I was groping and trying to feel things. There was definitely something emotional going on with me, I mean it was an anxiety or something that was there that was coloring the interaction. So then seeing it, I could see it there. I could see my father's responses also much more, in a much more detached way. I'm not doing a very good job articulating what, it was just a lot clearer.

Dr. F.: Watching it rather than being in the room.

Jane: Yes.

Commentary

The therapist now emphasizes the importance for Jane to stay with her story. By asking Jane how watching it alone and watching it with her husband would be different, the therapist is suggesting that one has to develop an ability to separate out other people's reactions to one's story from one's understanding of one's own story.

Dr. F.: Now, if you had watched that tape with Allan the first time, what do you think would have been different from watching it alone?

Jane: I'm not sure except that my immediate thought is that I would have felt the need to explain things to him, so stop it, and lest you hear such and such let me explain that in fact, this is sort of . . . catching him up on background. I don't know what but I would have felt the need to explain things, although Allan is exceptionally open. I wouldn't envisage him interrupting, I don't think he would do that. But I would probably want to, tend to explain things.

Dr. F.: It would have put your thinking at two different levels, Allan's understanding and what you needed to see.

Jane: Just see it and not worry about how other people would perceive it. That's true, but I am extremely eager to see it together.

Commentary

Jane's discussion about what she learned from the tape and her recognition of the importance of seeing it alone first are impressive. Her statement that she would like to view it with her husband to help him understand her family story is also significant. It appears as though Jane is ready to embrace more intimacy with her husband. One indication that partners are ready to be more intimate with each other is their curiosity about each other's stories. When partners defend or react to each other's stories, they create distance between them. However, when one is curious rather than judgmental about the partner's story, it is a sign that there is a marked decrease in the distance that self needs to feel comfortable and safe in a relationship. Jane appears to be ready to tell her husband her story without worrying about his judging it or being reactive to it.

Dr. F.: Why is that important, that you do that together?

Jane: To bring us closer.

Dr. F.: How would it bring you closer?

Jane: Because he will have that much more of a glimpse into who my father is, how that has shaped me, and it will just bring him into my family more.

Dr. F.: In a different way.

Jane: Yes. Because he will be learning about my grandparents, and more details about my father's situation and his responses, and his parents' responses and his own description, my father's own description of our immediate family with my mother and sister and myself and then watching my father and me interacting. I want him to see that. I think it's sort of obvious, but I don't know, maybe it's not.

Dr. F.: Just wondering. The thing about David and having this for him at a later date, what do you think about that?

Jane: Very glad, very glad to have it. There are so many things about David that I've wanted to bring up in the various sessions with you but I haven't. One thing just occurred to me that I hadn't thought since we left here the time that he was here. I asked him that night how it had been for him and he said, "Okay." Glad there were Legos to play with and stuff, and then he said, "You didn't talk about the Nazis." Blew me away!

Dr. F.: Isn't that interesting. That's a direct quote.

Jane: Direct quote, "You didn't talk about the Nazis." Now, I've been aware that this has been something that he's been aware of since we went to a seder the three of us. In April, we went for the first time as a family and part of the ceremony involved lighting candles for —

Allan: By survivors . . .

Jane: By children of survivors or survivors, and in fact there was a choir that sang a number of songs, including resistance songs from the Warsaw ghetto. There were slides that one of the women who was there had gone back and taken of Auschwitz.

So that was happening at the time among all kinds of other things. And he wasn't troubled at the time, although he really perked up during one of the resistance songs. They were talking about guns and fighting and he asked me about that. Guns have been an issue in our house with regard to him for a couple of years now. He's almost four, so about two years. He really likes to play with guns, and I have to face it. It's been an issue that I feel a lot better about now. Over the past half year or so, there was a time when it was extremely troubling to me. I mean he is not — how can I put this? — there is nothing about him that is bullyish and he's not cruel. There is nothing like that. So I have never been worried about that but he loves guns, makes guns out of Legos, out of Duplo, wants to buy guns, and I've always said, "Look, I don't want to spend money buying guns," and I've explained to him why I don't like guns and there have been battles around that. In a store where he told me once, "Please, Mum, buy me this gun!" and I said, "I really don't want to buy you a gun!" And he said, "Well, I'll just make them out of Duplo, I'm sick of it!" and he's doing this in front of the cashier and I just said, "I'm sorry." He gets an allowance now and I've told him if he really wants to save up his allowance and buy himself a gun, that's okay, but I just don't want to buy guns. Well, so there has been that sort of an issue and he knows why I don't like them and you know. . . .

Allan: I have an anecdote. Just this morning a friend was dropping in before both were brought to day care. On his lunch box was G.I. Joe, and David made a point of getting his mama to come down here and say, "See, look, he's got G.I. Joe on his lunch box!"

Jane: G.I. Joe on his lunch box, right. So I just, in a very relaxed way, I said, "Ooh, it's so violent, I don't like them." I said, "I know you kids like them, but I don't like them," and that was that. I let it go. So I'm very curious what is going on. I know part of David's desire is very much connected to my strong expression of dislike for that, I know that, but anyway, it feels basically okay, interesting but okay. So, this is taking me a long time. Oh, God, I hope I'm not doing what I saw myself doing on the cassette.

After that seder we rode the bus home and right away David, who was sitting next to me on the bus, said to me, "Are there Nazis in Vancouver?" I said, "There may be some people who have those ideas, but it's very different now." And he asked me something like do they look different, is there a Nazi on this bus, could I tell basically? Now I'm paraphrasing, but he was asking, "Do they look different. Do they look weird?" So I struggled to try and explain that being a Nazi was more what a person felt and thought and the whole issue of is it right to fight a Nazi, when is a gun appropriate . . . that whole thing came up. I was very aware of the struggle it created inside me about what I felt in fact about that. I can't remember exactly what our conversation was verbatim, but I remember saying, because I think he asked me, no, he said, "Well, I'd just kill 'em. I'd just get a gun and I'd just kill 'em if I saw a Nazi!" And I said, "Well, you may have to," except I said something first like "I don't think that would ever happen but maybe there would be a time when you would have to," and then I said something like "Myself, I would always try and talk to the person first because people can always change and you might be able to change that person's heart," something like that, and "I would always try that first, but you certainly have to be able to protect yourself." That basically took care of it and it was already late at night and I think he just fell asleep but there have been a couple of times when he has asked about Nazis, more or less out of the blue. I'm sure it's stuff that's going on in his head, and so having been able to hear from my father directly his own experiences for David when he sees these cassettes is going to be very, very important. As I'm speaking I'm also aware how much has been and still is unresolved in me about all this and it's showing up in him. It's inevitable.

Commentary

One of the principles underlying this approach is that an adult child who has begun to reposition in his or her family and become more aware of the powerful family themes, begins to reposition in all significant relationships. It follows then that there will be a difference in how the parents view their children. With this principle in mind, the therapist asks the parents about their concerns for their son. The parents mention that their son has become aware of the threat of Nazis. The therapist understands "Nazis" as a metaphor for an evil presence. However, he does not express this theory until the parents have had an opportunity to describe how they understand their son's issue. After the therapist has been able to assess what has shifted in the parents' reaction to this powerful theme he is able to introduce his hypothesis about the "Nazis" being a metaphor for being unsafe.

Dr. F.: What's your theory, each of you, about David's saying, "You didn't talk about the Nazis." What do you think he was saying when he asked that question?

Allan: Well, he knows that we accept just about anything he does but we draw a line about guns, so there must be something important about guns and that got to be fairly detailed by saying, "Well, it's okay, more or less, so long as it's playing, a water pistol or something," but Nazis are not, and G.I. Joe types that are realistic people are not. And my sense is that he has made a distinction, or we have helped him make the distinction between playing and playing for real. He knows that it's intimately connected with something in our past, something in ourselves. He senses that strongly, so that has much more meaning, hence the questions about the Nazis have much more meaning than about anything else. My sense is that he feels that something dreadful is associated with Nazis. He doesn't know enough, he doesn't have enough information to know, for instance, that he wouldn't walk across one on the sidewalk and that he might be threatened by that. And hence his question, I think, and the kinds of questions that he's been asking. He knows it's something that may in fact be occurring right now, although he does not know the details and that it has affected us and it may affect him. That's how I read all of that.

Dr. F.: And Jane, what's your theory about his association with this session and that question?

Jane: Well, I would just say that it's an anxiety for him and there is something unknown for him. He knows that why we come here is to talk about things that are troubling us and to help bring us closer together. I think that's basically how we talked about it.

Allan: In fact, I recall when we came with him riding back, do you remember he asked about Nazis.

Dr. F.: So Nazis for David would be a metaphor for what do you think?

Jane: Threat.

Allan: The unknown as well. We've gone to some efforts to describe something about it in a realistic way. I recall getting from the library a storybook that describes, tells the story of how a small Jewish kid is picked up and disappears and there is nothing more known about that.

Dr. F.: A metaphor for an evil presence. Nazis represent a metaphor for an evil presence that might affect his family and you're coming here as a way to get rid of that evil presence. Is that what you're saying that David was asking about?

Jane: Coming here to get rid of it . . .

Dr. F.: Or how he would understand your coming here.

Jane: Well, the other thing is that he knew that my father

was coming up here to see you and he certainly knows that the Nazis, I guess, were in power. I remember being so conscious of that as I tried to explain that to David, this is on the way back from the seder, what it means because when he said, "Are there Nazis in Vancouver," and I said, "There may be some," but I said something like "They are not in power now." I thought, God what does power mean to a 3-year-old? He has all these stories about people with powers, magical powers, right? So I tried to distinguish as best I could what it meant but that there was a time when there was an army of Nazis but not anymore. And that was a time when his grandfather was a young person so I think there is also that, more direct, that his grandfather was here talking about his past with you and that may have had to do with that but more symbolically, that we deal with troubles here.

Dr. F.: Well, I was curious. It's very interesting.

Allan: I was just going to say that I concur directly with what you said, that we come here to rid ourselves of the evil that Nazis represent.

Jane: Except.

Allan: Yeah, I wouldn't even qualify it.

Jane: Well, I have trouble with that because I think David sees Nazis as something outside of us, as well. I mean, you don't get rid of a bad guy by talking among ourselves.

Commentary

The therapist now attempts to take the couple to another level of understanding about how to free oneself from old themes. The therapist connects the theme of Nazis and the theme of grandfather as both representing loss. This idea is initially confusing to the couple. However, it stimulates their thinking about how these issues have gotten played out between the

generations. Their son struggles with the abstract notion of Nazis, the mother struggles with the meaning of the suicide of her grandfather, and the father struggles with the paradox of wanting to fit in yet be separate. Each generation has its own struggles. How they understand their struggles is to some degree, influenced by the multigenerational themes of loss, abandonment, and betrayal. In this family there are powerful themes of abandonment and betrayal. It is not surprising that their young son picks up themes about something scary and unknown. The son has his own way to gain control over his fears. It is important that the parents avoid overreacting to the son's attempts at mastery over his fears. If they can understand how these themes affect each generation, they can become more curious and less protective and defensive about the behavior of others.

Dr. F.: Well, that is why I said it's a metaphor for something more than a person or people. It's interesting to speculate on that. I just think that is such an interesting association. He can see that it's dealing with this thing called Nazis and it's such a powerful theme. It's like Grandfather was a theme, how he affected the family, but there was also what he represented about loss. I thought it was interesting how your father put into words the courageous act of his father, giving a whole different meaning to how his father chose to say goodbye.

There was one other thing I wanted to ask you that I had some reservations about. Have you watched the whole third session?

Jane: Yes, right to the end.

Dr. F.: I wanted to get your sense of it. Maybe your father made a comment to you when he watched it as well, about your grandmother. During that third session I debated about whether to raise this issue about how his mother somehow got to the sidelines and was dismissed as a psychiatric problem rather than as a creative person in her own right. I wanted to get your

thinking about the wisdom of that, and the impact it might have had on your father.

Jane: For my father I think it had a tremendously positive impact because what he said was you had raised the whole issue of his mother and how her competence got lost basically for the first time for him in that way. And as he said to me, it is something he wants to work on with his therapist. Now, were you asking me about the wisdom of your decision to ask that question?

Dr. F.: To raise it, to make his mother a competent person rather than keeping her an incompetent person.

Jane: Well, it's funny. There are a couple of thoughts I have. One is that I have a very strong tendency to keep her incompetent in my own mind. Although as a result of the sorts of questions and response my father gave it's more clear than ever that she had another side that people outside the family largely saw. So that she had quite a following of students even many years after. Well, I mean just the fact that she had a Ph.D. and was teaching and so on, speaks for itself, I guess. One thought is, see, I guess the way you phrased the question was something to the effect that my father didn't let her be competent because of his own perception somehow, that that was part of the dynamic there. One thing that struck me was that people can in fact behave very, very differently with different sets of people.

Dr. F.: Very, very important principle to remember. When you think about your sister, too, it's a very important principle to remember, but go on. We'll get back to that.

Jane: Right, I mean, so how much that whole interaction between my father and his mother and my grandfather and his wife and all of that, you know, the chicken and the egg. When she came to visit us in the States in our household she didn't behave like she did with her friends I'm sure.

Allan: It's probably true of Karol, too.

Jane: Yeah, I'm sure she's perceived by other people and behaves with other people very differently than she does with me, for sure, than with my parents. Yeah, I'm sure that's true.

Dr. F.: I'll ask you a very pointed question. It's one of those that you might think of a better answer to later. We'll come back to it. There has to be a loss, so this is a statement and a question. There has to be a loss in giving up the notion that Grandma is incompetent and also obviously there are gains to putting Grandma into more balance. Why don't you speculate for a second what the loss is to you in allowing Grandma to emerge as a competent person in the family. What do you give up?

Jane: I give up some kind of conceptual framework. It's the theory of, the picture of that family of my grandfather and grandmother and father and what it was like. Which is obviously what I am now trying to really understand freshly. But the other important thing which I was going to start to answer, the second part to your first question, before you asked this one, is that it very much has to do with my perception of my father, because although I never would describe him as not well, as the first words that would come out to describe him, unlike my description of my grandmother, I've seen him like my grandmother. I mean, he's gotten depressed and hospitalized like she did and all of that. I've never thought of my father as incompetent. On the contrary, but, oh, gosh, I'm sort of like blanking out. I guess I've thought of him as having episodes when he was depressed, episodes during which he was completely incompetent or completely disabled, not functional. I'm really blanking out . . .

Dr. F.: Well, I'll help you.

Jane: Okay.

Commentary

The therapist now begins to teach some systems principles. He is gently trying to provoke the couple to go further in their thinking about change and the cost of change. He focuses on the grandmother as a powerful example of how to stay safe around stories and suggests that letting go of their view of her as a sick person will cause them to rethink their entire relationship with the family. The therapist helps Jane understand that if her father gave up his old story about his mother he would have to mourn her loss all over again. Understanding this potential loss for her father helps Jane understand her own need to hold on to certain stories about him. If she changed her story about her father, then she would have to let him back into her life and run the risk of mourning all the years where she maintained distance from him. When the partners appreciate the ambivalence involved in giving up old stories about other generations they rethink their struggles to hold on to their stories about each other. The therapist can focus on any of the generations to illustrate how to initiate change between the generations. Sometimes it is easier for couples to think about change up a generation and then apply that wisdom to understand their own behavior.

Dr. F.: It's a speculation and then I want to ask Allan a few questions before we stop talking about this process. It's an interesting question. "What do you give up?" if you allow your grandmother to be seen as competent and what does your father give up if he allows his perception of his mother to change? Well, I think one thing your father would give up is what he said himself, that he needed safe distance from his mother. If you go back to the tape and listen to his story, you hear that it was a contest who went to bed first. I thought that was an interesting metaphor for getting safe from what he perceived as his mother's neediness.

Jane: His mother's neediness?

Dr. F.: Yes. That he perceived his mother's neediness,

which came out in what was called depression, because he knew his mother's competence. It was hidden from him as much as it was hidden from you. The emphasis was on what she wasn't, as he told his story, rather than what she was. And by focusing on what she was not, he was able, for whatever reason, to not let her be his mother, to take care of him. Now let's move over to you and your father. It's true I think you recognize always your father's competence but you, for some strange reason, told the story as if you were the caretaker, the emotional caretaker, and that you had to be very careful, tiptoe around your father 'cause you could kick him into a depression, kick him into suicide, or whatever. So the question, "What do you lose if you allow your grandmother to be seen as a competent person?" is the same question one could ask about you and your father. If you allowed yourself to truly see your father like you have more than ever come to see him, then you open yourself to his being your father in the fullest sense of the term, which means that you have to allow yourself to be fundamentally different with your father. It can no longer be the same with your dad, which produces a certain amount of safe distance because of the anxiety. It might sound a little confusing, but I think you've got the essence of the speculation.

Allan: I could add further, if you will, that to a large extent the way you've spoken to me about your father is how you would speak about your grandmother. I think that's pretty fair to say.

Jane: How I've spoken to you in describing him?

Allan: Yes. By emphasizing the incompetence. It's not a black and white thing because you continually extol his qualities but that's overshadowed by the negative characterization of him.

Jane: Which is what?

Allan: Well, you can't take what he tells you at face value because he might be high or he might be low. You can't tell him certain things, or you're cautious about telling him certain things because it might trigger off a depression or trigger off a grandiose thing and there's always a negative overtone about his state and his abilities that overshadows, the very positive things that you say about him. And I think it's entirely analogous. I mean, it's clear to me as you're talking about it that that's what it is.

Dr. F.: Well, I'll tell you why I raise it. Change is very delicate. We know how to be the same. I think you're very astute when you say you more or less hold on to this image of Grandmother. That is another one of those metaphors that are so powerful. So you immediately have to begin to ask how does it serve you to hold on to your stories, because that story was a story that you constructed, or your father constructed about his mother. And if we give up the story and we have to see the person in a different way we no longer can use the story to determine how we are with that person. We then have to become different because we can't say, "I can't be this way because. . . ." Most of us say it's that way because of the other, because of the consequences of what would happen to the other, or how the other would respond, that keeps us safely stuck and comfortably distant, and, I think, one-dimensional. It prevents us from being much more creative and increasing the range of our behaviors, emotionally, intellectually, and physically. Now, the other part of it is, and this is where the ambivalence about change comes in, most of us say we want things to be different. We want to be able to have a certain degree of intimacy and connection, yet most of our life we have only known how to be a certain way. So I think part of us doesn't believe we can deliver the goods by being different even though we say we want to be different. We haven't experimented with those behaviors.

Allan: Although in fact what you had said earlier when you spoke with your father following your viewing of the video is an indication that in fact you are changing.

Jane: Oh, yes, yes.

Dr. F.: The true telltale is not when there is cooperation. It's when the other person begins to appear to self like the old story and we are able to sustain a newness. That's what I wanted to work in here. That's what makes Grandmother such an intriguing one for you, because Grandmother and Father have similar stories. He danced around his mother, and you dance around your father. If he changes his story around his mother there has to be a whole bunch of sadness about his mother. The mother was there, he didn't allow Mother to come in. Well, that is going to be interesting as he tells you about it. You are going to learn something. There has to be some grieving and sadness about lost opportunities. This is without malice or intention. We lose our way around our mythology about each other. I think you two are doing a remarkable job of nipping this in the bud. It really prevents people in relationships from fully appreciating each other's complexity. But there are a few questions I want to ask you about this one, Allan, that would help me, too, with this process. I make an assumption that it is okay at any given time to spend more time with one person than the other because it generalizes. So how much of being an observer to Jane's work have you been able to apply to your own?

Allan: Well, just right now this conversation in two ways. One I could really see, when you talked about tinkering with the stories that's exactly what this has been all about. But moving beyond that and realizing that with me and my mother it's been exactly the same. Specifically when you spoke about Jane's father viewing his mother as being incompetent, I suspect that I have been much the same with my own mother and that I need to revise that. I don't have an awful lot of information to work on, but the parallel is entirely there. So I think that's one very obvious thing for me. Beyond that I can't say now.

Commentary

The therapist is now trying to assess how the husband has been affected by remaining on the sidelines of his wife's work on family of origin. It is prudent for the therapist to engage the uninvolved partner to ensure that he or she will not interfere in a negative way with the work. If the partner feels left out or ignored, his or her anxiety may intrude on the work. If the therapist is respectful about the partner's reactions and reaches out and solicits his or her thinking about the process, the couple is more likely to develop a partnership in which each supports the other in the family-of-origin work.

Dr. F.: Jane first watching the tapes by herself, rather than inviting you in, what did you say to yourself that was about?

Allan: Frankly, I was too preoccupied with other things to be concerned about it except to know that Jane was eager to see them, to see the tapes in spite of the real pressures for her to do nothing but write her thesis. So it's obviously drawing her with a tremendous pull and I don't think I've had too many thoughts beyond recognizing that. I mean, clearly I would like to see the tapes and I feel that more strongly now than I did before. Before it was sort of minute but I sort of hold off, ward off any of these temptations by the realization that it's too busy now. I couldn't do it justice.

Dr. F.: If it weren't too busy, if there were not as many demands, at what point would you have felt secondary or pushed out of the process?

Allan: I'm not sure I understand the question.

Dr. F.: Well, you were saying because of the demands on you it works for you. I'm just wondering if you didn't have all these demands, with this focus on Jane, do you think there would have been a point where you would have felt that your agendas were not being attended to enough? Your part in the process was being ignored?

Allan: I don't know. Let's put it this way: I can only base my experience on the time that we actually spent here and, as in this morning, most of the session has been dialogue between the two of you. So using that as a basis, it can't help but be one where I'm directly and primarily involved if only because of the fallout of the process; the change is going to affect us. I guess another way of saying it is that I feel that my job for Jane is to empower her, to support her, to be there for her as much as I can. If it means going through that process for her, that's what it means. So even though it may be totally concerned with Jane it's also my job to be fully attentive and fully participant. I trust, as an act of faith, it will have an impact on us. I don't know if that's really what you mean but it is more or less—

Dr. F.: No, no, that helps. Now, for you Jane, do you begin to think about Allan, and his being more on the sidelines. Does it worry you?

Jane: That Allan is on the sidelines? It doesn't worry me, but I am actually, well, if I say longing, it's a bit too strong a word, but I very much want the same for him, and that goes back years. Wanting some of that to be explored and wanting some of the stories to be explored, although when you first asked Allan at what point would he have started feeling like his own agenda wasn't being met I remembered that when it was more focused on Allan around the time of his trip to Ottawa and so on, there was a point where I said, "I want to go back to Dr. S. and I need to meet more than every two weeks because I got all this stuff and I'm having dreams" and so on. Certainly, I hope and I trust that when your turn comes, which should be soon, that that will not be the response that I have. Many of my needs have been met but that did happen to me, that's for sure.

Dr. F.: A lot of people would say, "Well, why do you even bother with the couple when you could see one person and do this? Why have the two people here?" But there is the power of the spin-offs from it. It's like keeping it really connected without the other person doing something apart from the relationship. But I have to be very attentive to the ebb and flow of that sort of thing. It has to be in balance. Now, I think the two of you are really wonderful with each other because you give each other a lot of room to work on that and you do think about it for yourselves. You've come a long way on that one.

Allan: We've made a commitment to each other, as in Jane looking after David until I finished my thesis. That was a two-year commitment. That was difficult for Jane. And I've made the reciprocal commitment, and you know, it states how we want to relate with each other. That's just an extension of that idea.

Dr. F.: I guess the important thing to always remember is where you end up, not being concerned with any one point in the process. A lot of people really have trouble with that because when your needs kick in, you're not thinking about where you're going. It's what's happening at this moment that really stirs up a hornet's nest. Sitting here I have to be attentive to that. I know where we're going, but at any point in the process it's always good to make sure that the assumptions are the same on that notion. So I did introduce that concern. That had to be addressed. I just can't say, "Well, believe in the process."

Jane: Yeah. There will be times, I hope less and less, but anyway there will be times when there will be urgent needs, I mean, things will come up and so on. Certainly if Allan had urgent need at any point during the past month or two months when it's been more focused on me, I hope I would be able to say, "Deal with it because the other stuff can wait."

Allan: Well, look, I do have a thought that I want to bring up but I'm not in a hurry to bring it up, either. Nor is there time, really. Well, the thought won't go away. If it's postponed to the next time I can live with that.

Dr. F.: Let's stop here.

Commentary

The therapist discusses the importance of both partners being involved in the process. He makes the point that although both partners work on self issues, it is crucial that they bring the new learning back into the relationship. One of the major objectives of the family-of-origin exercise is to produce deeper and more solid connections between the generations. Each adult child must develop the ability to be more connected with significant family members. As well, the partners must be able to bring wisdom and caring to each other and, together, to their children. The therapist's task is to encourage the individual to introduce the solid part of self in all important relationships. This is the vision the therapist tries to impart to the couple.

9

Ending Family Therapy with Couples

The Termination Process

The therapist should be alert to indications that a couple is ready to terminate therapy. Once a couple has progressed through the middle phase of therapy, the partners have begun to assume more responsibility for change. Partners who have repositioned themselves in significant ways with their extended-family members speak of their accomplishments with a sense of ownership. They consistently use the sessions as an opportunity to discuss their repositioning moves. There is a noticeable decrease in conflict. The partners have become their own experts and no longer turn to the therapist for problem resolution. They consistently discuss what they have learned from their own families. They demonstrate increased interest and enjoyment around family contacts and no longer need distance to get emotionally safe. They seldom shift into blame and disappointment over the behavior of other family members. The degree of emotional intensity decreases and the partners present many more stories about being creative and spontaneous with various family members.

The partners also report about changes in other systems in their lives. For example, they may have rethought their work situation or find that their friendships have taken on a different meaning. It is important for the therapist to elicit information about change in other systems. If there has been a significant repositioning of self with extended family, there will be changes throughout a person's social network. There is a general sense of being the master of one's own fate. Individuals who have moved into this phase of therapy consistently take responsibility for their own choices and are not easily defeated by other people's reactions to these choices.

Prior to terminating therapy, the sessions should be reduced in frequency. In the initial stages of family therapy with couples, the sessions usually run weekly. After the couple has shifted into the middle phase of the work, the sessions should be twice monthly. During the end of the middle phase, approximately one session per month is appropriate. During this phase the partners themselves are responsible for experimenting with being different in their families. Time is required to set up visits, conduct the visits, and then attend a session to discuss the visits. By the time a couple has moved into the end of the middle phase, it is appropriate for the sessions to be less frequent. Less frequent sessions encourage the couple to take more responsibility for their changes, as well, they will be less likely to see the results as connected with the therapy itself. During frequent sessions, couples have a tendency to give the credit for their change to the therapy. When the frequency of the sessions is reduced and each partner is asked what he or she learned between sessions the therapist is sending the message that any changes are a result of the partners' hard work rather than the process of the therapy hour. This message is central to the ending process. The partners should terminate with a solid sense of their own power, expertise, resources, and wisdom.

When the therapist sees that the partners have consolidated their gains and are generally able to use problems and crises as opportunities to learn about self and to experiment with being different, termination is indicated.

Planning for the Therapy Session

When the therapist and couple have decided, after consultation, to end therapy formally, it is wise to plan a termination session. The session offers a unique opportunity for the therapist and the couple to learn, in greater depth, what the overall process has meant. It is helpful for the couple to reflect on the overall process, to appreciate how far they have come. It is a unique opportunity for the therapist to learn about his or her theory and what approaches made a significant difference to the couple. The couple, being consumers of the service, are the experts on how this particular work has affected them. It is wise for the therapist to use the learning and experience of the couple either to modify his or her approach and/or gain greater confidence in various strategies, procedures, and general interventions. Only by listening to how clients experienced the therapy can one truly develop a model relevant to couples' realities.

In preparation for the termination session, the therapist should ask the couple to reflect on the overall process so they can come to the session prepared to discuss it. Prior to scheduling the termination session, the therapist should ensure that neither partner is ambivalent about ending therapy. If any ambivalence is expressed it should be discussed and worked through prior to setting up the last session. It is important that both partners agree that the timing is right for ending. If the therapist has taken the couple through the three stages of the middle phase, for the most part they will have already emotionally terminated the therapy process. The final session allows the couple to have a ritual that formalizes the ending. It also provides the therapist with additional information about how people say good-bye.

Structure of the Termination Session

The purpose of the termination session is to review and assess the therapeutic experience.

There are three parts to the termination session. The first part focuses on the learning that has come from repositioning with extended family members. The therapist will ask questions about what has changed in significant relationships. He or she will inquire about the remaining problems and how self has learned to deal with them. He or she will also identify the remaining pockets of anxiety and examine how the connections between family members have changed over time.

The second part of the termination session focuses on the couple describing for the therapist the highs and lows they experienced in the therapy. The therapist asks questions such as: What were some of the disappointments? What areas would the couple have liked the therapist to deal with more effectively? What would they have liked to focus on in more depth? Was the therapist's timing appropriate? What aspects of the work were most meaningful to the couple? These types of questions help the therapist understand the power of his or her model. It is very helpful to hear from a couple what aspects of the work were especially meaningful or helpful to them in developing a different appreciation of themselves, each other, and their relationships with their extended families.

In the last part of the termination session the therapist communicates to the partners that if they find they become emotionally stuck they can return for consultation. It is important to convey that returning is not an indication of failure. Many times just one session around a difficult life event frees the couple to move in more creative directions. It is helpful to emphasize that the therapeutic process is about mastery over life's problems, not the solution to all problems. The goal of therapy is to help couples become more masterful in the way they deal with life events. Their problems are opportunities to learn about self, not indications of failure.

Termination Session and Commentary

The following termination session concerns the same couple discussed in Chapter 8. Initially this couple entered therapy because of the wife's affair and the couple's concern about whether the marriage was viable. After approximately one year of therapy the couple was ready to terminate. Each partner was asked to consider the overall process in preparation for the termination session.

The interview begins with the husband notifying the therapist that the wife is pregnant. The therapist uses this opening to begin a discussion about new developments. He also encourages each partner to review significant changes in his or her life since the commencement of therapy.

Brian: Well, there's a third party to our relationship. Sally is pregnant.

Dr. F.: I must admit, when you presented your family, I said to myself, I am surprised she didn't put on her diagram a little dotted line. I don't know why I had that image, that you were pregnant then.

Sally: It's funny because I actually miscarried at least once, and I thought to myself, after, I thought that I was pregnant. I know that you suggested that we put miscarriages and abortions on, but I couldn't bring myself to put that down because I dealt with it as a gynecological problem and I still don't think of it as a child. So I am throwing up all the time, in shock. So we'll see.

I'm being low-keyed about it because I miscarried once. My sister is here right now. I don't plan to tell anyone because the first time I did, and it wasn't our disappointment, it sort of became everyone else's. This time we will keep it cool until it is well on its way.

Dr. F.: Any other developments?

Brian: Things have been very comfortable and pleasant. We had a big trip at Christmas for a couple of weeks. We went down to Death Valley, and it was nice to get away together from other pressures at work, whatever. I guess in my own situation, I feel a lot more at ease at work. I guess after a while you develop a certain reputation, capability, and more work comes in. So that's entering my life. I have had some ongoing discussions with people I work with about partnership, relationships, and I think we see areas where a lot of work has to occur between ourselves. I know that's on my mind a fair amount, actually. And now that a third party is coming in, it will be more important.

It was interesting having Sally's mother for a visit. It was the first time she had been out here on her own. We got into some very interesting discussions. One of them was new to me, and that was her perception of Sally. I had always felt that I was the only guy who had gone astray in the eyes of parents, but apparently there was a period in Sally's parents' eyes where they were concerned that she was going astray. That was a surprise to me because I always had the image that she was very solid with her parents and that would never be an issue.

Sally: Brian always thought he had a monopoly on that.

Commentary

The therapist hears that the partners have a heightened curiosity and openness about each other and the family stories. When partners are ready to end therapy they talk about their families in significantly different ways. They are more open to

various stories and less reactive to criticism or shaping-up maneuvers by family members. In this brief part of the interview it
is clear that both partners have shifted position with their
families. There appears to be more balance. Brian points out he
is now open to the idea that Sally was not the perfect child in her
own family. The therapist picks up on this point and emphasizes
that they will now have to share the role of being difficult in
their own ways in their respective families. The purpose of this
statement is to encourage the partners to evaluate further how
they have been able to deal with old issues in new ways.

Dr. F.:Now you have to share that role with her.

Brian: It was interesting to hear her mother describe, particularly after World War II, their perception of working hard
and generating a prosperity and all of a sudden a generation like
ours comes along. And at that time, the total incomprehension.
It was interesting to hear. Also on her part expressing a great
concern and trepidation of the times that we seem to be in. So it
was very nice to talk to her. She was really a positive force.
Helping to organize this and that. It was a week, eight to ten
days. Our house has been quite busy. We've had people from the
East, people that I work with, staying with us. They are also
personal friends. Sally's sister. There are a lot more family
coming.

The other thing that I did, that I didn't mention to you . . .
at Christmas I had been planning to write all of my brothers
and sisters, and I think I wrote only to my oldest brother, about
whom I talked to you. We had a lunch on my last visit in
Montreal. I sort of picked up on a couple of points on that
lunch and wrote away. That letter took on remarkable
proportions and made the rounds to the family. I got a very nice
letter back and my father was saying it was so nice to see that his
youngest son could have such a nice rapport with his oldest
brother. And I sure hope he has a similar rapport with the rest
of the family. . . .

It's been interesting to see all of these things. A lot of things that were valuable to me over the last couple of years, like reading and time to myself, I feel I'm having to reassess that, the energies or feelings that I associated or may still act on, I feel that time for that is getting less. I'm going to work harder to structure time for myself. It was really nice this weekend because we went to our first inaugural outdoor trip. I sort of felt like we were coming out of hibernation.

Dr. F.: What about the issue of where to live?

Brian: I think it has certainly settled in these parts in terms of trying to look for a more permanent place. There's been a concern with house prices and interest rates, and yet it would appear to be a good time in terms of the cost of housing. But with payments, it isn't such a good time. So I haven't really made any direct moves in that way. We take drives and look every once in a while. I'm slowly getting more motivation as the landlord in the apartment we are living in is making increases there.

In terms of this town generally, I'm feeling quite positive about it. More and more people are coming to visit us. I think people generally enjoy themselves when they come here.

Dr. F.: Sally, what are your thoughts?

Sally: I was just thinking of when my mother was here. We had gone through a few weeks where we went out on Sundays looking at houses and I had more of a sense of urgency about it than Brian. In fact, I thought he was still resisting it because of the money, I guess. But when my mother was here it was interesting to talk to her about it. In fact, she really put it into more of a perspective for me, in terms of the expectations of what her parents had and what she had and really how enormously high our expectations are. And in terms of the way things are likely to go, it is fairly unrealistic. She actually was sort of encouraging us to wait and not feel pressured into feeling that we have to buy something now but to wait until we felt financially comfortable and also emotionally comfortable with it. I'm at a point right now where I would like a house because to me it has to do with the symbolic part of settling, wanting to have a garden, and I'm sure with this pregnancy I will be nesting. I'm already feeling like nesting. I'm sure by the end I will be like a hen.

Brian: It's amazing what a change a few weeks can make.

Sally: I'm prepared not to rush into it and also the other reality is the importance to me in spending time with a young child. I am not prepared to give that up to have a house. So, anyway, that will have to work itself out.

I enjoyed having my mother here. When she was thinking of coming, she had said, "I will send you your plane fare." I said, "That would be great, that's nice, but in fact it is important for me to have you involved in my life here." She was really surprised and, I think, delighted. I think that my mother is such a matriarch, and things revolve around her at home to the point that she is used to behaving like that and she found . . . she and I spent quite a bit of time alone. She also spent time with the three of us, my sister too. In the time that we had by ourselves, I really realized that . . . She talked about her own situation at home, and in fact, in a sense she really loves her position; in another sense she feels restricted by it. There is enormous expectation in terms of my father and my family in what she's going to do, and to continue to do. She's 60 years old now. She's very energetic, and would never tell anyone not to come, but in fact what happened over Christmas, for example, was that enormous numbers of family just came and came and came and basically stayed and expected to be fed. Afterwards she was practically ill, she was so tired, so she's looking at gradually changing. She realizes she has to do it. I think for her coming out here, she sees this as a place where she can be herself, and in a way that's quite outside the rest of the family. She feels very good about coming to me in that way, which I think is lovely. I think in a sense that my repositioning has allowed her to reposition herself.

Commentary

The therapist checks to see what pockets of anxiety remain. Although the couple is ready to end therapy, it does not mean there is no anxiety. There are still challenges for each partner in his or her family. During the termination session the therapist assesses whether the partners have developed sufficient wisdom about how to deal with anxiety to allow them to be proactive consistently in their families. It is important to remember that the parents have not changed. Rather, the adult child has begun to be different with the parents. The therapist asks questions to determine whether the partners are able to remain open and curious about their parents even when their parents are critical and reactive.

Dr. F.: Could you explain that to me?

Sally: She will always be my mother and I will always be her daughter, but having moved away and established my own space in life, not without pain and problems, but nonetheless, there it is. There is something that is very much my own that she feels comfortable with. I think she can feel really the supportive family without having to be the center of it, the supporter herself. It allows me to support her without mothering her. We have an equal friendship. I think her ability to really tell Brian and me what she thought of us when we were in our hippie days, I thought that was great. She really let us have it one night. . . .

Brian: You started to react immediately. I thought you should have let it go.

Sally: Yes, I know, and you were right to do that . . . but that's what I mean. It's a different position to take, instead of reacting. In fact, I find it interesting that we were perceived that way. Obviously you are very much in your own . . . you take a point of view and you become that point of view and to be able to move off that point of view . . . There is great strength to be gained from that. Also, a real interest in what other people's situations are. I enjoyed that.

My mother has moved up to the country now. My father is completely happy up there. He has everything he wants. He has his family coming when he wants, but basically he is alone much of the time, which he prefers. He has his dog. But it's my mother who realizes that she's going to have to agitate the thing a little bit to get more of what she wants and needs. I was encouraging her to do that. I think she needs that encouragement and will accept it from me and probably accepts it more readily here than if I were there. Because I know from having talked with my sister, my sister sees it as well, but she doesn't feel that Mother will listen to her because my mother is very much the "mother" with her, and also the grandmother. But it is interesting; she continues to change.

Brian: In her observation of how much work and effort went into keeping a relationship with your father going, she had to be very strong. Then it was interesting she reflected back on my mother. She really admires my mother and feels she does a hell of a lot more work than she in fact did, given that my mother had to move away, go and establish a home in a different location. The fact that we may have perceived my mother as being strong-willed but that only proves the fact of how strong-willed my father in fact was, and that she had to put a lot of effort out to maintain her position and interests. I thought that was interesting.

Sally: They have strong support for each other now, Brian's mother and my mother.

Dr. F.: This has been on the increase?

Sally: This has been increasing in the relationship. It has certainly increased since we have been out here. I think that their contact with each other is in a way contact with us. They get news from each other. In fact, they are very good friends. They respect each other. I think they understand each other. Especially Brian's mother, she doesn't have many close women friends. She doesn't have a sense of that, where I think my mother does.

Commentary

The therapist now asks about other family relationships. If the adult child has repositioned in the family, that child should talk about relations with siblings in a new way. Sally had been very reactive to her sister in the past. When the therapist asks her about her reaction to her sister, he is again checking to see if she has been able to develop a different position and a deeper sense of connection with important family members. Siblings are important resources in the family. If the adult child has repositioned, he or she should be able to embrace siblings in a new, more positive way.

Dr. F.: What about the visit with your sister? Did you notice any differences there?

Sally: She has just been here a couple of days and will be here to the end of the week. Her daughter has come to see me before. I think in a sense . . . so far it has been catching up on news, which takes a while, to get a sense of where everyone is at.

I think she was very excited about coming, and also I think she was a bit nervous. I think because I get along so well with her daughters, it was as though I had an easier closeness established with her daughters than I had with her. So now I think there were good intentions on both sides but I feel we're still sort of exploring each other as adults. I'm delighted she's here and especially, just having found out that I am pregnant. She, of course, has three kids—she has all this information for me, which I think is really useful because I'm not going to tell anyone else right now, and it's helpful for me to know all these things.

Dr. F.: This is the first time she's come out alone?

Sally: That she's ever visited me on her own. In terms of not having the sort of ongoing involvement, when you're living closer, I can sense that same sort of . . . In fact, it's nice to have someone somewhere that you can go and see, and you are still in family, but you are somewhere else, not home. She's been delighted, getting up in the morning, not having to deal with her husband and children asking "Where is this?" "Where is that?" Basically, she's been a wife and mother this whole time. She's also just started working. She finished her M.A. last year, and she's gotten her second job. She's excited about working. She enjoys telling me about that. I think it's great that she's gone ahead with that. So I've been giving her a lot of encouragement to go on.

But, in a sense, I feel that relationships are really lifetime and they are just going but I sense some changes already in a couple of days. There is no unfinished business or problems that I need answers for. I just want to know more about her and the way she is now. Although she herself has brought up several things already about when we were children. Without my asking she told me more about my maternal grandmother and her parents because she was much older, five years older, so she remembers a lot more than I do. She just seemed to be in a mood to talk about that. I didn't ask her. It's good because it's more information for me that I didn't have. It's intriguing.

The other thing. Actually, Sheila went over to the island this morning to see my aunt and uncle and will come back tomorrow. It's interesting to see how that extension of the family has sort of slotted itself in now. Now that there is no problem or animosity there between myself and them, it has allowed for a free exchange. My cousin picked Sheila up this morning, and I think that will be really nice for them. I was pleased that they went over together, but a couple of years ago it would have bothered me.

Commentary

The therapist has moved into the second part of the termination session. To learn about how the couple understands their own change, he begins to ask them questions about when they began to notice changes in their respective families and their relationship. Whom do they hold responsible for the changes? What do they need to have happen in their families to know that change has occurred? The answers to these questions help the therapist learn more about the process of change. It is quite enlightening to know how people understand their change. Do they credit their partner, or a change in an extended-family member, or perhaps some change in the life of a friend? Do they credit their own wisdom, or do they credit the therapy and, if so, to what degree?

Dr. F.: I was just wondering, looking back now, when the breakthrough with that family occurred?

Sally: Well, it's funny. You always hear about family issues that become big issues—the issues themselves are hazy in my mind. There was a lot of misunderstanding and I know some specific things on both parts, but in terms of the breakthrough, I have trouble saying exactly when that was.

Brian: That visit with Eileen last fall sometime. I remember you coming back and saying that you were feeling much more positive.

Sally: That's right. The way I look at it now—I know how the loyalties are in my family, and this other family is also very strong with loyalties. They were also isolated. They were referred to by one of my other cousins as "country cousins," which unfortunately stuck. This rankled my aunt, who is actually quite a sophisticated woman and was quite disgusted and enraged that she would ever be thought of in that way. But I think their loyalties were very strong. I think the rift between my cousin and me developed basically . . . when I started to think about it differently was when I felt that if that had happened to me, what would my family have done? I know damn well they would have lined up with me, as I would have expected them to. In fact, I think that is what they did.

But they were also very uncomfortable about it because basically I know that my aunt has always really liked me and Brian, and so does, my uncle, my father's brother. So I think they had a lot of discomfort with it, but nonetheless, that was the way it came down. I went out one evening with my aunt and I let her know that my position was different, that I didn't necessarily expect her to understand it, or even . . . I wanted her to know that there were two sides. I did let her know some of the strains that I had been under, some of the reasons why I behaved the way I did. But never feeling really proud about it because I felt, well, I'm not going to go over there and apologize but at the same time I felt responsible for my part of it. I wanted to let her know there were two sides to it. Afterwards, she replied really well to that. She acknowledged that there had been bad feelings and that they had been very upset about it and uncomfortable but that they hadn't known what to do.

And the other thing, my cousin and I cleaned up some of our stuff together. There has always been basically very good will there and I know she loves me the way that I love her. Both of us were very uncomfortable with the way it was. Also, her life has smoothed out a great deal from what it was a few years ago. Her relationship that she was in before is finished and she is now in another relationship, but her life has changed considerably. So she herself is in a different position than she was then. She was dreadfully hurt by that previous relationship, but she got herself out of that. In a way we were both in a new enough position on our own so now it's like the old days when we are together.

Commentary

The therapist pushes the adult child to see how he or she understands change. It is important that the adult child credits himself or herself with the change. If the adult child still gives others the credit for improvement, then he or she will be more vulnerable for disappointment later. It is essential that prior to terminating therapy each partner understands his or her own power to sustain change.

Dr. F.: This is like a rich resource that was available to you when you moved here, but these issues stopped you from getting involved. So if I follow what you're saying, you did something to reach out in a different way, which opened up the potential that was there.

Sally: I think so.

Dr. F.: I was just wondering if you know what got you to reach out in a different way at that time?

Sally: I think looking and becoming involved with family systems and what they are about—they are part of my system. I realized there was more energy going into my denying that than I wanted there to be. I don't know whether I wanted to renew those relationships or not, but I knew that they were causing me a lot of unhappiness. My thought at the time was that I wanted to clean up my side of it and then whatever happened was okay. If that hadn't happened, gotten back together, because there was good will there, I would have at least felt that I had done my part of it but, in fact, it has worked out very nicely.

Brian: It's a bit like Ontario and the rest of Canada. There is this sort of strong central clan around which everyone else focuses . . . and on the periphery. So that family, if you came out to the West Coast you were a country bumpkin.

Dr. F.: Was that one of the concerns you had about coming out here, that it would cut you off in that way from the family?

Brian: Oh, no. In my own case I delight in the misconception about it all. I'm not sure about Sally.

Sally: I had a lot of fears about being cut off from the family. The thing is basically for me my relationships with my family were so supportive that any change and so far away seemed like a major upheaval. I was afraid of that. It's been upheaval, but it has settled down, and I'm happy about it.

Brian: But the geography aside, though, even in the families in Quebec, I always get a sense that it's your family that is the center of all the activity, Christmas, etc. They are the hub of it because they are still . . . everyone is in a lesser light . . . my impression from the outside. So that family has been a very powerful influence regardless of whether you are back East or out West. So there is that and there has been tension between your mother and me as unfinished business from an older generation as well that has a bearing on it.

Sally: That is the other thing that I was pleased about. It isn't that I want to do my mother's work for her. I don't. But I want her to do well. She is actually recognizing that it has been there. She understands what I'm talking about, but she has her own blocks and resistances, and when she was here . . . that's the other thing. I took her over to the island and I left her there. I know she was a bit nervous about it because my aunt can be a real pain or she can be delightful. I knew in the past things have happened. The first day my mother was ready to write her off, but she stuck it out for another day and night and day, and I said, "I think you should stay there on your own and get to know them a bit. If there are things you want to bring up, bring them up!" She did that. She doesn't have the intellectual support that I would have with Brian or by studying this; she just went in there. And she said they actually did straighten some things out.

She enjoyed spending time with her brother-in-law. In fact, she is looking forward to the next time they'll be visiting, and planning out what they will do. Which doesn't have anything to do with me. It pleases me that they would have other things that would bring them out here so that when they do come, they'll stay longer. They will come with reasons of their own as well as being with me. I think it's helped my mother.

Right now her younger sister's husband has been diagnosed with a large malignancy and he has lost his job. He's had very little contact with the family in the last two years, yet he himself phoned my father from the hospital and asked if he could come down when he had the operation because he wanted someone there. He felt powerless without a doctor he knew there. My father said sure. They are there now. I'm sure it must be difficult for them, but at the same time, it's probably good because it's her youngest sister and I think she needs to spend some time with her. I'm pleased for her that that is happening.

Commentary

Brian and Sally appear consistently proactive in their relationships with various extended-family members. They not only perceive their family differently, they also embrace each other differently. There has been a definite shift away from reactivity toward openness.

The therapist now moves to the third part of the termination session: evaluating which aspects of the process were most useful to the couple. He turns to the partners as the experts and asks them to help him understand the overall process. He wants to pay particular attention to their disappointments. Knowledge about what they would like to have done differently can help the therapist in his work with other couples. It is important that the couple understand that the therapist is not looking for validation or a pat on the back. Rather, he is seeking vital information that can help him modify his model to provide a better quality of service to other couples.

Dr. F.: Sounds like a lot of big changes going on in the family. Since this is the last session, it would be helpful to me, and I hope you as well, for each of you to spend a few minutes sharing the lows and highs of the experience of therapy itself. What made a difference, and what were some of the disappointments? Some of the things you hoped would happen that didn't, and some of the things that did make a difference. Sally, I'm going to start with you and hear some of the things you hoped would happen that didn't. Take yourself back to the very beginning. Evaluate the highs and lows.

Sally: When I look back, I think there was a lot of anxiety in the beginning and I think that's the bottom line for most people coming into any new process, the thought that they might end up separating. I think that you have to address that. I think that we did do that and we decided obviously against that, but I think that's something that's a real strain on people. Especially if there is a lot of ambivalence . . . I think that is a major anxiety, and I think if I ever got into this line of work I would be aware of that one because it's quite strong. Initially it might color what you get from people because they are reluctant to give out the words in case someone will advise them not to stay together.

I see it as a very positive experience. There isn't anything that I can think of that hasn't happened. Except that I see it as obviously a process that doesn't stop here or ever. And I think the danger is that. I'm sure new situations will come up and hold new complexities that would seem just as bad as the first one. I can see there would be a need to search and keep talking. Learning that is more important than anything else and I think we have learned that.

I realize that you have to do the work yourself. I think that if you weren't prepared to do that you wouldn't get very far.

Because it strikes me that this kind of system works when the person internalizes it and begins to try and look at themselves differently. Basically it's been really positive for me. I've appreciated the direction you have given us. You have been very much involved, but you haven't really tried to steer us in any direction.

Commentary

The therapist now encourages the couple to reflect further on the overall process and what made a difference in their beginning attempts to reposition. He is especially interested in hearing how they experienced not being permitted to react to each other in the sessions. This lack of interaction is a strange experience for many couples, particularly if they have been in therapy before where they were encouraged to react to each other. In family therapy with couples the partners are blocked from defending or justifying their positions. It is useful to hear how they evaluate the experience of sitting on the sidelines, listening to each other's story.

Dr. F.: Can you think of any experience that made a difference to you?

Sally: I think it was helpful to me. . . . During the first few sessions I remember feeling quite anxious about everything. I don't think I took in very much. But after that, after you had the information about us, I thought it would be helpful to hear the other person's point of view and observations about us. Especially relating it to times before. Like times when we were first together and understanding that some of those things had not been worked through, because I was tending to focus on the present problems. I think that view, sort of looking back, the view of unfinished business was revealing to me and finding out what it was.

Dr. F.: What did you think of the format of each of you talking to me with the other observing?

Sally: I think it's a good way to go because it interrupts whatever dynamic that's going on between the two people and in fact, you're just sitting there and you may be trying not to listen or may not like what you're hearing or you may be happy, but you're forced to listen. I think giving the other person the freedom and free range of talking about the circumstances the way they see it is very helpful. I didn't find it threatening. In the beginning I guess we really didn't relate to each other very much, but in a sense we really did. I was aware of everything Brian was saying. And hopefully Brian to me. I think the structure is very good.

Dr. F.: Okay, Brian, how about you? If you took yourself back to the beginning, how would you evaluate the process?

Brian: On that last point, I think what it does is that it gives you that breathing space so that . . . you know, you're only here for an hour and then you're back. One of the things that I did notice is a number of cases where I could see myself responding in certain ways, but in a situation like this I would just observe. I think the breathing spaces just fit in with the ongoing relationship anyway. I know in the past when the idea had been raised by Sally about going for help, I really balked at it, at a fear level. Why confront things that I didn't want to confront? What's interesting about that is that I think you're always able to anticipate thinking that you're going to uncover worse things about yourself. Even through this process I can't say that I have had real discomfort. I've had to try and describe things and talk about things, but what's interesting is that the problems that you come up with in the end aren't personal problems in a sense. Here, the situations that my family found themselves in or what their families found themselves in, you think gosh, that is interesting . . . the parallels there. It seems to me this fear thing is that you're going to uncover a funny side to yourself. That it's terribly personal and private and your own fault. A sense of it's all my own doing.

So I didn't come with any expectations. I found it really positive. What I found really positive was being able to see Sally in the context of family and problems that she perceived and with problems that I had actually never been able to place. And also to see myself in relationship to my family and what initiating explorations in my own family sort of generated. An interest on their part so that the process goes beyond just the two of us sitting here. That breathing space seems to work back into the family. I agree with Sally, the field is constantly moving, so there is work always and the pressure may come from somewhere else. But I think that going through this process . . . there is a way of working through things, be it together or with others. Which leads me back again to the idea of less of a sense of isolation that I may have been operating under previously.

I can't really come up with any expectations that I had or describe low times because it has been interesting.

Dr. F.: Anything that you would like to have happened or dealt with, that didn't?

Brian: I think part of the exploration that Sally and I have still is a . . . a sexual plan. I think even coming here that that has initiated that sort of exploration, greater comfort. And willingness to explore.

Dr. F.: Let me ask you questions about it because you reminded me of something. I recall it was dealt with in a more indirect way than a direct way. What are your thoughts about the wisdom of that?

Brian: Well, I'm not sure how one would deal with it in a direct way. I think we put a fair effort into changing our sexual relating and attentiveness and so on. I think there is still a lot of work we need to do. Like I recall our trip at Christmas. There were certain nights when we had a lot to work through and it was very deep down. So that's why I say that I think that if the exploration continues . . .

Dr. F.: Do you think you have developed a handle to be able to deal with that in the way that you want to in the relationship?

Brian: I guess I wouldn't know of a direct way of how I wanted to. . . . I would certainly want it to be a satisfying relationship. How to deal with it I can't say without a specific image for it.

Dr. F.: How would you have approached it five years ago?

Brian: Oh, yes, I think in that respect, four or five years ago we would have avoided it.

Commentary

The termination session is coming to a close. Before concluding the therapist wants to raise two other points. One is to emphasize that the partners have to become masters of their own lives. He asks them how they have understood this process and encourages them to remember that they have to be their own heroes. As part of the theme of being their own heroes, the therapist also asks about other systems in which they have effected change, such as work and friendships. The therapist would expect to hear that there have been significant changes in these areas as well. The therapist concludes with the suggestion that the couple can return for a consultation if they become stuck over certain dilemmas. He purposefully raises this possibility so he can emphasize that future difficulties are opportunities for learning, not signs of failure.

Dr. F.: Let me throw something out to you and get your reaction to it. This process, as I see it, is about mastery over life's problems, being able to deal with concerns in life in a new way. It is about developing a framework or approach to deal with life's problems in a creative way. So, for me, therapy is successful when people develop that mastery. When you raise this issue of wanting more intimacy sexually or a different type of sexual connection, how masterful do you see yourself in terms of being able to make that happen for yourself?

Brian: I think I have a long way to go on that one. I think there is a recognition where I have probably not been willing to recognize the fact that I am partly responsible for being the master of my own destiny for whatever reason. I see that in a number of fields in my own endeavor. That there is a long way to go there. It's very easy to become fatalistic about that. I think it's ongoing. For me, it's a beginning to see it, and I think there is still an even bigger jump from beginning to see it and doing it. Anyway, I see that. I see it in other things, my work relationships, and in our own relationships.

Dr. F.: How would you view it, Sally, problem-solving versus mastery over one's destiny?

Sally: Again, I think that this difference of looking at it can put you in a strong position because as long as you're trying to eliminate problems, then it's very unlikely that that is ever going to happen so you're always going to be failing at what you see as problems, or else denying that there are problems or being taken over by the problems, however you are going. But I think that is actually a wise way of looking at it given that they are going to be there. I actually feel much more masterful myself. Not just in the marriage but outside the marriage as well. In fact, probably as important to me, outside the marriage as well. I think somehow, although you haven't said it in so many words to us, that idea has come across.

Dr. F.: Any last words that may be helpful before we stop?

Brian: Just keep up the good work.

Dr. F.: One last point: Sometimes life events get us bogged down and we find some of the old reactivity kicking in. If that happens, a brief consultation could be useful. I want to leave the door open for that.

Sally: That's a good idea. It's useful knowing that is available just in case we get stuck again.

Brian: I like the idea as a consultation. It gives it a different meaning if we need to come back.

Dr. F.: You've been an enjoyable couple to work with. Good luck!

Commentary

It is not unusual for a couple to raise an additional problem just before terminating the therapy process; there is usually some ambivalence about ending. The therapist should not become too anxious about it or use it as a reason to extend therapy. The therapist must reframe that concern as an opportunity to continue work on life's problems. When the husband raised the issue of sexual concerns, the therapist used it as an opportunity to talk about how important it is to embrace these problems in new, creative ways. The husband talks about his ability to think about some of these things differently, although he is not certain about his ability to do too much about them. The therapist reconfirms the principle that the partners have become their own heroes. He does not accept the expression of a problem as an indication that the couple needs more therapy; rather, he defines it as an opportunity to apply the principles they have learned to this area and others.

10 _____

Special Issues Concerning Family Therapy with Couples

This chapter discusses a range of special issues that a systemic therapist encounters when applying the principles of family therapy with couples. It is not possible to do justice in one chapter to all the possible complications, dilemmas, or unique situations that arise in this work. This chapter touches on a few of the more important ones. The principles the therapist develops to deal with these dilemmas and others must be consistent with the overall philosophy, values, and goals of his or her model.

Should the Therapist See One Partner in a Relationship?

It is not unusual for one partner to call a therapist and request individual therapy for a relationship problem. On occasion the caller will say the partner refuses to attend. The therapist's handling of this request is crucial to the reframing of the problem. If the therapist accepted the caller's request for individual therapy at face value, it is likely that he or she would see the individual alone. After the therapy commenced the individual would use the time to complain about the marriage and the partner. An emotional triangle would quickly develop. The therapist and client would have a special relationship at the expense of the client's partner.

The therapist's philosophy and theoretical framework will influence how he or she receives a request by a family member to be seen alone. If the therapist's orientation is individual psychotherapy, there is no reason not to see the family member alone. However, if the therapist has a theoretical framework grounded in systemic thinking and believes individuals need to rely on their own resources—their internal wisdom and their family—for help and understanding, then he or she will be reluctant to see an individual alone.

Seeing an individual alone can undermine the integrity of the relationship. The individual will use the therapist as the primary resource, not only for understanding the dilemma but also for confirming his or her story about the spouse or other family members. It is safer and more respectful to engage the couple for at least the first session. By forming a relationship with both partners, the therapist can be seen as a resource for the marriage, the family, and the individuals.

The therapist should avoid aligning with one family member against another. When the therapist sees only one family member, the absent partner has to make some sense out of what is occurring. Usually the uninvolved partner will feel at some disadvantage. When the partner in therapy takes home information about the therapy, or expresses new ideas about how the family or the relationship could be improved, the uninvolved partner can experience this as criticism, lack of support, or lack of understanding and may develop negative feelings about the overall therapeutic process in general and the therapist in particular. Therapy can then become another battleground for the couple. If the partner is involved at this point it is difficult to balance the therapeutic relationship. The outside partner will likely attend the session in an angry, defensive mood and be quick to feel left out and misunderstood. The therapist needs tremendous skill to involve the outside partner in the therapeutic process so that he or she feels understood, honored, and appreciated.

These difficulties can be avoided when therapy is started with both partners. It should be recommended to people who ask to come in alone that they begin the therapy process with their partner. It is common for the caller to express reservations; however, it is important to encourage him or her to reconsider the wisdom of starting alone. It is helpful to say something along the following lines to the caller, "It is far more respectful and healthy to start together. My job is to honor your relationship and to be open to both stories. If I see one person without the other, I am violating some important principles about relationships. I seldom see it work when one person starts without the other." When there is discomfort with this idea it can be helpful to suggest that the couple come in together for a consultation, after which a decision about who will be seen can be made. Labeling the first session as a "consultation" seems to alleviate the anxiety of the caller and allows him or her to approach the partner in a positive way.

The basic principle is that one should not start therapy with one partner when he or she is involved in a significant relationship with another. The therapist wants to improve connections and build on resources within the family. He or she does not want to develop a special relationship with one family member at the expense of the other. However, there are rare times when it is necessary to see one person alone. The therapist may begin with the couple in the first session and discover that one partner is unwilling to continue. It is then appropriate to continue with the other partner. There are a number of reasons a person may opt out of attending with the partner. For example, one partner may be too anxious, reactive, or emotionally stuck in a series of other relationships that he or she does not want to explore. At times one partner may be so reactive that it is intolerable for him or her to sit through a session listening to the other partner talk about dilemmas. Some people have decided privately to end a relationship and are not willing to invest anything more in that relationship. When one of these situations arises, the therapist must see the more motivated, functional, less reactive partner. However, when a therapist has made this decision, it is still important that he or she avoid participating in a triangled relationship with that partner against the unmotivated or reactive partner. The sessions should remain focused on the individual's working on self issues. The client should be discouraged from raising issues about the partner. Although the client may be frustrated about not being able to use the session to ventilate complaints about the relationship, at some level he or she will appreciate that the therapist demonstrates respect and neutrality, reducing the potential for dysfunctional triangles to develop. When a client sees the therapist alone, he or she has more of a tendency to idealize the therapist and use him or her as a major support. He or she may invest more emotional energy in the therapist and the therapeutic process than in significant relationships in his or her life. The therapist should guard against this tendency and continue to encourage the client to work on his or her most significant relationships in a new way. The therapist should reduce the importance the client places on the therapist and therapy and help the client become his or her own hero by working on repositioning moves with the client's partner and other family members.

When the therapist stays detached from the client's story and avoids triangled relationships it leaves the door open to involve significant others in the therapeutic process in the future. In contrast, if the therapist had bought into the content that an adult client had presented, it is unlikely that the therapist could later be a positive connecting force for the family. Even when family members refuse to come in initially, they may be more open to it later. The therapist never knows when other family members will be ready to work on self issues. It is crucial that the therapist stay neutral about family stories at all times. The therapist should stay curious and questioning, with the overall goal of encouraging the client to achieve better connections with all types of family members. It is easier to do this when the couple works together; however, this can also be done when one partner only attends and learns how to be a positive force in all his or her relationships.

Dealing with Divorce and Separation

A common question is how to operationalize the principles of family therapy with couples when there has been a divorce or separation. Many therapists will not see the couple together after they have decided to separate. Others believe that the family is no longer viable after couples separate. These attitudes should be reconsidered. First, divorce is not family breakup but a restructuring of the family. If there are children, the parents still have to work out some arrangement to parent them effectively, and need to maintain a certain degree of partnership in this task. Furthermore, when a couple separates, they may need to clarify whether they want to divorce or work on continuing as a couple.

In either case, therapy should continue when a couple is separating. How people separate, how they understand their separation, and how well they are able to maintain some connection with each other during the separation process will determine to some degree what they are able to learn about themselves; how they will honor their history together; whether they will find their way together; and, if they decide to divorce, how well they can do so in a less painful, scarring way.

When an adult presents the problem as one of separation or

ongoing difficulties in handling a divorce, the therapist should assess the degree of reactivity in the relationship. Often couples in a second marriage will ascribe difficulties to that marriage when the real difficulty stems from unresolved issues in the first marriage. This area is a complex one. Over the course of therapy partners will often raise issues they had with their former spouse. Individuals who have not been successful in working through the loss of their first marriage tend to bring those old issues into the second marriage. Second marriages are quite vulnerable. Many fail for a number of reasons, two important ones being that couples who have not learned their lessons from their first marriage hope that the second marriage will make up for their earlier losses, and couples try to make the dream they were not able to realize in their first marriage come true in their second. Both these struggles can seriously undermine the potential of a new relationship. The therapist needs to understand what happened for each partner in previous significant relationships and identify the unfinished business from the first marriage that is being acted out in the second. Individuals who never really understood their part in the first marriage and who blamed their former partner for the failure of that marriage, are more likely to bring the same themes into the second marriage and quickly experience disappointments and loneliness.

The therapist should help each adult sort out the lessons to be learned from the first marriage. It is helpful to ask previously married couples, "What positive lessons have you learned from your first marriage?" When couples answer "Nothing!" or place all the blame on the former partner, this is an indication that the second marriage is vulnerable and that old areas of reactivity will be evident in it.

The therapist should also assess the type of connections individuals have with their former spouses. Do they talk to each other regularly? Do they discuss concerns about the children? Do they need to maintain distance and separateness from each other to feel emotionally safe? When there is a comfortable relationship among all the adults, there is greater potential for work on positive connections. However, if individuals are angry, conflictual, or judgmental about their former spouse and/or their partner's former spouse, then the work on family connections will be more difficult. It is important that children in families have access to all the important adults in their lives. If parents are reactive to their former spouses or if their new partners demand that little or no connection be maintained with former spouses, then the children will have to choose between or among family members. We know that divorce is difficult for children, but the more devastating aspect for them is being cut off from significant adults in their lives. If a parent, because of unfinished business with the former spouse, blocks the children from connections with the other parent, the children can feel abandoned and betrayed by both parents. This type of separation from parent is one of the most significant causes of unfinished business for children. The family therapist should help the adults work through their unresolved issues from their former relationships so they can embrace people in their lives with minimal past residue.

One way to help adults begin to let go of old issues is to encourage them to mourn the loss of their original dreams. Most adults' dream for their first marriage is that they will marry their true love and be happy forever. When young people marry, they expect that they will finally feel loved, accepted, and safe. When the marriage unravels, they feel abandoned, betrayed, and bewildered. The partners then begin the search for a new partner to fulfill the dream. Unfortunately, they carry the old resentments and a degree of caution into the new relationship. At the first sign that their dreams will not be realized with the new partner, they begin the slow but steady process of distancing and withdrawal. Individuals have to develop a new dream with their second partner; second marriages are different from first and are based on a different type of emotional contract. Many individuals go headlong into a second marriage trying to create what was missing in their first marriage. If this is the emotional agenda, the second marriage is vulnerable from the beginning. When therapists ask couples how they said good-bye to their first dream and question them about their expectations for their second marriage, it frees them to begin the process of letting go of the original dream.

It can be helpful to invite former spouses to the session to facilitate this process. It is healing when former spouses come together, each talking about how difficult it was during the divorce, how sad each felt about not being able to make the marriage work, what they have learned about themselves in intervening years, and how each needs to say good-bye in the proper way. Many divorced people used anger to say good-bye. These individuals need to revisit some of that history to say good-bye properly. As long as we stay angry or need anger to justify leaving, we do not learn from the experience. The therapist should gently shift people out of anger into sadness. Individuals need to experience the sadness about the loss of their first dream. Out of sadness can come better connections. If individuals hold on to the anger about their first marriage it is difficult for them to be truly open to their new partner. They need to understand this so they can begin to think about the rituals and ceremonies they need for healing.

The concept of mourning the loss of the original dream is new to many individuals. Most have seen parents or friends use anger and hurt to justify leaving. It is important for children to see their parents say good-bye the right way. If they do not have proper guides for dealing with conflict, they will have only negative messages about how to deal with differences. Revisiting the old marriage and encouraging individuals to rework the old themes in a positive way leads to healing between the generations.

Dealing with Affairs

One of the greatest challenges to a marriage is the emotional/sexual affair. Individuals engage in different types of affairs.

There are strictly sexual affairs. There are emotional affairs. And, more commonly, there are sexual/emotional affairs. For many people the purpose of an affair is to form a relationship with someone when one feels unloved, disconnected, estranged, or basically alone in a marriage. Reaching out to another person is an attempt to feel safe, loved, appreciated, understood, and emotionally connected. When couples first come for therapy it is not unusual for a partner to hide the fact that he or she is having an affair. When the therapist asks questions about significant people in the couples' lives and inquires about how they try to feel safe when they are anxious or feeling unloved, the partners begin to privately question the wisdom of keeping the affair secret. Gradually the story of the affair emerges. Other couples, at the initial contact, present the affair as the central problem. One partner is involved in an affair and the other is enraged by the betrayal. Other couples begin therapy fighting over an affair that has just ended.

When there has been an affair the therapist should ask the partners about the meaning each has attached to it. The therapist should always bear in mind that the affair is a metaphor for something that has not worked in the life of the couple. Couples can form greater connections with each other when they understand the symbolism behind the affair. Initially partners may fight about the affair and use it to maintain emotional distance. One feels injured, the other is contrite. Each takes a position vis-à-vis the affair, and the battle lines are drawn. The job of the therapist is to reframe the meaning of the affair, to help each partner understand that he or she could use the affair either to learn more about self and the other, or to justify distance and end the marriage. When the therapist defines the affair as a metaphor for something deeper and more significant, he or she gives the couple permission to let go of focusing on the betrayal and to begin the process of understanding how each has gotten into this situation.

At times a couple uses the affair to maintain distance in the relationship. For example, the therapist may help an individual feel a little closer to the partner, and the partner will respond by introducing the affair again. It is as though the affair is a ghost in the room—it haunts the process, but no one is able to do anything about it, because it is inaccessible. The challenge for the therapist is to bring the ghost into the open. One way to achieve this is to involve the third person in the therapeutic process. By asking the partner having the affair to invite the third person to the session, the therapist begins to exorcise the ghost. Giving the third person a name and making him or her a real person facilitates the process of detriangulating the affair from the relationship. Once the therapist makes the suggestion that the third person be involved in the session, the couple can no longer use the affair to distance. The partner must decide whether to make the invitation and involve the third person in the process, end the affair because it is too painful, or leave the marriage because the third person is too important. In any case, the affair will no longer stabilize the emotional distance between the couple. The balance shifts within the relationship after the therapist suggests the third person be involved. This powerful intervention should only be made when the therapist is convinced that one or both partners will persist in introducing the affair to maintain emotional distance.

When the third person attends the session, the therapist must honor that person as a legitimate member of the system. He or she should be given an opportunity to express his or her needs, expectations, dreams, and vision. When the therapist honors this third person as an equal member of the system, most of the fantasies about the affair are dispelled. After a session of this type the relationship is different. There can be a number of outcomes: the third person, after listening to the stories of the other two, may feel that his or her dreams will never be honored and may end the affair, the couple may rediscover each other, or it may become clear that the commitment between the partner and his or her lover is so great that the marriage is no longer viable. The job of the therapist is not to negotiate the affair but to bring it to the surface. His or her goal is to provide the partners with an opportunity to use the affair to clarify their positions and to learn about self and the unfinished business that each brings into current life events. *Many people use relationships to distance from their own sadness, loss, and vulnerability.* They deal with their unfinished business by getting lost in affairs.

Occasionally one partner will attempt to swear a therapist to secrecy about an affair. It is crucial that the therapist never become a party to secrets. If the therapist joins one partner in a secret, the therapist violates his or her role in the family. Secret-keeping is a negative process and profoundly separates people from each other. A therapist who joins a person in a secret is playing out his or her own unfinished business. The therapist must tell the family member that he or she cannot be party to any secrets and that it is important that that person introduce the secret in one of the sessions. The therapist should ask questions based on his or her hypotheses and understanding of the family themes. A therapist who is a party to secrets restricts the types of questions he or she can ask and the range of themes the therapist feels comfortable dealing with. I know of no other process that can undermine family connections more than a therapist joining a family member in a secret. For further elaboration on how to deal with secret-keeping in families, see Freeman (1991, pp. 367–369).

When Should Children Be Involved in the Therapy?

There is some confusion about when to involve the children in the therapeutic process with couples. Many couples present their problem as resting within their relationship. The therapy is focused on helping each partner gain a clearer sense of self and the issues each has brought into the marriage. Other couples raise concerns about their children, but still see their major problem as their relationship with each other. Some couples are preoccupied with the behavior of their children and seek therapy for the purpose of focusing on these concerns. These different configurations require different approaches.

Couples who present with problems in the relationship and who only peripherally mention concerns with their children are not anxious to involve the children in the therapeutic process. However, there is a time when it is appropriate to see the children. They have important stories to tell, and they need to hear certain stories from their parents. It can be a connecting experience to have several sessions in which the children and parents are together, each telling his or her story. These sessions are more appropriate in the middle phase of family therapy with couples. The children are invited not because they are the problem but because the sessions can allow for learning about connections between the generations. It is also helpful for the therapist to gain a sense of the family through the children's point of view. Nevertheless, the primary goal for inviting the children to attend the session is to give them an opportunity to experience generational storytelling. In the middle phase the parents are not reactive toward each other; they have learned a great deal about themselves and their own stories about family and are ready to tell their stories to their children – important stories for the children to hear and record. On the other hand, the children have their own stories to tell. Now that the parents have developed a healthy amount of curiosity about each other, they are more open to their children's stories as well. The focus of the sessions is not on family problems but on family legacy and history, and how each generation can teach the other about its needs.

The therapist must use a different approach when couples seek therapy because of their worries about their children. These parents tend to be quite anxious about their children and often label one or more of the children as "dysfunctional." In the early stages of therapy the therapist has to put considerable energy into reducing parental anxiety, shifting the focus to the parents' own learning about self, and helping the parents become more curious about, rather than reactive to, their children.

Parents who begin therapy with high anxiety about children have difficulty talking about issues other than their preoccupation with their children. At times it is necessary to involve the children in the therapeutic process as a way to get them out of it. When the children attend and tell their stories in such a way that it reduces their parents' anxiety, then a shift in therapy occurs.

There is a time and a place for involving children in therapy. They should never be defined as the source of the problem; rather, they should be seen as potential resources for learning about family and what each family member needs from the other. The therapist must not label, triangle, or collude with the parents around the children. The therapist's goal is to find a way to connect the generations. The children need to have an expansive sense of family. When parents are not able to help their children stay connected with grandparents, uncles, aunts, and cousins, then the sense of family is diminished in the children's eyes. When the parents develop a more positive sense of their own family and better connections with their extended families they provide their children with greater resources in their own lives.

Related to the issue of involving children is the issue of when to involve other family members in the therapy. Adult siblings of parents, parents of parents, and adult children of parents all have the potential to help redefine the sense of family and add to family stories. When the couple becomes excited about rediscovering family it is time to consider involving other family members. This is not possible at the beginning of therapy when the couple is far too anxious about their problems with each other. However, as the therapist gradually shifts the focus away from the relationship problems to self issues and the need for more stories about the family, the partners become more curious about the stories of other family members. The sessions with other family members take place in the middle phase of the family therapy process.

What Do You Do about Concurrent Therapies?

Multiple therapies create numerous difficulties. Many individuals who begin family therapy already have a therapist he or she is seeing individually. Sometimes children in the family are seeing child psychiatrists or school counselors. These other therapies present problems for the therapist who is trying to operationalize the principles discussed in this text. The major goal of family therapy with couples is to place responsibility for change with the couple, to encourage them to rely on their own wisdom and family resources. When the family members see other therapists they have a tendency to use that therapy to support their point of view and confirm their stories and mythologies about the family. This makes it difficult to get them excited and motivated to rethink their family stories. One of the greatest obstacles to increasing people's curiosity about themselves is professionals and friends who reinforce their stories. It is important for the therapist to get a clear understanding of what therapies and other special relationships the partners rely on to deal with their problems.

Other therapies are also used on occasion by one partner to distance from the other. When individuals are anxious or feeling misunderstood and vulnerable in their relationship, they will usually search outside for support. As was mentioned earlier, some people do this by starting an affair, others by starting a therapeutic relationship. There are times when the other therapies are so powerful that it is not wise to begin a new therapy. If other therapies are in progress, it is wise to express reservations about initiating yet another therapy. The systemic therapist must assess whether he or she would be a positive influence in the life of the couple. If the systemic therapist decides that there are too many other professionals involved in the family's life, he or she should opt out. Alternatively, the couple may decide to terminate their other therapies.

Cotherapy?

Cotherapy is a popular technique. There is some thinking that opposite-sex therapists can serve as positive models for couples. The approach in this text does not encourage the couple to use the therapy as a model for relationship development. The task of the therapist is to encourage the partners to go back to their families and learn their own lessons from their own history. However, there are times when it is helpful to have a cotherapist. One can ask only so many questions. When a cotherapist has a similar theoretical approach he or she may inquire into areas that the other therapist may have overlooked.

In building a cotherapy relationship it is productive for each therapist to observe the other at work over a period of time without intervention. After each session the cotherapists should discuss what occurred in the session and the bases for the questions asked. Over a period of time the observing cotherapist will begin to anticipate the types of questions that the cotherapist asks. At this point, the cotherapy team is ready to become more spontaneous and interactive with each other. It takes approximately a year for two people to be able to anticipate each other's questions. Once this ability is acquired, the cotherapists become a team and can contribute greater depth to the therapy.

To have a cotherapy model that honors the above procedures, the cotherapists must share a similar philosophical and theoretical point of view, a similar value system, and respect for each other's integrity and professional competence. Having a male/female team is not as important as having two individuals who share a theoretical point of view and who are respectful of each other.

Occasionally therapists will join together as a way to deal with their anxiety about seeing couples or families. This practice is unwise. It is difficult to learn to be a systemic therapist by depending on a partner to help one through an interview. One of the most powerful learning experiences for a student is to have the opportunity to conduct numerous sessions on his or her own. Consulting on the interview afterwards and observing it, if possible, on videotape identifies areas where the student may be blocked and consolidates learning. If someone had been in the room to "take over," the student would be less likely to be spontaneous and get through the hour in his or her own creative way. It is important for student therapists to believe in themselves. If they have this basic belief they will be open to using other people's ideas in more creative ways.

Epilogue

To learn how to be a systemic family therapist one must be open to new ideas and uncomfortable situations and remain curious and nonreactive about anxiety within others and oneself. Each clinical situation can teach one about self and about how people's lives unfold. One should develop a method for learning that allows for wisdom to increase. Being invited into people's lives and letting their stories touch you will add to that wisdom. The challenge for the systemic therapist is to remain open to new ideas and always remember that one does not have the answers to the human dilemma.

References

Bank, S. P., and Kahn, M. O. (1982). *Sibling Bond*, New York: Basic Books.

Bowen, M. (1978). *Family Therapy in Clinical Practice*. New York: Jason Aronson.

Bowlby, J. (1969). *Attachment and Loss, Vol. I: Attachment*. New York: Basic Books.

_____ (1973). *Attachment and Loss, Vol. II: Separation, Anxiety and Anger*. New York: Basic Books.

Carter, B., and McGoldrick, M. (1988). *The Changing Family Life Cycle: A Framework for Family Therapy*, 2nd ed. New York: Gardner Press.

Erikson, E. (1964). *Childhood and Society*, 2nd ed. New York: Norton.

Erikson, E., Erikson, J. M., and Kivnick, H. O. (1986). *Vital Involvement in Old Age*. New York: Norton.

Freeman, D. S. (1981). *Techniques of Family Therapy*. New York: Jason Aronson.

———— (1991). *Multigenerational Family Therapy*, Binghamton, NY: Haworth Press.

Kerr, M., and Bowen, M. (1988). *Family Evaluation*. New York: Norton.

Lerner, H. G. (1989). *The Dance of Intimacy*. New York: Harper and Row.

Levinson, D. (1978). *The Seasons of a Man's Life*. New York: Knopf.

Malone, T. P., and Malone, P. T. (1987). *The Art of Intimacy*. New York: Prentice-Hall.

McGoldrick, M. and Gerson, R. (1985). *Genograms in Family Assessment*. New York: Norton.

Osherson, S. (1986). *Finding Our Fathers*. New York: Fawcett Columbine.

Richardson, R. (1984). *Family Ties That Bind*. North Vancouver, British Columbia: Self-Counsel Press.

Thomas, A. (1968). *Temperament and Behavior Disorders in Children*. New York: New York University Press.

Thomas, A., and Chess, S. (1977). *Temperament and Development*. New York: Brunner/Mazel.

Toman, W. (1969). *Family Constellation: Its Effects on Personality and Social Behavior*, 2nd ed. New York: Springer.

Index